Since I've met my cousin Anna, she's been a force of inspiration. Reading her memoir, I now fully understand why. Anna's childhood struggles could've been anyone's, and were certainly similar to my own, but her brave and passionate spirit shines as a bright reminder that no matter what happens in our lives, what lies within us is stronger and more powerful than our circumstances.

RUTH WARINER
Bestselling author of *The Sound of Gravel*

Anna's personal story is riveting, captivating, and heart wrenching all at once. You will be startled by this true-life tale and also amazed at the profound ways Anna brings comfort and strength to so many journeying with her. You will be mesmerized by this book and deeply touched by her ability to mount up above her challenging life. Great job, Anna!

SALLY CLARKSON
Author of *Own Your Life* and cofounder of Whole Heart Ministries

The Polygamist's Daughter reads like a taut suspense novel, only Anna's story is terrifyingly real. I rooted for Anna, experiencing her unstable, uprooted, crime-laden childhood alongside her. This memoir reminds us all that no one is beyond the reach of Jesus, and He loves to pursue the broken in broken places.

MARY DEMUTH
Author of *Thin Places: A Memoir*

The Polygamist's Daughter is a heart-wrenching account of my niece Anna's extreme neglect, fear, and abuse inflicted by the very ones meant to protect her. Readers will be astonished by her powerful testimony of surviving danger and terror while growing up in the cult of her infamous father, Ervil LeBaron. This account of Anna's resilient spirit, strength, and courage brings hope to others—many of whom, through fear, have remained silent for too long!

IRENE SPENCER
Author of *New York Times* bestseller *Shattered Dreams: My Life as a Polygamist's Wife* and *Cult Insanity: A Memoir of Polygamy, Prophets, and Blood Atonement*

The Polygamist's Daughter is a crazy read, full of things almost unimaginable in this day and age. And yet it's real, and Anna LeBaron went through it. *The Polygamist's Daughter* is a riveting narrative, but even more, it's a story of redemption. Read it for the ride, but settle in for the hope.

SARAH MAE
Author of *Longing for Paris*

As remembered through the eyes of a child, certain aspects of *The Polygamist's Daughter* seem at times more like adventure than inhumane living situations. You will be captivated as Anna LeBaron's life circumstances weigh heavier and heavier upon her, culminating in the brave decision to escape from the grip of a horrific family situation. Carrying insurmountable grief, she eventually finds peace and wholeness in Jesus. Anna has woven a tragic yet redemptive telling of her childhood that will leave you wrought with holy emotions right up until the last page.

JULIE PRESLEY
Author of *Stones of Remembrance* and *Nor Forsake*

The Polygamist's Daughter

Anna LeBaron *with Leslie Wilson*

a memoir

TYNDALE
MOMENTUM™

*The nonfiction imprint of
Tyndale House Publishers, Inc.*

Visit Tyndale online at www.tyndale.com.

Visit Tyndale Momentum online at www.tyndalemomentum.com.

TYNDALE, Tyndale Momentum, and Tyndale's quill logo are registered trademarks of Tyndale House Publishers, Inc. The Tyndale Momentum logo is a trademark of Tyndale House Publishers, Inc. Tyndale Momentum is the nonfiction imprint of Tyndale House Publishers, Inc., Carol Stream, Illinois

The Polygamist's Daughter: A Memoir

Designed by Nicole Grimes

Edited by Bonne Steffen

Published in association with Jessica Kirkland of The Blythe Daniel Agency, doing business at P. O. Box 64197, Colorado Springs, CO 80962-4197.

The stories in this book are about real people and real events, but some names have been omitted or changed for the privacy of the individuals involved. Dialogue has been recreated to the author's best recollection, and some events have been compressed for brevity.

For information about special discounts for bulk purchases, please contact Tyndale House Publishers at csresponse@tyndale.com or call 800-323-9400.

Library of Congress Cataloging-in-Publication Data
Names: LeBaron, Anna, author.
Title: The polygamist's daughter : a memoir / Anna LeBaron, with Leslie
   Wilson.
Description: Carol Stream, IL : Tyndale House Publishers, Inc., 2017.
Identifiers: LCCN 2016052538 | ISBN 9781496417558 (sc : alk. paper)
Subjects: LCSH: LeBaron, Anna. | LeBaron, Ervil M.—Family. |
   Mormons—Mexico—Biography. | Polygamy—Religious aspects—Church of the
   Firstborn of the Fulness of Times.
Classification: LCC BX8680.L48 L43 2017 | DDC 289.3092 [B] —dc23 LC record
available at https://urldefense.proofpoint.com/v2/url?u=https-3A__lccn.loc.gov_2
016052538&d=DgIFAg&c=6BNjZEuL_DAs869UxGis0g&r=iAtpRRBtLgEtrNg
RnTpsAGWJLbzzaIiqo9CoIHsjDQ4&m=3gtQ6rvNtve3fkqV12krNImHsnNH
JCI5-td-eN6kH5o&s=hZhVlV3L-dprVcGP—HQ7gqxyblxQrjwAy5Xz-KCZW8&e=

Printed in the United States of America

23   22   21   20   19   18   17
7   6   5   4   3   2   1

To my brothers and sisters—
all the sons and daughters of Ervil LeBaron.
I'll never get tired of rehashing our stories.
It's the best therapy.
The stories yet to be lived and told
will be the best of all.

NOTE FROM THE AUTHOR

THIS MEMOIR WAS written from memory, with many details corroborated by close family members. Some names have been changed for the privacy of the individuals; some scenes have been recreated to the best of my ability; and some of the events described have been compressed for brevity. Various details not known to me at the time of the events have been added to the story to give context to the reader.

Except in certain circumstances when the words were seared in my mind, the dialogue is not verbatim. It is, however, in keeping with the spirit of the events surrounding them. The same is true of the people. I describe them to the best of my recollection, based on my age at the time these events occurred, our circumstances and experiences, and my impressions of them at the time.

I also want to make it clear that my father took the basic tenets of Joseph Smith's teachings, including polygamy, that had been practiced for generations in my family and radically twisted them. My father promoted an extremism that shattered so many lives. The modern-day LDS Mormon church officially disavowed polygamy in 1890.

Within these pages, I tell my story. I hope one day the others involved will tell their own.

FOREWORD

WE ALWAYS MEET people somewhere in the middle of their stories. I met Anna LeBaron somewhere around chapter 34 of the book you are holding, and I had no idea of the unfolding story that I would become a part of.

Her narrative begins with "At age nine, I had forty-nine siblings," and ends with "He knows my name. He knows my story. And He has set me free." What happens in between is a shocking and powerful account of a young woman becoming herself, while others wanted her to be anything but herself.

Starting as someone who was just one among scores of siblings, Anna has emerged as a one-of-a-kind human being. For someone who was surrounded by demands to obey, comply, serve, and disappear, Anna has done an amazing job of "showing up." If you were to meet her now you would be taken by her kindness and her generosity, by her smile and her positivity. And you would never guess the specifics that you are about to read.

I first heard about Anna's journey during a series of conversations between us. I watched her fight, and I watched her learn. I watched her pursue fearlessly (or at least it appeared that way from my chair) the kind of truth that would make her free. I watched her write her story in her heart, not knowing that one day she would write it for your eyes.

But she almost couldn't help it. It is consistent with the generosity of her life that if she found hope, she would also do whatever it takes to give it to others. If she found life, she would do whatever it takes to offer it to others.

Prepare to encounter situations that few of us could actually imagine. Fleeing in the dark of night, pursued by the FBI, protected by SWAT teams, and traumatized by multiple murders in her family—all of these experiences were part of Anna's life in the cult. But that is not the real story here. While those details may keep your eyes open, the real story will keep your heart open.

The real story is about a child born to an evil tyrant, a child who endured far more than just fatherlessness—she endured wickedness. And yet, this young woman, in the darkest of conditions, found the light of fatherhood to be real and profoundly healing.

Her discovery unveils a fundamental truth for every human soul: Regardless of your circumstances and your family history, you are made for more. You are more than the sum of your experiences and more than the sum of your humanity.

Anna's story meets you in the middle of your story. If you find nothing else in *The Polygamist's Daughter*, you can find the hope that you, too—whether now or later—can breathe the words of Anna's friend in the last chapter, "She has overcome!"

Bob Hamp
Founder of Think Differently: Counseling, Consulting, Connecting
Author of Think Differently Live Differently

PROLOGUE

At age nine, I had forty-nine siblings.

I didn't play hopscotch with my school friends at recess or watch *The Brady Bunch* on television with my siblings. My mother didn't pack my school lunch and my dad didn't give me a hug at the door, wishing me a good day. Instead, my parents, who were on the run from federal authorities, abandoned me in Mexico for about a year, leaving me with a family I didn't know. A family that included a man named Rafael.

I was fed each day and had a foam pad to sleep on at night. But I found it difficult to sleep in this strange place, so far from my mom. Why couldn't I stay with her and the rest of my family in the United States, instead of in this dingy, dusty apartment south of the border?

Even though I had grown up in polygamy, I had no idea of the truth.

I was auditioning as a potential wife for Rafael.

My father, the notorious Ervil LeBaron, had promised Rafael several of his daughters in marriage. If Rafael, a recent convert to my father's polygamist sect, was still in favor with him when we girls reached marriageable age—typically fifteen—it would happen. My sisters and I were pawns to be auctioned off to the highest bidder, those followers willing to do whatever my father asked, no matter what it involved.

I understood from watching my mom, along with her twelve sister-wives and my countless siblings, that no one was allowed to question my father's authority. So, like the others, I obeyed.

And even though this life made my stomach ache, I never said a word.

ONE

"WHAT WILL WE DO without you?"

I stood in the driveway of our Dallas home, clinging to my mother as the sun rose higher in the sky, and begged her through my tears not to go. I couldn't imagine life without my mother. So great was my grief that I barely noticed her two sister-wives saying good-bye to their own children.

We had been living there only a short time, having moved yet again on short notice. I'd be sent off to school that day with no explanation as to why my mom had to leave—again. Usually she left without notice and would come back in a few days, or sometimes weeks. This time was different. She didn't know when she would be back.

I'm sure Mom felt like she had no other choice—she was obeying my father's order. Ervil LeBaron led The Church of the Lamb of God, a radical offshoot of the Mormon Church, and Anna Mae was the fourth of his thirteen wives. Like the other wives, she learned early on to do as she was told.

My mom, raised in Arizona, had met and married her second husband, Nephi, when they were both part of the traditional Mormon Church, known as The Church of Jesus Christ of Latter-day Saints.

Nephi attended one of Ervil LeBaron's exhaustive talks and eventually bought into my dad's more radical offshoot of Mormonism. He hurried home to tell my mom that the way they'd been living out Joseph Smith's teaching was all wrong. When she remonstrated, Nephi invited Ervil to their home to convince my mom that they needed to convert and follow this new prophet. Ervil was powerfully persuasive—so much so that Nephi and my mother not only converted, but agreed to relocate to Colonia LeBarón in Chihuahua, Mexico.

Nephi stayed in Arizona to sell their home, but my mom went ahead with their five children. During this transition, she spent an inordinate amount of time with Ervil, who—while tall, handsome, and charismatic—was also narcissistic, entitled, and manipulative. He proclaimed that he had a revelation that it was God's will and plan for my mom's life that she leave Nephi and marry him instead. She fell madly in love with Ervil, and like the other sister-wives before and after her, she succumbed to his potent influence. They married and she had seven more children with him, including me.

"Please, Mom, don't go."

On the driveway, I wrapped my arms around Mom's waist, my tears dampening the front of her faded denim dress.

"Anna Keturah," she said firmly. Like most mothers, Mom always included my middle name when I stirred up trouble. She named me, her tenth child, after herself, but insisted on a different pronunciation (Ah-nah) that she heard while pregnant with me.

"Stop crying! You're seven years old. Crying doesn't do any good." She bent over and kissed my cheek. I placed my hand over the spot to hold in her warmth as long as possible.

Helpless, I watched her get into the beat-up Chevy with three of Dad's other followers. Along with the other kids and a few remaining adults, I watched them drive away, hoping Mom would turn around and wave or smile at me one more time. She didn't. My thirteen-year-old sister, Kathleen, took my hand, pulled me into the house, and did her best to comfort me. This wasn't her first time being left in charge of the kids in my mother's absence.

Those of us left behind in Dallas were supported by the adult women in our group who worked at the family's used appliance business, although the majority of the income generated from the family business went to my father. The sister-wives, even nursing mothers, spent long days—often twelve to fourteen hours of back-breaking labor—at the store, just one of many abuses they endured under my father's control. We children witnessed some of the other abuses, but all of us had been conditioned to keep silent.

While the women were gone, Kathleen cared for me, Adine, Hyrum, Celia, Marilyn, Manuel, Virginia, and other children of my mom's sister-wives. To pass the time, Kathleen played games and read to us, activities she preferred over the never-ending housework. Though Kathleen did her best to scrape together meals to feed us, when the sister-wives got home, they would scold her for not cleaning up the messes made by so many toddlers and young children.

When we were all together, I quietly observed the interactions between the sister-wives. Some had petty jealousies, and a few spoke cattily behind each other's backs. Others got along well, especially biological sisters married to the same husband. As teenagers, two of my mother's daughters, Ramona and Faye, were given in marriage to Dan Jordan, my father's right-hand man. Ramona became Dan's sixth wife at age seventeen.

Later, Faye was "sealed" to him following her sixteenth birthday, along with my step-sister Amy. Since the "blessed event" making them wives number seven and eight took place on the same night, Ervil flipped a coin after performing the double ceremony to see which of the girls would share the marriage bed with her new husband that first night. Faye was relieved when Amy was chosen to spend that first night with the forty-plus-year-old man.

These hurried ceremonies were performed in secret; in many cases, the other wives knew nothing until after the fact. Even if the girls in our group dreamed of being courted, dating, or marrying different young men, they never experienced that kind of happily-ever-after; those types of relationships were seldom allowed. The older men in Dad's sect preferred younger and younger wives, and they managed to get their way with each successive marriage. At first, group members frowned upon underage unions and quietly protested when the older men began to court teenage girls, but the leaders became ever more emboldened, and the disapproving whispers and looks from the older wives did nothing to stop this practice.

x x x x x

A few months after my mom left us in Dallas, Kathleen roused me from a deep slumber. "Wake up, Anna. It's time to go."

As usual, no one had told me that we were moving again. But I knew the drill. I gathered a couple of items within reach and padded down the long hallway behind my older siblings. None of us had many personal possessions, since we left behind most of our belongings with each move. What we did have, we kept in small cardboard boxes, which, if we were lucky, we could grab before leaving the house. An extra change of clothes and a few special trinkets were treasures that we would keep well-hidden so other siblings wouldn't take them, claiming them as their own. We felt rich when we had a full deck of cards for a card game, a diversion that would keep us entertained for hours. Speed, War, and Slapjack were my favorites.

When we got outside, I blinked several times, then wiped the sleep from my eyes as I tried to see my surroundings under the heavy cloud cover.

"Keep moving," a husky voice barked.

I felt someone thump me on the back of my head. I turned slightly and stuck out my tongue at my brother Arthur, only because I knew he couldn't see me in the inky darkness. I was wearing flip-flops, and with the next step, I stubbed my toe on a piece of the crumbling driveway and nearly fell. My rubber sandal fell off, and I had to scurry back a couple of steps to retrieve it. Another man, Alex, helped herd us kids as well. Clearly, they were in a hurry to get on the road.

"Anna?" cried the thin, fearful voice of Celia, my sister closest in age.

"I'm right here."

She took my hand, and I asked her to help me find my sandal. We felt around in the dark until she found it just off the driveway in the weed-ridden yard. I quickly slipped it back on, and we fell back in line with the others.

"Do you know where we're going?" Celia whispered again.

"I heard Arthur say something about Colorado."

"Oh, I hope so. That's where Mom is." We clung tightly to one another, and to the hope of seeing our mother again.

"I can't see anything. Where are the cars?"

We both knew we would need at least two vehicles to transport all of us kids on the eight-hundred-mile trek from Dallas to Denver. Just as I opened my mouth to say I didn't know, the clouds parted slightly, and a full moon revealed a large box truck sitting at the end of our cracked driveway.

"We're not going in that, are we?" My surprise and disgust carried my words slightly too far, reaching Arthur's ears at the front of the line.

As he directed everyone to the open back of the box truck, he hissed at each one, "Get in. Find a place to sit, and be quiet. Absolutely no talking!" Then he spun around and headed toward me. He yanked my arm hard, and held me in place while the line of siblings marched on toward the truck. Celia could only watch, her countenance filled with compassion mixed with confusion. Arthur leaned down, his face only inches away from my own. I could smell the peanut butter on his breath.

"Shut your mouth and get in. You know we're doing this to build God's kingdom. Do you think I need to hear you complaining?"

"N-no," I stammered, trying to wrench free from his firm grasp.

He tightened his strong fingers around my upper arm until I felt certain they would leave a mark—or worse, a bruise. "Then I'd better not hear another peep out of you." He quickly released my arm and shoved me in the middle of my back, propelling me forward once more. I stutter-stepped but managed not to fall or lose my flimsy flip-flop again and climbed in the back of the truck.

The space inside was dimly lit by a couple of flashlights held by older siblings. Someone had spread a few moving blankets across the floor of the truck, but these did little to soften the hard wood floor. I wrinkled my nose at the pungent odor of mothballs mixed with the greasy residue on the blankets. Scanning the truck for Celia, I quickly spotted her midway back. She patted the floor next to her, indicating she had room for me beside her. Even the slight movement of her hand echoed throughout the empty space and garnered startled looks from the older siblings.

I scurried next to Celia, sat down cross-legged, and leaned up against the metal wall behind me. We sat quietly for what seemed like an eternity. Even a sigh or heavy breath brought worried glances from other siblings because Arthur had told us not to make any noise. I didn't even want to imagine what the adults might say or do if one of us younger ones actually spoke up about our confusion or fear. Celia and I clutched one another, and that small reassurance helped me keep my rising whimpers at bay.

Finally, Arthur appeared at the back of the truck. He grabbed the door handle and pulled it down, and the door rattled shut, leaving us in darkness, except for the faint light of the flashlights. Moments later, the tired truck sputtered to life. The way it squeaked and groaned around every turn, I worried that we wouldn't make it out of our neighborhood, much less anywhere else. It bounced in and out of potholes as we made our way onto a Dallas freeway en route to Colorado.

After a while, the noise provided enough covering for me to safely whisper to Celia, "What do we do if we have to go to the bathroom?"

Celia only shrugged her shoulders, but I could see dread in her eyes.

Thankfully, Arthur and Alex, who took turns driving, made scheduled, reasonable potty breaks. They even gave us a loaf of bread and jar of peanut butter along with a butter knife after one stop at a gas station and convenience store. It was all we had to eat, but still it was something. I gobbled up my sandwich in mere moments. We played guessing games about where we were headed and told stories to pass the time.

I managed a fitful sleep, but when I woke I was stiff and sore from lying on my side. It took me a moment or two to get my bearings. My ears were buzzing from the constant noise of the motor and the grinding gears that were mere inches from where I'd rested my head.

But ringing ears and stiff muscles seemed a small price to pay to see my mom again. I hoped the truck would hold together long enough to get us to our destination.

Finally, the loud, constant hum of tires on pavement traveling at highway speeds lessened. The truck careened one direction, then the next. We held on to one another for stability when we weren't lying down. One of the older kids turned a flashlight back on. "I think we're almost there. Gather up your stuff." All I had with me was a worn stuffed rabbit and a ponytail holder—we called them *bolitos*—around my wrist. Celia held her prized possession, a worn Raggedy Andy doll, to her chest.

When we finally came to a stop, the rolling door was opened with a deafening rumble that reverberated off the metal walls. Celia and I squinted in the bright sunlight, thankful to hear nothing but relative quiet. I saw a figure just outside the back of the truck—something familiar about it made me sit up.

"Mom!" I yelled, as the tears started welling up in my eyes and the ache in my heart began to ease. I clambered over my siblings to get to the edge of the truck bed, lean over, and hug my mother's neck. "I never thought I would see you again!"

"Anna Keturah, stop being so dramatic." She held me tightly for a few seconds, then peeled me off and searched for her other children who needed hugs as well.

x x x x x

Celia, my other siblings, and I experienced a few blissful days— blissful only in the sense that we were reunited with our mother, not in less work or more comfortable living conditions. This new "home" in Denver was completely run down, like all the other barely affordable houses we rented. The cramped three-bedroom, one-bathroom house sheltered about twenty of us, which meant constantly crowded conditions. Mom, her children, and the other children in her care shared this home with Teresa and Yolanda, two of my mother's sister-wives, and their six children.

I didn't realize it at the time, but Mom shouldered enormous responsibility. She cared for her own seven children, the ones who were still minors, as well as four other children who belonged to Beverly, Mom's sister-wife who was in prison. But that wasn't all. Mom was given charge of her sister-wife Mary Lou's children when Mary Lou lost her short battle with cancer.

I don't remember ever meeting Mary Lou, but I do recall the day that two of her six kids showed up at our house when Mom was gone for a couple of weeks and Kathleen was in charge of us children. The newcomers, technically my half-brother and half-sister, spoke little English, and I could see the fear and worry etched on their faces. I remember my mom taking us aside after returning home and instructing us to be kind to them because they no longer had a mother and they were separated from their older siblings. They lived with and were cared for by my mom from then on.

Even though we all had our own mothers, we were expected to obey all of the sister-wives. Teresa and Yolanda meant well, but if you got on their nerves—as children tend to do—they'd pick up any nearby object to administer a spanking. Their go-to items included a long-handled spoon, the back of a hairbrush, or even their shoe, which they'd remove in a pinch if we misbehaved or didn't do what we were asked to do.

As always, my sisters and I spent hours washing dishes—plastic margarine tubs that served as our only bowls—and doing laundry, while Mom, Teresa, and Yolanda were working at the used appliance store. We took our time with the household chores we were assigned in the absence of the adults.

My life in Denver brought many challenges, but being

separated from my mother was not one of them, so it seemed nearly perfect to me. I recall a few happy moments in the Xavier Street house, playing Monopoly and card games inside. In the backyard, we played tag or caught grasshoppers to see who could hold on to one the longest, squealing in horror as they wiggled around in our hands.

At night, we each spread our threadbare blanket on the living room floor and lapped half of it over ourselves to create a thin makeshift sleeping bag. As usual, I snuggled near Celia, thankful to be away from the large cockroaches we'd come to fear in Texas. We giggled and whispered about playing house and dreamt of having new dresses, all our own.

While in Denver, I first heard a phrase that I didn't understand but didn't dare ask about: "hot lead, cold steel, and a one-way ticket to hell."

What I didn't know then was that nearly two years later, hell would be unleashed right on our doorstep.

TWO

On September 23, 1977, I had just nodded off when the front door burst open and bright lights filled the room.

"FBI!" yelled several voices as half a dozen federal agents ran through the door.

Then a deep voice boomed, "Stay where you are, and show us your hands—slowly."

From the blanket cocoon I shared with Celia, I enlarged a tiny hole and peeked out. A tall, lean, red-haired FBI agent was holding his arms out straight like sticks, gripping a gun in his hands. He continued shouting into the room, which was crowded with children who had been wakened abruptly. "Nobody move! And let me see those hands—now."

Fortunately or unfortunately—depending on your perspective—I'd been taught how to react during an FBI raid. We were told that our dad had enemies who wanted him arrested, or worse, dead. We were taught that we were being persecuted because we were God's chosen people. Knowing his enemies might tip off authorities as to his whereabouts, my dad instructed my mom and the other sister-wives about the importance of training all the children for this and other scenarios. They coached us to keep silent under all circumstances, and if for some reason authorities forced us to speak, our only answer would be, "I don't know."

I can recall first the adults and then our older siblings drilling us on this multiple times, acting out potential scenarios we might face with different types of law enforcement. Other kids our age played make-believe cops and robbers or cowboys and Indians. We did that, too, but we also played FBI agents and fugitives. The sad reality was that we weren't playing—we were rehearsing for situations that could likely occur.

"What do you say if they ask you if you're tired?" Arthur's face pressed close to mine. He was the drill sergeant, and I was the new recruit.

"I don't know."

"Good. What do you say if they ask you if you're hungry?"

"I don't know."

"Good. What do you—"

"But what if I *am* hungry?"

Arthur glared at me, then rolled his eyes. "It doesn't matter. Listen, this isn't rocket science. You never, ever tell them anything except 'I don't know.' Do you understand?"

"Yes." I bowed my head in shame for my stupidity and tucked away this thought for future drills: never ask questions.

"Those men are bad guys. They hate us for what we're doing. Just because they don't understand the Lord's work, they think it's okay to persecute us. But it's not okay, is it?"

"N-n-n-no." My lips quivered so much I could barely form the word, as I thought about the hateful FBI and their eagerness to hurt—even kill—my family.

"Just do what we tell you, and everything will be all right." The red-haired agent repeated his directive, his voice low and controlled this time. I didn't show my hands or pull off the blanket, but I did sit up so I could better see the action through my peephole. I scooted closer to Celia, trying in vain to calm my fears. Red kept an eye on us kids, while the other agents fanned out through the house, some cautiously heading into the kitchen and others down the long hallway to the adults' bedrooms. They moved stealthily and announced themselves before they opened any doors.

After a few minutes, they herded all the older kids and the mothers they had found into the cramped living room with the rest of us. We huddled together in silence while federal agents searched every inch of that house, both upstairs and downstairs. They dumped out cardboard boxes with our few articles of clothing in them. From the noises in the back of the house, I imagined they were doing the same in the bedrooms and bathrooms.

One of them shouted from the detached garage, "Hey, come get a load of this."

Immediately, two agents disappeared, heading outside.

I could hear their muffled voices outside, deep and low. Moments later, they reappeared. A stocky man with a bald patch down the center of his head said, "I've been doing this for more than twenty years, and I've never seen anything like this."

Agent Red, now more relaxed, with gun holstered, asked, "What's that?"

"They probably have two hundred loaves of bread, donuts, and snack cakes stacked up in that garage."

Red's jaw dropped at that news, replying to Baldy as if we weren't there at all, "With as many of them packed into this house, it probably won't last long."

While they poked fun at our family's ways, I whispered to Celia, "I hope they leave soon. I wonder what they are looking for?" I felt an elbow in my ribs, a painful jab from one of my older siblings. I muffled a cry in protest.

"Shhh!" Red narrowed his eyes, looked in our direction, and walked over to us in a show of authority. I could see red bumps on his neck from razor stubble. I felt sure I was in trouble. But a moment later, he returned to his post near the front door.

Baldy set up a makeshift interrogation station at the kitchen table. The adults were questioned one by one. I strained to hear, but they spoke in hushed tones, and the activity of the other agents drowned them out. I knew my turn would come.

It seemed as if several hours passed, which is a long time for a nine-year-old to remain silent in the midst of such stress. But still, I knew sitting on the floor huddled with Celia was better than being questioned. So I waited and watched.

Baldy finished questioning the adults, though he didn't get any helpful information. He jotted down a few notes, then stood and headed toward the front door in the living room where Celia and I had sat since the men first descended upon our home.

I'd never been more grateful for my big sister, older than me by two and a half years. We continued clasping hands under the blanket during the entire raid. Her presence strengthened me and gave me a confidence I didn't know I had.

If we had been interrogated, we would have done fine. We were extremely well coached. Thankfully, they left all of us kids alone—this time.

After what seemed like hours, the FBI agents left, and we began cleaning up the mess they had made.

x x x x x

The majority of our religious teaching came from my dad's prophetic revelations. However, my mom and the other sister-wives allowed those of us who wanted to go to Sunday school to board a church bus that came down our street every Sunday morning.

At the local church, teachers handed out prizes to kids who took home handouts, answered the questions, and then brought them back the following week. I didn't always know the answers, but I sure wanted the stickers and little plastic dime-store toys they handed out as prizes.

One Sunday morning, our teacher asked my age-group, "Who is God's Son?"

I had no idea what the correct answer was. After attending Sunday school a couple of times, I caught on to the fact that no matter what question they asked, answering "Jesus" meant I was right about half the time and would get rewarded for getting the answer right. I never spoke that name at home, though. The sister-wives and other adults only spoke that name with derision, if it was spoken at all. The difference was stark, and the kindness of the Sunday school teachers and the bus ministry workers stuck with me.

In January of 1978, all us kids went back to school after Christmas break. Though school tended to be a blur of faces and places because of our many moves, I recall this month clearly. The entire city had worked itself into a frenzy about the Denver Broncos playing in the Super Bowl against the Dallas Cowboys. My sister Kathleen was a huge Denver Broncos fan. We owned an old television, and adult family members would gather around to watch the football game each week, even though the poor reception made the image grainy and hard to see. The younger kids were shooed away.

One morning at school, our teacher stood before the class and announced, "The Denver Broncos organization has asked our school to make a spirit banner. Everyone who wants to can write something on it to help spur on the team and the fans. They're actually going to hang our banner along one of the hallways of the stadium."

The class buzzed with excitement about this project.

At the appointed time, our teacher led us into the hallway where the banner hung along the wall that backed up to the library. I stood and stared at the banner, not really knowing what to do next. A girl in my class handed me a brown crayon and said, "C'mon, don't you want to cheer on the Broncos?"

I stared at the brown crayon, then back at the banner. Suddenly, I knew I didn't want to use a plain old ugly brown color. I walked over to the bin of crayons atop a desk someone had pulled into the hallway, and I selected bright orange instead. I knew enough to know the Broncos' nickname was the Orange Crush.

I had no idea what to write, so I simply copied what another student had penned much further down the banner from where I stood. Though I'd never even watched an entire football game in person or on TV, working on that banner helped me connect with the other kids in my class.

Participating might sound like such a little thing, but the act made me feel normal and included. It gave me the opportunity to be part of something bigger than myself. Truth is, I couldn't have been more ignorant of what a Super Bowl was. I didn't know anything about football. But I didn't care about any of that. I cared about feeling like I belonged. Working on that banner gave me something in common with my fellow students. I'd felt like an outsider my whole life, constantly hearing in my head the sister-wives' warnings against making friends outside the family. "Never fraternize with the enemy," they said.

Worse, we felt conspicuous when we were singled out as different because of our faith. In fact, mere weeks before the Super Bowl hype, the faculty at school sent all of our family's children to the library during the class Christmas parties. They told me my mom had directed them to sequester us "because we don't celebrate pagan holidays." So, as silly as it may sound, the Super Bowl excitement allowed me to be a chameleon. I didn't stick out in my ratty, outdated clothes or because of my unusually large family. For the first time in my life, I found something outside of the cult that allowed me to safely and inconspicuously participate. And oh, the joy of blending in!

THREE

THE JOY OF BLENDING IN continued for me even though the Denver Broncos lost the Super Bowl that year. I always did my best to adjust to our new homes and schools. In Denver, I had even met a couple of girls I secretly hoped might become my "at school" friends, since we were not allowed to bring friends home or go to their homes to play. Unfortunately, one night my hopes were quickly dashed again.

Someone was shaking me, and I woke with a start. "What's going on?" I said as I sat up, rubbed my eyes, and tried hard to resist my beckoning pillow, however thin and flat.

"Shhh! Don't ask any questions. Just get your shoes on quickly," Teresa whispered. She and Yolanda made their way around the darkened room to wake all the children. "Hurry, we need to leave in two minutes."

I joined my brothers and sisters (six that I remember) in the back of a station wagon and tried to find a comfortable position.

"Where are we going, Mom?"

Her look clearly said not to pursue that subject. My half-brother Ed rode shotgun; he was old enough to drive, so he and my mom took turns at the wheel.

I hoped to get a little more sleep during the drive to who knows where.

Moving unexpectedly and often was a way of life for us that I accepted. But that didn't mean I enjoyed leaving a familiar place for someplace unknown. Just the fact that it was always done in the middle of the night was disconcerting. Continual moves across thousands of miles prevented me from ever feeling settled anywhere. Our lives were characterized by fear, chaos, and insecurity, with my mother's presence, love, and care the one constant source of comfort and stability.

We drove and drove and drove. It's funny the things you remember. Texas is a big state, and we drove straight through it. The landscape left much to the imagination, being mostly flat and dry in the heat of a Texas summer. I occupied my mind by reading the road signs along the way and couldn't figure out what BBQ was. We didn't go out to eat, and I had never experienced the taste of barbecue, so my mom had to explain what the letters meant.

We passed much of the time playing made-up road trip games. The stops for gas were quick, with several of us crowding into the women's bathroom at one time. The grown-ups would get coffee to stay awake, but no other treats were purchased. When we got to the border, we were told to stay quiet and let the grown-ups do all the talking.

All told, that trip—heading south from Denver right into the heart of Mexico—covered more than 1,700 miles. We finally stopped in front of an apartment building in Catemaco, Veracruz, and began unloading the car. The heat and humidity was stifling; it caught in my throat and made it difficult to draw in a deep breath. It felt like walking into a sauna compared with the dryness of the Mile High City we'd left behind. My clothes stuck to me when I walked, and sweat trickled through my hair and down my neck and back.

What happened next was a blur. Strangers greeted us at the door, kissed our cheeks, then quickly ushered us in and closed the door behind us. The adults talked in whispered tones in the crowded kitchen, leaving us kids to guess what was going to happen next. *Who are these people?* I wondered. They smiled, but the gesture seemed hollow—forced. *What are we doing here?*

Then suddenly, the worst thing imaginable happened. My mother, who held my baby sister, Adine, on her hip, headed for the door. Avoiding my gaze, Celia followed them. With a slight wave of her free hand, Mom said a quick good-bye. I stared at the three of them, my mouth agape. I knew not to make a scene, after doing so two years before on the driveway in Dallas and being chided for it, but as I looked at Adine, I envied her and wished I were still the baby, the one who got to stay with Mom. Mom always insisted on keeping the youngest child with her when she traveled for my dad. I remembered going with her on long trips before Hyrum and Adine came along and ousted me from that coveted position.

I vividly remember one trip in particular. It was just my mom and me in her old, baby-blue Volkswagen Beetle. I remember we were driving on a mountain switchback and when I looked out the window, I could see that there were no guardrails on the edge of the road. I was frightened that the car might plunge over the precipice and couldn't stop shaking.

I shuddered at the memory. The confusion I felt now didn't help the shaking. I knew why Mom had to take Adine, but I didn't understand why Celia had to be taken somewhere else. *Why can't Celia stay here with me?* In Celia's absence, I would be the oldest of my siblings left there. I watched as the station wagon pulled away, leaving behind our small group made up of Hyrum, a few other siblings, and me.

Rafael and Antonia, strangers to me but recent converts to

my father's church, cast surly looks our way, so I quickly glanced around our new home. Their second-floor apartment had tile floors and was sparsely furnished, but it was a nice place by Mexican standards, especially when compared with the hut behind the apartment.

The neighbor's home was built out of sticks and had a thatched roof. The door was open, and I could see that the floor was just hard-packed dirt. Someone had fashioned a broom from a long stick with twigs tied around the bottom, and the mother was using it to sweep out trash from the house.

As the weeks went by, I noticed a grown man, who had legs that didn't work, living in the hut, along with a few small children. I wondered if he was their dad. He walked around on his hands and kept his useless legs folded up Indian-style. I was fascinated with how quickly he could get around walking only on his hands. He needed that skill to dodge the dogs, chickens, and pigs that scurried in and out of the hut as they pleased.

I spoke up for myself and my siblings, feeling the weight of responsibility of being the oldest, even though I was just nine years old. "When's my mom coming back?"

"Stop asking questions! That's how little girls get into big trouble. You don't want trouble, do you?" Antonia stood with her legs apart and stared at me, hands on her slim hips.

I bit my lip. Of course I didn't want trouble. But I didn't understand how asking a few questions about my mom fell into the category of causing trouble. Still, I shook my head. My questions remained unasked but never left my mind. Where did my mom go? How long would she be away? And most important, would I ever see her again? The stability and comfort she provided, which I'd known and depended on all my life, was gone. What I didn't know then was that it would be more than a year before we would be reunited.

I found some comfort in having Hyrum and a couple of other siblings there. But I desperately missed Celia, who I learned had been sent to another home in Calería.

It didn't take long to realize that Antonia didn't appreciate caring for and feeding more children than her own, Gabriel and Rosa. As the weeks went by, it seemed as though she seized every opportunity to shame and humiliate my siblings and me. *Why did Mom leave us with someone who seems to hate us so much?*

I retreated inward. Though I'm certain there was nothing wrong with my hearing, everything felt off kilter and sounded far off, as though I had cotton in my ears or the way sounds are muffled when your ears are plugged with water. It was as if I were hiding in plain sight. I learned to be seen and not heard in those close quarters. The dwelling always felt crowded, especially since many other members of the cult came and went from Rafael and Antonia's apartment, usually in the night. The overcrowding only exacerbated my intense loneliness. I felt alone, silenced, unseen, and invisible—unless I caused a problem.

I clung to little things to feel a degree of normalcy. Not long after I arrived, I was tasked with copying from the *Teachings of the Prophet Joseph Smith* (the *TPJS*, for short) as part of my education. I'm sure Antonia came up with it to keep me occupied. At first, I hated being stuck at the table while the younger children played. The subject matter was boring and the content way above my comprehension, and no one explained anything to me. What I actually learned about the religion I was born into came through observation and by regularly overhearing adult conversations, which was inescapable in the crowded quarters.

But as time went on, I found solace in copying word for word what the self-proclaimed Mormon prophet had written. Over time, I filled three spiral notebooks with the prophet's words. The monotonous activity not only helped pass the time, but it also enabled me to tune out some of the chaos going on around me. It quieted my fears and aching heart as well. I particularly liked it when others praised me for my dutiful attention to this religious task, so I kept at it long after I had completed my assigned schoolwork.

I remember the day my Bic pen ran out of ink and needed to be replaced. At first, I feared asking Antonia for money to buy a new pen. She didn't easily part with the meager money brought into the house. But I was pleasantly surprised by her response. Some fanfare went into the fact that Antonia handed me pesos specifically intended to replace the pen when I did that day's shopping. I didn't often experience such a sense of pride and accomplishment, so I reveled in this unusual feeling.

Rafael and Antonia required us to earn our keep. In addition to the chores I did around the apartment, they arranged for me to work for the woman who lived in the apartment below ours. She and her husband had artwork and photos on the walls and decorative items on the tables, all luxuries to me. My family had never owned anything more than the basic necessities.

Each morning I knocked on the woman's door to begin a day's work. I did her laundry regularly—hand scrubbing on an old-fashioned washboard until my skinny arms ached. Then I took the heavy basket of wet clothes up two flights of stairs to the rooftop, hanging them on the communal clotheslines to dry. I swept and mopped her entire house every day and helped peel and chop vegetables and make tortillas. Sometimes she would let me taste the delicious food we prepared, though not often.

Our neighbor paid my meager wages directly to Antonia, and I never saw a single peso. Though I didn't particularly relish working for the woman, my part-time job did get me out of the house, an opportunity my younger siblings didn't have.

Though I seldom had time off from my grueling workdays—and when I did, I rarely had time to myself—I do remember standing at a bedroom window one day and looking out at a mountain range in the distance. *If only I could just get over that mountain somehow, I'd find Mom, and we would be together again,* I thought. Sadly, that mountain was farther away than my legs could take me, so the impossibility of the task weighed heavy on my heart. The mountains taunted me with their majesty and mystery—and their distance. I fantasized about leaving the apartment and walking toward the mountains, but my fear was stronger and I stayed put.

Because I didn't want to be given harder work or be separated from my siblings, I didn't dare cry openly about missing my mom, even though the ache I felt was overwhelming. Each night, I struggled to fall asleep as images of my mom flashed into my brain. I wondered where she was and what she was doing. Did she miss me? Did she know what Rafael and Antonia made us kids do? Would she ever come back to get us? But my thoughts stayed just that—thoughts. I was helpless to change my circumstances.

Thankfully, the woman downstairs tired of me after about a month. I worked hard for her and did my best, but my best efforts must not have suited her high standards. After she dismissed me, Rafael capitalized on my unique looks. With my long blonde hair and fair skin—an anomaly among the dark-haired, dark-skinned Mexicans—he reasoned that I would be a great marketing tool, so he sent me to the streets to sell items door to door.

At first I sold handmade paperweights—rocks we found and painted designs on. I especially liked painting a picture of the sun on mine—a design that worked even on oddly shaped rocks. Rafael rehearsed a script in Spanish with me until I memorized what to say. He instructed me to stop at each house and deliver my sales pitch. Most of the town's residents couldn't afford frivolous purchases any more than we could.

I went out alone, and at first I stayed close to the apartment. As I familiarized myself with the streets, I ventured farther out each day. Thankfully I was good with directions and could retrace my steps back home based on the landmarks I passed along the way. I did get lost a few times, but I somehow managed to figure things out and find my way back.

I did everything possible to sell as many items as I could in a day. I paid no heed to the looks of pity I received from my buyers because—bottom line—pity translated into more pesos. Each day, I wore one of the two outfits I had. Each night, I washed and line-dried that day's clothes. Even though my clothes were worn from scrubbing, they were clean when I started out each day. But the dirt I kicked up from the dusty roads stuck to my sweaty face and body, leaving me a sight to behold, I'm sure.

On other days, Antonia and I baked cakes, which I sold by the slice. I carried a whole cake on a plate, along with a knife to cut slices. Each buyer had to bring his or her own plate to the door for the cake slice. Because we made the frosting the same way every day, if we had leftover cake, we used food coloring to give it a different color than the day before and sold it as fresh. Anything to put food on the table. We weren't allowed to eat the cakes we made, but occasionally we'd get to lick the bowls if Antonia was in a good mood. On my route, I would sneak a taste of the icing on the edge of the plate between houses, hoping nobody noticed the swipe mark left by my finger.

Because I provided a source of income that was necessary both to pay the rent and to feed the constant stream of people who came and went, I felt pressure to sell every day. Each day, both Rafael and Antonia reminded me how important it was that I do my best to sell every slice of cake or every painted rock. Still, I was the little *gringa* or *güera* (the fair-skinned, blonde-haired foreigner) whose heart raced and stomach churned every time she approached a different house.

Every afternoon as I walked the streets, fear consumed me because I was terrified to go home with unsold items, afraid of Antonia and Rafael's disappointment. Sometimes I was late getting home because I'd gotten turned around and lost my way in the dusty Mexican streets, but the adults responsible for me didn't care about my well-being at all. I had heard about American children occasionally being kidnapped in Mexico, and I knew I was at risk being out by myself.

When I wasn't selling our homemade goods, I ran errands. Almost daily, I shopped the outdoor markets and the tortilleria, where the aroma of hot, fresh tortillas made my mouth water as I neared the shop. Shopping got me out of the house without the pressure of selling. I wanted to feel useful and helpful, and enjoyed the rare praise I received.

FOUR

"HURRY UP, ANNA! Your father will be here any minute." Antonia swatted me on the behind with the broom as she herded us kids out of the kitchen. "I need you to collect the clean sheets from the clothesline and take them to Rafael."

My father was coming? I was eager to do anything for the father I only had vague recollections of seeing before. I scurried up the steps to the rooftop clothesline to retrieve the dark blue sheets, which were a little thin but in decent shape overall. The oppressive Mexican heat had barely cooled, though the sun had gone down over an hour before. I decided to surprise Antonia by making the bed in the back bedroom myself. I guessed that this would be where my father would be staying. When I was halfway through, Antonia entered the room.

"What are you doing?" Her screeching voice reverberated off the walls.

"Wh-what do you mean? I'm putting the clean sheets on the bed." I stared at the floor, my cheeks hot with embarrassment.

"Did I tell you to do that?" Antonia stood over me, hands on her hips.

"No."

"That's because I don't want those sheets on the bed. The ones that were on the bed were already clean. Take those darker ones back off, and give them to Rafael. He's going to use them to cover the windows."

"Why do we need to cover the—"

"Anna! Stop asking questions and do as I say. Do you hear me?" With that, Antonia left the room.

I turned back toward the bed and began stripping off the sheets, still not understanding why the windows needed to be covered.

Since my father rarely came to any house where my immediate family lived, having him visit was a special treat. Rafael took my siblings and me aside to remind us to always refer to our father as *Tío* (uncle), if anyone asked about him. Though I didn't know it at the time, this was for my dad's protection. He and his followers didn't want to take the chance of him being recognized, since the police and FBI were always looking for him.

Excitement filled the house, as everyone anticipated a visit from our religious leader. We knew he was a very important man, with a growing flock of followers to consider. As a prophet called by God to lead his people, he constantly traveled to the various places his members and wives resided. None of my father's wives or children were permitted to question the critical and secretive nature of his work or the spiritual call of God on his life. Still, every one of his visits energized each household as they prepared for his arrival. Antonia took care to make special foods, as Rafael took the sheets I gave him and hung them over the windows to hide my father's presence from outsiders.

My father! I trembled with anticipation. Though I may have been around him at other times when I was younger or he might have slept in a house where I happened to live at the time, I couldn't recall interacting with him at all, not even to greet him.

What would he be like? Would he play with me? Would he even know who I was?

I did my best to stay awake, but I was fast asleep by the time he arrived. The next morning I woke up to the wonderful smell of fried steak and potatoes. I tiptoed to his bedroom, and peeking around the doorway, watched him eating breakfast at the writing desk in his room. He looked like a giant with his long arms and his long legs.

Antonia caught me peering at him and grabbed my arm. "Leave him alone and let him eat," she hissed at me in Spanish. "And don't expect to get any of this for breakfast." I followed her to the kitchen and ate my refried beans wrapped in a tortilla.

Still, I soaked him up during his visit. I studied him—what he looked like, what he sounded like. It struck me that he was so tall that he had to duck his head to walk through a doorway.

One afternoon, I tiptoed into the room where he sat writing at a desk. I imagined he was busy drafting a sermon or a long letter to his congregants in the United States. I climbed up on the bed and sat watching him until late into the night. He never once acknowledged my presence. I knew I had to stay quiet so as not to be shooed out. He was handsome and had a deep, booming voice. His receding hairline left him with a significant forehead. His eyes were dark, and his brow was usually furrowed. He wore a size 13 shoe, proportionate to his 6'4" height.

He spent most of his time either writing, reading his sermons out loud, or sitting still—deep in thought. I recall the studious way he hunched over the desk while he feverishly wrote in longhand, filling page after page of yellow legal pads. His words flowed continuously, and I could hear the pages turning at a regular pace as he filled each one. Those pages would be taken by one of his wives and typed out. The faster the typist you were, the more he liked having you around to transcribe his poor handwriting into readable pages.

Eventually, my tired body and heavy eyelids took over, and I fell asleep on the bed that on other occasions I wasn't allowed to sleep on. I slept soundly in the comfort of the coveted bed. At some point during the darkness of night, I felt someone gently shaking my foot. It took several moments for me to fully awaken. And when I saw my father there, looking down at me, I could hardly believe my eyes.

"Do you know how to make coffee?" he asked.

"Yes," I said. I had never made coffee in my life. But my father had just spoken to me for the first time. I would do anything he asked.

"Would you mind making me some?" His eyes crinkled at the corners as he smiled warmly at me. When he relaxed his cheeks once again, I could see lines of white on his tanned face. He looked so strong and regal and important. I was in awe of him. Being sent on this important mission felt like quite the honor. I knew I couldn't let him down. I felt chosen and special to be able to serve him in this way.

"Sure." I hurried to the kitchen to do his bidding. I stood in front of the stove and bit my lip. I'd watched others make coffee numerous times, so I imitated what they had done. I boiled a pot of water and added several teaspoons of Nescafé, the Mexican brand of instant coffee. Once the air filled with the aroma of coffee, I figured it must be done.

I stood on a wooden stool to retrieve from an upper shelf a *jarrito*, a little Mexican clay cup with a handle. I tried my best not to spill the steaming liquid as I carefully poured it from the scalding pan. I proudly carried it back to my father, who still sat at the desk consumed by his work. I placed the coffee next to his right hand and waited. After a few moments, he picked up the jarrito and took a sip. He didn't rave about my coffee-making skills, but he didn't complain, either, so I hoped I had done reasonably well.

I crawled back under the worn blanket on the bed in that room and watched him write until I fell asleep again. Several times during the night, he roused me to ask me to make him more coffee, which I gladly did. Though we spoke fewer than twenty words to one another, I'd never felt closer to my father, nor more needed as a daughter, as a person. Knowing I played a critical role in helping my father accomplish his important work gave me such a sense of belonging and fulfillment. Plus, I got to sleep in a real bed, not the chunk of foam on the floor.

The next morning, he woke me at daybreak and asked me to make more coffee. I went to the kitchen, where Rafael and Antonia were sitting at the table. Rafael glanced at me. "I hope you know how blessed you are, Anna. You are one of the celestial children. You are born of the prophet Ervil LeBaron. He is a great man who hears directly from God. I hope you appreciate that blessing and call on your life."

I believed his words wholeheartedly. We had been taught all our lives how special we were to be Ervil's children, to come from such a godlike man. I nodded slowly, then turned to make the coffee.

But all the while, I pondered what Rafael had said. Was I really blessed? I lived in a strange country without my mother, and with a father who acknowledged my existence only when he asked me to do his bidding.

Right now, a true blessing would be to have some of the steak and potatoes prepared for my father's dinner, instead of the beans and mush that my siblings and I had day in and day out. It was the first time I had ever questioned whether the "blessing" of serving my father was truly enough. It felt like blasphemy, and I could hardly admit it even to myself.

Later that morning, Dad came into the kitchen where Celia, Hyrum, and I sat with Antonia's kids. A few days earlier, Celia had been sent from Calería to live with us. We ate the *atole* (hot liquid cereal) Antonia made for breakfast. As we finished, he leaned over the table and looked directly at me. "Anna, how would you like to go with me on a mission trip?"

"I'd like to." I felt important and noticed. I paused and bit my lower lip as I pondered whether to ask him a question. "But what's a mission trip?"

His laughter rang out and filled the tiny kitchen. "It's where we teach the gospel to the Lamanites, so they can go to the celestial level of heaven, instead of being stuck on the telestial level in the afterlife. It's our duty to go and tell them."

A cold, hard stare had taken over the laughter and crinkled eyes. "Go get ready. We need to leave in a few minutes." And just like that, his laughter pealed once more.

Celia helped me brush some of the tangles out of my long, unruly blonde hair. Then she helped me braid my hair into two long plaits. "Want to see?" She carried the wooden stool from the kitchen into the bathroom so I would be tall enough to see my reflection in the dingy mirror. I turned left, then right. "Wow, I love it. Thanks!" I hugged my older sister before I changed into my best outfit—in truth, my only other outfit—a skirt with an elastic waistband and a matching blouse with a print of brightly colored flowers. I hurried back to the kitchen, so as not to keep my father waiting.

"Anna!" Celia hollered from the bedroom.

I returned quickly. "What?"

Celia held up my *chanclas* (flip-flops).

"Oops." I quickly slipped them onto my feet.

My sweet sister hugged me and whispered, "Have a fun day preaching."

"What's preaching?"

"You'll find out."

I padded back to the kitchen, eager to spend the day with my father. When I got there, he was already gone. "Where is he?" I asked Antonia, who banged pots and pans around loudly, probably irritated that she'd had to dirty so many to make us breakfast.

"He went to the car. Hurry!" She swatted at the back of my thighs with a dish towel.

I jumped out of the way and hurried out the front door to find my father in the driver's seat and Rena, the youngest of my dad's thirteen wives, sitting on the passenger side of the front seat in his long, beige Lincoln Continental. I hadn't realized we would have company with us. Still, I'd never had the opportunity to spend this much time with my dad. I needed to take advantage of it. I opened the back passenger door and crawled inside to sit behind Rena. Without a word, Dad started the engine and headed toward the highway. Soon after, the skies opened and started pouring rain.

Rena remained quiet during the drive, except when Dad asked her a question. I didn't want to be a nuisance, so I didn't speak either. Dad droned on and on, but most of his religious talk and words were way above my understanding. After all, he needed to prepare to preach or whatever God had called him to do that day. We finally pulled off the main highway into a village with one main street and smaller dirt roads crossing it. Dad parked on the main road. "We'll have to walk from here. It's too muddy to drive the car; we might get stuck."

We walked down one of the dirt roads lined with small huts on either side. I tried to avoid stepping in puddles or mud, but the rain was really coming down, and I had a difficult time keeping up in my chanclas. Dad stopped in front of one hut that had only plywood for walls. He went into it, and Rena and I followed. We spent what seemed like hours in that house. I tried to sit still on the end of an old couch as I listened to Dad drone on and on in Spanish about "the civil law of God," or whatever he was preaching about to this poor, captive audience. I slowly realized that going on a mission trip was not the glamorous event I'd imagined. But I did get to spend the day with my father and Rena—away from Antonia and her resentful glares. And I didn't have to clean or sell anything that entire day. However boring, it offered a welcome respite.

Without warning, Dad finished talking. When he bowed his head, so did everyone else in the room. I bowed mine, too, though I couldn't help but squint my eyes and take in the scene. Dad's bushy eyebrows worked up and down as he practically preached another sermon during that long prayer. Finally he stood, shook hands with all of the adults in the room, and we left.

I felt so thankful to be out of that house and away from the boredom of listening to the adults. The rain had stopped, and the air smelled of damp earth. I breathed in deeply and closed my eyes for an instant. We headed back down the narrow road on the long walk back to the main street where Dad had parked the Lincoln.

I ran ahead to climb in.

"Anna, stop!" My dad's voice boomed as loud as thunder behind me.

I did as he said. In fact, I stood so still I began to shake, though I don't know if that was from fear, from holding my body rigid, or from the chill of being damp. He reached my side in seconds and grasped my shoulder, none too gently. "What have you done?"

What had I done? Whatever it was, I hadn't intended to be a nuisance, which I clearly was being.

Rena reached my side, leaned down, and spoke softly. "Anna, you have mud all over you."

I hadn't realized that with every step I took, I had accidentally flipped mud onto the back of my skirt and blouse. By the time we reached the car, my entire backside was covered in mud.

"O-oh no!"

"You're not getting in my car with all that mud on your clothes." Dad spat out the words, then glanced around us for a solution to the problem. "Rena, fix this." And with that, he trod off to a little café on the main road.

"I'm so sorry!" I began to sob.

"Don't cry. We'll wash it off. Don't worry." She handed me a handkerchief, and I dabbed the corner of each eye. Rena dragged me all over that little town until we found a house whose owners allowed us to use a chopped-off piece of rubber hose attached to an outdoor spigot in back. Rena hosed off the mud, but that still left me all wet. I had to turn my blouse and skirt around so I could sit on the driest part of my clothing to avoid ruining the seat of the car. That meant I stared at the wet, mud-stained back of my outfit all the way home. Doing so relieved me somewhat—it seemed like penance for being such a bother. I felt certain my father would never ask me to accompany him on another mission trip.

My father had many meetings during his stay in Catemaco. Couples or burly, rough-looking men came to the house regularly, and Antonia showed them to the bedroom where Dad continued to write at the desk. The rest of us went about life and work as usual, the only real difference being that we saw Dad when he occasionally emerged from the bedroom. But he never acted like Rafael did when he gathered his daughter on his lap, cuddled her, and called her "Rosita," the endearing form of her name. I didn't feel an affinity for my father like I had hoped I would. Yes,

I wanted to please him, but that was more out of a need for self-preservation than anything else. Plus, he had far more important work to do—writing sermons and keeping his followers in line.

One day Antonia caught me listening at the bedroom door where my father was conducting a meeting. "Anna? Don't you have work to do? I guess you must have already finished your chores if you have time to stand around waiting for your father and eavesdropping on his meetings. For shame! If you don't have enough to keep you busy, I can come up with additional chores for you. Come with me."

I mumbled an apology and followed her to the kitchen. She opened the small window, and a light breeze greeted us. I wondered why we didn't keep the window open all day. She handed me a can of evaporated milk and asked me to open it.

"Yes, Antonia." Since we didn't have a can opener, I dragged the step stool in front of the refrigerator, where she kept the hammer we used, along with a knife, to open cans. I grabbed the hammer from the top of the fridge and pulled it toward me. When I did, the claw of the hammer hooked on a bit of a broken plate sitting on top of the fridge. As the dish fell, it slashed the side of my left calf. Blood gushed down my leg, then my ankle, and onto the stool.

I stepped off the stool immediately, grabbed a rag off of the counter, and tried to stop the bleeding. Though I knew she'd be furious with me, I finally called out, "Antonia, I'm hurt, and I need your help."

Antonia washed the blood from the rag and held it to the cut once more. I hopped on one foot to a chair at the dining table, and Antonia pulled another chair close enough for me to prop up my hurt leg. She leaned over and examined the wound. "It's pretty deep. Stay here."

Moments later, Rafael returned with her to take a look at the cut and offer his opinion. Between them, they decided I needed only a "butterfly" bandage. Antonia cut an adhesive strip, shaping it into a butterfly shape, and placed it over the wound. Based on the depth and length of the gash, even I knew I needed stitches. I didn't see how such a small bandage would be able to hold the two pieces of skin together, especially on this moving part of my body. But taking me to the doctor was not an option. That cost money and took time we didn't have. I would just have to hope for the best.

Later that afternoon, Antonia approached me as I sat at the kitchen table copying from my book, my leg throbbing from the pain of the gash. "Anna, here are a few pesos." She opened her hand to show me the coins. "I need you to run to the pharmacy."

I lifted my face toward hers and beamed. Antonia understood. She acknowledged my pain and the fact that I needed medicine so the cut wouldn't get infected. They still weren't sending me to the doctor to get stitches, but this simple acknowledgment meant so much to me. She must actually care about my welfare.

"Anna, are you listening to me? I need you to go pick up some aspirin. Your father has a terrible headache. He's been writing all day, and he can hardly see straight because of the pain. You need to hurry. Can you do that?"

"What?" I stared at her in disbelief. I slowly came to realize that neither she nor anyone else in that house cared about the gash on my leg. She had already forgotten about my gaping wound, further confirming that my needs were unimportant and not likely to be acknowledged.

"Anna!" Antonia pressed the pesos into my hand. "Run! Run fast, and bring back the medicine for your dad!" I heard the urgency in the sound of her voice.

I limped down the concrete steps from our second-floor

apartment and down to the dirty street that kicked up dust into my open wound, past the houses where I'd pounded on doors day after day trying to sell painted rocks and slices of cake. My mind raced. I had a gash on my leg the size of a stick of gum, with nothing but a tiny strip holding the two pieces of flesh together.

Antonia's words echoed in my brain, "Run fast, and bring back the medicine for your dad!" Did my dad know that Antonia would send me to the store to get something for his headache? Did he even know my leg had a gaping wound that was getting dirtier by the minute? If he knew, he must not care. I couldn't be very important to him. And after listening to Rafael go on about my father's greatness, I knew I existed only for the greater good of the kingdom of the prophet Ervil LeBaron. Still, that thought was more tolerable than believing I was only a nuisance and a bother.

FIVE

MORNING DAWNED with the promise of another scorching hot day, offering no relief from the oppressive trifecta of Mexican heat, sun, and humidity. The air was stifling, limiting our breath and energy. Still, chores beckoned. We couldn't wait for pleasant temperatures or a cloudy day to work.

Antonia ordered us to help her clean house, which we did, no questions asked, no complaints issued. We kids knew better than to voice dissatisfaction with any of the adults in our lives—or with any circumstances in our lives, for that matter. God had granted us what we were supposed to have. We couldn't argue with our lot in life.

I squeezed water out of an old rag and began wiping down the kitchen table and chairs. Out of the corner of my eye, I watched as Antonia picked up the thick slabs of yellow foam the children used as bedding. One by one, she shook them to remove the dust. As she shook the pallet I slept on, some dirt fell to the floor.

Antonia gasped—not a surprised, spontaneous utterance, but a calculated, overly dramatic response intended to garner attention and show her utter disgust. In a loud voice, she proclaimed for everyone in the house to hear, *"¡Mira qué cochina es Anna! ¡Ni si quiera quita la tierra de su cama antes de dormirse!"* ("Look what a pig Anna is! She doesn't even remove the dirt from her bed before sleeping in it!") Then she burst into cackling laughter as she continued to scrutinize my little sponge "bed."

Shame flooded me. I felt blood rushing to my cheeks, and I instinctively covered them with both hands. I wished I could run and hide, perhaps joining the disabled man next door so we could compare our inadequacies. I didn't realize I was dirty, but of course I was. I spent the greater part of the day on the dusty Mexican streets, trying desperately to sell homemade items. Though lush greenery grew wild in the tropical humidity, the poverty-stricken area we lived in had little grass or foliage at all.

Most of the roads I walked were nothing more than dirt and dust that would cling to me and my clothes as I got into bed at night. But Antonia had no compassion for a little girl sent to live far away from her mother. She didn't quietly show me the dirt and offer to teach me how to shake the foam clean each morning or evening. She didn't unobtrusively brush off the dust, allowing me to keep my dignity.

x x x x x

My one prized possession that I had managed to hold on to through all of our moves was an Indian-looking leather purse that Teresa and Yolanda, both sister-wives of my mother, had given me for my ninth birthday. I didn't care that they'd spent only a few pennies on it at a flea market. The purse was the one thing I owned that had value to me.

One day, Antonia asked to borrow the purse. She never returned it. I longed to ask her to give me back my purse, but I didn't dare. I felt like I had no right to do so. After all, I played Cinderella to her Stepmother. Whether she eventually gave it to Rosa or tossed it in the trash, I'll never know. I just remember feeling that she had taken from me the only pretty thing I possessed.

The weeks went by with the same routine. Then one day I had a fortunate turn of events. The wealthy woman who answered the first door I knocked on took pity on me and bought the entire cake. She told me it would be her family's dessert that night. I couldn't imagine a meal that was followed by dessert. We rarely had anything to eat other than beans and tortillas, sometimes with Spanish rice, at every meal.

I skipped back to the apartment, cheerful for the first time in days, as I imagined the praise I would receive for my quick work. I climbed the stairs, entered the apartment, and noticed that the house seemed far too quiet. *Where was everyone?* I walked in, dug the change out of the pocket of my polyester skirt, and plopped it on the rickety kitchen table.

"You're home early."

I turned, surprised to see Rafael standing there with an odd look on his face, like he was hungry.

"A woman bought my whole cake today." I beamed at him as I showed him the pile of pesos on the table.

He quickly crossed the floor toward me and petted my hair. "You're a good girl, *Anita* ("Little Anna"). You know how to get into people's hearts, don't you?" He twirled several strands of my long, blonde hair in his slender fingers.

"I, well, I guess I'd better go clean up and start warming up the beans."

"What's the rush? Antonia and the kids won't be home for a while. They went shopping at the *mercado* (open-air market). Come, let's sit and talk."

An intense heat spread up my neck to my cheeks until they felt ablaze. I hoped Rafael wouldn't notice.

"Ah, you like that idea." He grabbed me by the hand, his thin, clammy hand swallowing my tiny fingers. "Come with me."

"I can't. I have work to finish before Antonia gets home." I tried to pull my hand out of his, but his grip held me tightly. Instead, I stumbled along behind him as he led me to the bedroom and then toward the large bed he shared with Antonia. The tattered bedspread was faded and threadbare.

"Antonia's not here. I'm the boss now, and I'm saying you don't have to work right now. I want you to sit and rest for a while." He picked me up and plopped me on the bed beside him. My feet didn't reach the floor, so my legs just dangled over the edge.

I scooted to the far end of the bed, but he quickly shortened the distance between us by moving to the middle. My instincts told me to run, but I feared what this forceful man might do to me if I did. I didn't dare defy him. I knew better than to refuse a direct command. Deep in my gut a burning and churning commenced, like it had the first few times police had raided one of our homes. Something was off, something had interrupted the norm, and I felt powerless to do anything to stop it. I just wanted to get out of that room and as far away from him as possible. *Where is everybody?* I thought.

"Such a beautiful girl." Again, he reached over and touched strands of my hair and allowed them to slide slowly through his fingers.

I pushed his hand away, but he wasn't easily deterred. He moved closer to me. Without warning, Rafael placed his hand on my thigh. His breathing got heavier, and his voice lowered as he spoke. Frozen by fear, I gave only short, cursory replies. My body stiffened, and the blood from my beating heart pounded between my ears.

"Let's talk about love," he said.

He leaned in close to me until his mouth was mere inches from my own and I nearly gagged on his rancid breath. I turned my face from his. I closed my eyes tight, and willed him away with every fiber of my being. I wanted to run away from him, but my body remained frozen. I could scarcely breathe. "I-I don't want to talk about love."

"But you're so beautiful. Someday you'll be my wife. Your dad told me so."

His wife?

My stomach churned as his words sunk in. I had never imagined becoming *anyone's* wife. My days were spent trying to scrounge enough to eat, to help care for my siblings, to serve the kingdom. I had never truly had a childhood! And now, it seemed, I would have no future because my father had promised to give me away to this man. To Ervil LeBaron, a daughter was a commodity to be bought and sold. I wasn't worth even being told about his plan.

I mustered my strength and courage—from where, I don't know—quickly ducked under his outstretched arm, jumped off the bed, and fled out the apartment door, preferring the streets of Catemaco over being alone with Rafael.

After that horrible encounter, whenever the two of us were alone, Rafael started in again. He never forced me. Instead, it seemed he was genuinely trying to woo me by rubbing my back and shoulders or stroking my hair. He believed his touch and whispered affirmations would draw me to him.

Rafael wasn't my only "suitor." In the months that followed, more of my dad's followers began to casually—and routinely—approach me about becoming one of their wives. Once I began to realize that these grown men only initiated advances to me when Antonia wasn't home, I did my best to avoid being at the apartment alone. As a young girl, having my dad's followers casually

and routinely approach me about being one of their wives confused me. Still, I knew deep inside I would someday have to marry
one of them, thus fulfilling my duty to my polygamist father.

The women in our family were never allowed to make up their
own minds. The girls had even less freedom. We were commodi-
ties; others ascertained our value and traded us at their discretion.
I was too young to understand the leering, touching, and sexually
motivated overtures. I just knew how inappropriate the situations
felt and how uncomfortable they made me. Sadly, I couldn't get
away from that place. And I had no dad or mom to protect me.

SIX

MY DEEP SLEEP WAS INTERRUPTED by a repeated jostling on my arm. "Who's that—what?" I blinked, trying to adjust my eyes to the morning sunshine streaming through the front windows of Rafael and Antonia's apartment.

"Get up." Antonia always sounded sharp and annoyed, and this time even more so.

I tossed back the thin sheet and sat up on my little foam pallet. "Yes, Antonia. What's happening?"

"You're going to Calería. They want you there. The bus leaves in an hour, so you'll need to hurry."

"Okay." I stood up and padded off to the bathroom. I tried to run a comb through my tangled hair, but gave up as it snagged on several matted sections. When I returned to the kitchen, Antonia was standing at the small cooktop making mush for the family. She turned around and glared at me, not offering me a bowl of mush. I wondered what I'd done. It seemed awfully early in the day for me to have gotten into trouble.

"Here are five pesos. Don't lose them. You need to go—now."

"I—you're not taking me?" I stared at her in utter amazement, terrified at the thought of making this journey all by myself.

Suddenly the idea of missing breakfast paled in comparison to traveling on a bus by myself to another town. I'd been to the house in Calería before, but I had never traveled there all alone, and the idea of boarding a bus with total strangers frightened me.

I hated knocking on the doors of houses where people I didn't know lived and trying to entice them to buy the cakes and other items we made, but at least in that situation, I had the advantage of talking with just one person.

What if someone on the bus took a liking to the little blonde American girl and snatched me? I'd heard stories of American tourists disappearing during Mexican vacations. "I don't know if I can do that by myself."

"You can, and you will. I don't have time for this today."

I knew that what she really meant was that she didn't have time for me today. She never had time for me. My heart ached for my mother, for her warm embrace and gentle voice. I missed her so much and wondered when she would come to Mexico to get me. I looked up to see Antonia staring at me, her eyes narrowing.

"Yes, Antonia. I can do this."

Once I left the oppressive house, I tried to embrace a sense of excitement about the day ahead. Something rose up inside of me, and in my mind's eye I could see myself traveling alone, making this trip without any problem. I didn't have to stay home and clean house under Antonia's critical and disapproving eye. I didn't have to sell cakes door to door. I didn't have to wash clothes until my arms ached. Instead, I got to embark on an adventure that most kids would only dream of. The gash in my leg had healed, so after I left Antonia's house, I skipped much of the way to the bus station, slowing to a walk when my calves started to cramp up.

I drew upon my previous experience traveling by bus with others. I boarded the bus and put my pesos in the square metal can under the watchful eye of the leathery-faced driver. I grinned at him to show him I wasn't afraid, that I was starting my adventure. He smiled back, revealing stained teeth. I found a seat, where I sat up perfectly straight and stared out the window.

The trip felt like it took a long time, when in fact it probably took less than thirty minutes. The bus jerked to a stop in front of a large broken-down building with cracked plaster walls. The driver called out, "Calería!" I stood and exited, along with other passengers. Though I scanned the crowd, I didn't see a single face I knew among the few people waiting at the station.

My fear of being among strangers in a foreign country threatened to override my sense of adventure, but I looked one direction, then the other, and started walking down the main road in the direction of *el centro* (the town square). After walking about a kilometer, I arrived at the center of town, which had a roundabout marked by a wooden gazebo, its paint peeling off. Vendors with small carts milled about. Some had long lines of customers, but I had no more money for tacos or *paletas* (popsicles).

Instinctively, I turned to the right. I recognized the street where I needed to turn. On the corner was a little store that sold necessities and treats like bottled Coca-Cola and other indulgences we never got. I remembered buying toilet paper there one day.

I continued down that street and arrived at the concrete house where I had stayed once before. Though it was one of the nicest and cleanest on the block, it still had cement floors and rats that would come out at night, scurrying the length of the ledge at the top of the wall. The wall did not go completely up to the ceiling; instead, there was a narrow space for ventilation between the wall and the roof. I opened the door and called out, *"Hola . . ."*

A woman I recognized as Teresa's and Yolanda's mother came from the kitchen into the tiny front room. She wore a long skirt and a white, long-sleeved button-down shirt, buttoned all the way to the top of her neck.

"Anna? What are you doing here?"

"Antonia sent me. She told me to come here."

"No, no, no." She rattled off a long rant in Spanish about how Antonia didn't know what she was doing and how much of a burden it was to have to handle so many children. "You have to go back to Catemaco. Right away." She took some pesos from the center pocket of her dark skirt. "Here. Now go right back and wait for the next bus."

Though utterly confused, I didn't think it was my place to question her authority, so I did as I was told and walked the kilometer back to the bus stop I'd just left. I waited for another bus to take me back to Catemaco. By now, the sun blazed down on me, my tummy growled, and I couldn't stop licking my lips because they were so dry. *Why didn't I get something to drink while I was in Calería?* Thankfully, the bus arrived soon, and I again found a seat—and shade from the noonday sun. I smiled and tried to find adventure in going back. Once the bus arrived back in Catemaco, I disembarked and headed for the apartment of Rafael and Antonia.

I opened the door only to hear Antonia shout, "What are you doing back here? Did you not understand me when I sent you to Calería? Where are the pesos I gave you?" implying that I had spent them on myself.

"May I please get a drink of water? Then I'll tell you the whole story." By that time, Rafael, Gabriel, and Hyrum had joined us in the tiny kitchen. I felt more gawked at than I had been on the bus. I shared my tale and then cowered as I waited for the anger to erupt from Antonia's lips. But though I could see that she and her husband were highly annoyed, they didn't direct their anger toward me. Instead, Rafael and Antonia talked about the crazy lady in Calería who had sent home the little girl who'd only just arrived.

This time, Rafael handed me pesos for yet another bus ride. He squatted down in front of me, his breath hot on my face as he sternly said, "Go to Calería and stay there. Do not come back to Catemaco, no matter what they tell you. Do you understand?"

I gulped and nodded, not trusting my voice to answer him aloud.

Any remaining sense of adventure had left, any enthusiasm vanished, any joy about my day dried up like the hot, Mexican sun. I trudged back to the bus stop and waited for the next bus to Calería. The bus was much more crowded this time. I joined workers on the way to their menial jobs and had no choice but to stand for the entire trip. My legs ached, and I felt weak from hunger.

Once I arrived back in Calería, I returned to the concrete house and experienced the same surprise and annoyance that Rafael and Antonia had greeted me with in Catemaco. I waited for the adults to stop talking—and shouting—to explain myself. "Rafael said, 'Go to Calería, and stay there.'"

Ultimately, they agreed to let me stay, for which I felt grateful. I don't think I could have faced another bus ride. No one ever explained their reasoning to me, so I never found out why they had shuffled me back and forth from Calería to Catemaco over that long, hot day. But the experience helped me understand my worth—or lack thereof—to all the adults around me.

I felt unloved and unwanted, a little girl who was nothing more than a nuisance. With no father or mother around to protect me or see to my needs, I felt like I didn't belong anywhere, especially where I ended up that day. I hadn't eaten anything the whole time, during any of the bus rides or the short stops before being turned around. I was starving. But that physical hunger paled in comparison to my hunger for someone—anyone—to care for me and want me.

x x x x x

In Calería, the adults sent me to the little store nearby on a regular basis. At the time, I thought they trusted me to do a good job, when in actuality they couldn't risk being seen in public for fear of the authorities tracking them to my father and other outlaws in our group.

Being light-skinned, fair-haired Americans, we really stood out. Mexican residents always noticed our comings and goings because of that. Plus, our neighbors must have thought it strange that we had so many people crammed into two houses next door to each other. Rena and her family lived next door to Lorna, another of my father's wives.

On one of my shopping trips to the little corner store, the teenage daughter of the store owner showed a special interest in me. She was so pretty with her long, brown hair, and she seemed so *normal.* I had quietly observed her going to school on the city bus carrying her books in her leather *mochila* and envied her life I could only dream about.

In Spanish, she eagerly greeted me when I entered the store. "Well, look here, it's little Anna. How are you today?" She grinned and waved.

I told her I was fine and headed for the aisle with coffee.

"Wait, come talk to me."

I eyed her suspiciously and stayed rooted in place.

"Silly girl. I'm not going to hurt you. Come on. I'll give you a free Coke." She held a glass bottle of soda, something I'd had so rarely that I could count the times on one hand. I couldn't resist.

I hurried behind the counter, and she picked me up and placed me next to the cash register. "So, tell me about your family."

I took several gulps of the glorious liquid and enjoyed the fizzy bubbles. My delay tactic gave me time to think. I knew better than to answer her questions, and I deflected them with short, abrupt answers.

My heart raced and my face flushed. "What do you mean?"

"Where are your mom and dad?"

"I don't know," I said truthfully.

"What is your dad's name?"

"I don't know," I lied.

Thankfully, she stopped questioning me.

Mom would be so proud of me. The girl's gift of a Coke to bribe me into revealing family secrets had been wasted.

It was the first time I recall lying to avoid someone finding out about our family. But doing so became easier as time went on.

SEVEN

I LISTENED TO RENA'S SOFT ALTO VOICE float a melody through the tiny house in Calería. I was lying on a thin mattress on the floor, with no pillow, staring up at the underside of the metal roof and trying to imagine happier times and places, such as when I was with my mom. *Why did we have to be apart?* Rena finished singing "Oh, You Can't Get to Heaven" in hushed tones. Then, in a voice barely above a whisper, she told us the story of attending high school in the United States. For a few brief moments, I imagined a world far from my own living nightmare.

The days here weren't any different than they were in Catemaco. I earned money to buy food for the family by selling cake slices, and I scrubbed clothes on an old-fashioned washboard, hanging them on the clothesline out back to dry. At any given time, we might have anywhere from nine to twenty of my father's followers and children living under the same roof. That many people produced tons of dirty clothes.

"Good night, kids." Rena slowly got up off the floor where she had been sitting, leaning against the concrete wall. I could hear fatigue in her grunts.

In my heart, I willed her to stay, hoping against hope that

she wouldn't leave us alone. But she undoubtedly had work to finish—laundry, perhaps, for her own two children and the rest of us who lived there. I sighed quietly as she left, taking with her every trace of safety and protection. I feared the night even more than the day.

After the lights went out, I covered my entire body, even my face, with the threadbare sheet I had been given. Though I couldn't get comfortable on the thin mattress, that wasn't what was causing my uneasiness. I couldn't put it into words other than a growing fear of the unknown that weighed heavily on me. *What was going to happen to me and the people I loved?* This uneasiness accompanied my fear of what I knew would happen during the night ahead, and it pressed on my chest like one of the cinder blocks from the walls.

Within minutes, I could hear them. I peeked out from under the sheet and saw giant rats scurrying along the top of the wall below the thin metal roof above us. They were beginning their nocturnal habit of scavenging for any errant morsel they could find. The rats had easy access from the outside to the inside through the ventilation gap at the top of the concrete wall. I plugged my ears, a feeble attempt to drown out the clickety-click of their tiny toenails on the cement overhead.

"Are you asleep?" I whispered to my little brother, Hyrum, lying closest to me.

No response.

I knew I couldn't handle the terror of the night alone, so I crawled stealthily to a mattress fifteen feet away where Celia was also wide awake. "Can I sleep with you tonight?" I asked, knowing full well neither of us would actually experience restful slumber. She didn't answer, but pulled back her sheet and scooted over to make room for me on her mattress.

We lay quietly for a few moments, and then I whispered, "I hear the rats."

"I know. Me too."

"I'm afraid one's going to fall off the ledge and land on me."

Celia snuggled close and said, "I'll protect you."

I nuzzled my face into her neck and felt her warm breath. I cuddled closer to her and stroked her long, blonde hair, a simple act that calmed me. Oddly, I felt something hard.

"You have a knot or something in your hair," I whispered.

Celia brushed her long, blonde hair daily until it felt silky smooth, so I was surprised to feel a knot. I sat up and tried to see what it was in the dim light.

Suddenly the "knot" moved, burrowing half an inch into her locks. I shivered—the "knot" was alive—and then I screamed, a deep shriek of both shock and terror. "It's a beetle!"

Mexican beetles aren't like the tiny June bugs or beetles we typically see in the United States. These beetles could be as large as a walnut.

Celia bolted upright, her muffled screams joining mine. I tried to part her hair and find the beetle that had nestled closer to her scalp, but it was difficult in the dark.

As I watched helplessly, Celia frantically dug her fingers into her mass of hair. I felt a cold shiver start in my spine and tingle all the way to my neck and down to my fingers, almost as if the beetle were crawling on me. Finally, I saw something catapult through the air over the two mattresses where Hyrum and others were still asleep, bounce off the wall, and fall back onto the floor. It lay still for a few seconds—stunned or perhaps just getting its bearings— and then the giant black beetle scurried off to softer, friendlier surroundings. Probably another mattress. Or worse, the hair of another of my sleeping siblings.

Celia whimpered uncontrollably, and I did my best to soothe her. "Here, let's lie back down under the covers." The threadbare sheet was a poor barrier between us and the beetles and the rats, but it helped with mosquitoes. It was certainly better than nothing.

A few minutes later, I felt another beetle land—hard—on top of the sheet near my stomach. It began to crawl slowly toward my head. This time I was prepared. I flicked the sheet underneath the beetle's body, but it didn't budge. I hated to move my hand or any part of my body out from under the sheet because I feared other beetles would scurry into my safe cocoon. But I had no choice. I poked my arm out from underneath the protection of the sheet, reached on top of the thin fabric, and grabbed the beetle. I could feel its body twitching, which scared me, but I managed to hold on to it and toss the bug as far away as I could.

Celia and I looked at the room full of our siblings, sleeping peacefully. We were both exhausted from battling the beetles. "I don't think I'll be able to go to sleep," I said.

"I know. Me neither," she whispered back. "I'm afraid the sheet will slip off and one of them will crawl under here." She paused, then shuddered. "Or in my mouth."

"We could take turns, like army men on watch." I didn't relish the idea. After all, we both desperately needed sleep with a long workday ahead of us tomorrow.

"Okay, let's do that."

"You go ahead and sleep first." I stroked her hair once more, shivering as my hand passed over the area where I'd felt the beetle only moments ago. Before long, I heard deep breathing and felt her body relax. Thank goodness someone could sleep. I lay listening for scratching sounds, my beetle and rat alarm on high alert. The room stayed blissfully silent, except for the deep breaths around me. I turned over and lay with my back toward Celia.

Suddenly, someone cranked up the music from the cantina down the street. What had been a soothing melody, a mix of voices and guitar, became a noise fest of Mexican *ranchera* music, with the familiar *gritos Mexicanos* (a Mexican shout during a popular song or celebration) that kept me awake. I actually yearned for the long, hot workday, which would be minus the bugs, rats, and raucous music, as I finally fell asleep.

It turns out, I didn't have to endure another night of the pulsing beat. The next day, Rena took her kids along with me and Hyrum back to Catemaco. My dad needed her to type up his lengthy sermon and book notes. Celia had been sent to Mérida to help our older sister Lillian and her husband, Mark, with their small children. Antonia was none too pleased with our intrusion back in her small apartment.

x x x x x

We had been in Catemaco a few weeks when, on Halloween night in 1978, we were awakened in the wee hours of the morning by a sharp and insistent knock at the door. Six-year-old Hyrum, who didn't know any better, groggily got up from his pallet on the living room floor, walked over to the door, and opened it. Suddenly, five or six *federales* (Mexican police) herded him out of the way and filed in, spread out, and began searching every room while we watched in terrified silence. They were carrying automatic weapons, so we didn't dare argue with them. I heard loud and gruff orders directed at the adults, and soon all of them were standing up with their hands in the air.

I had no idea what was happening. Why were they bothering us? The police held up wanted posters with pictures of people I knew—my father, Mark, Rena, Ramona, and others. Despite Antonia's protests, they began removing items from the apartment.

Hyrum and I avoided the men as much as possible and answered with *"Yo no sé"* ("I don't know") whenever they questioned us. We had been well trained to give that response to any and all questions from authorities. I was asked to identify the people on the posters, but I didn't give them any information. Hyrum and I couldn't figure out what was going on or why the officials were looking for people we knew.

Through the slightly open door of the back bedroom, we watched the policemen push Dan Jordan, Ramona's husband, roughly onto a sofa and begin questioning him.

"Are you Ervil LeBaron?" A tall, gaunt officer with a huge mustache stood over him.

Dan hung his head low and mumbled, "Yes."

Why isn't Dan telling the officers his real name? I knew my father was in a back room of the apartment, and I watched the policemen go into his room and come out a few minutes later. Apparently satisfied with Dan's answer, the police arrested him and Rena and led them out of the apartment in handcuffs.

Three of the federales stayed in the apartment for several more hours. None of us were allowed to leave during that time. I could feel their stares as I did my chores. They frequently demanded that I make them coffee or quiet the little children. And I could see Antonia's added stress as she prepared food for them. Naturally, she took out her frustration on Hyrum and me. He and I stayed close to one another, barely speaking about the terrifying events, even after the authorities vacated the ransacked apartment.

The authorities completely missed the fact that Ervil LeBaron had been within their grasp the entire time. Our family called this a miracle of God's protection on my father, since there was no other viable explanation. We all believed he was supernaturally spared from being arrested.

EIGHT

A FEW WEEKS LATER, Gamaliel, the brother of sister-wives Teresa and Yolanda, arrived at the house to take me to Mérida to stay with other relatives for a while. As usual, I didn't protest; I merely gathered my few belongings and put them in a sack. I ran alongside Gamaliel to reach the bus station, desperately trying to keep up with his long strides. He didn't slow down for me at all. When we arrived, he got in line to purchase our tickets while I waited in front of a *carnicería* (butcher shop) across the street.

My mouth watered as I watched several patrons exit the carnicería with brown paper bags filled with *chicharrones* (deep-fried pork rinds). A bacon-like aroma wafted past me each time. I fantasized that a kind Mexican woman might take pity on a little girl with matted blonde hair and offer to share her snack. But none did. My stomach growled so loudly that I quickly crossed both arms over my tummy to quiet it.

I spotted Gamaliel waving at me from the bus station and trotted across the street to him. "*Tengo hambre*, Gamaliel." ("I'm hungry.")

"We don't have time to eat, Anna." He grabbed my tiny fist in his large, brown hand and pulled me toward the bus marked

"Mérida, Yucatán." Passengers who were already on the bus had lowered every window. I wondered whether their attempts at lessening the stifling heat had been successful but later discovered they had not. I stumbled alongside Gamaliel, trying to keep my feet underneath me.

We boarded the bus, and Gamaliel handed our tickets to a toothless driver whose long handlebar mustache reminded me of one of the Mexican policemen who had raided Rafael and Antonia's apartment.

"We're lucky we made it." I didn't know whether Gamaliel was speaking to the driver, to me, or to himself, so I kept silent. We walked down the center aisle and looked for an empty seat, but there were none. I was thankful I didn't have to ride on Gamaliel's lap. We passed dozens of people, a complete cross section of Mexican society—men and women, old and young, professionals, farmers, and street vendors—as we made our way to a place where we could stand together.

After several stops where people got off, we managed to find two vacant seats next to each other. Gamaliel pointed out a few landmarks along the way as the bus traveled on the winding highways to Mérida. I was staring out the window, lost in my own thoughts, when suddenly Gamaliel elbowed me in the ribs and pointed at a highway sign to Guatemala. "If you follow that road to Guate*mala*, and then keep going, you'll eventually get to Guate*peor*. Get it? You'll be going from *mala* (bad) to *peor* (worse)."

I gave him a wry smile. Intense fatigue and hunger kept me from humoring his joke any more than that.

"What's wrong, little one?" He lifted my chin with two fingers, so I had to meet his gaze.

"Well . . ."

"Go ahead. What is it?"

"I'm hungry." I looked down at my filthy chanclas, ashamed that I'd given in to complaining. I felt embarrassed for feeling weak and needy, having to beg for something to eat, but the thin, watery oatmeal I drank for breakfast had long since been digested.

"Ah, yes. That makes sense. It is well past lunchtime, and you haven't had anything to eat since early this morning." He stood there and glanced around the bus, seeing a street vendor in the throng of passengers behind us. Gamaliel quickly made his way to the man, bought two apples, and returned to where I was sitting, holding on to the vertical metal poles to steady himself as he walked. The bus bounced in and out of potholes along the highway. "Here you go, Anna."

I could hardly believe my good fortune. I hadn't had an apple—or hardly any fruit—since leaving the United States months earlier. The truth was, my siblings and I were all malnourished, and we'd been battling diarrhea the entire time we'd lived in Mexico. We had no choice but to drink the water, and parasites attacked our unsuspecting systems with a vengeance.

I stared at the delicious fruit, turning it over and over in my hand, before taking a first crunchy bite. The sweet juice trickled down my chin, hands, and even my forearms. Something primal took over, and I closed my eyes and gobbled up the fruity goodness like my life depended on it.

Moments later, I opened my eyes to see a boy watching me from the opposite side of the bus. His loud voice announced to the entire bus, *"¡Miren! ¡Come la manzana como cochina!"* ("Look! She's like a pig with that apple!") The words stung, reminding me how Antonia had used the same description of me.

I stopped eating momentarily and glanced around to see dozens of faces staring back at me—many were laughing. Shame washed over me. Shame that I was looked down upon, even among the poorest citizens of a third-world country. Shame that my desperate hunger drove me to attack food like a wild animal. I wanted to dive under my seat and never come out again. But I couldn't move. And there was no place to hide anyway. So I sat there, flooded with embarrassment, the splotchy redness and heat from my humiliation rising from my chest up my neck and cheeks.

Still, I continued to eat the apple. I felt compelled to finish it because I didn't know when I'd get another chance to eat, or if I'd ever see another apple again. But every bite I swallowed had to work its way around the lump in my throat.

NINE

GAMALIEL AND I FINALLY ARRIVED in Mérida, Yucatán. When I found out that the "other relative" I was going to live with was my oldest half-sister, Ramona, I was thrilled. I got more and more excited as we walked from the bus station to her house.

Just the thought of living with Ramona was like a soothing balm to my raw, vulnerable heart, since I had such a strong, maternal attachment to her from all the time she had spent caring for me from the time I was born. In our large families, the oldest girls often were secondary mother figures to their younger siblings. Ramona had taught me my favorite card games and played endless rounds with me. If she ever grew tired of playing the same games with me over and over, I never knew it, and she probably let me win too many times. I remember the day we were going to Olan Mills for a rare family photo session. Ramona entertained me for hours after my mom bathed me, fixed my hair in loose curls, and dressed me up.

I was glad Ramona wasn't in Catemaco when her husband, Dan, got arrested—a primary reason husbands and wives in our family rarely lived together or stayed in the same place for very long. I didn't know it at the time, but many adult family members, including Ramona, were hiding out in Mexico because they had carried out the orders of my father or were involved in other ways. Some were even awaiting prosecution for murder. But that wasn't the Ramona I knew and loved.

Ramona lived in a small efficiency apartment with her three daughters and cooked on a small propane-powered camping stove. She had no pan to "refry" the beans, so she pureed them in a blender. The final texture was smooth, not like the mashed beans that I was used to eating in Catemaco and Calería. She had to add enough liquid from the boiled beans to allow the blender to work, so they came out runnier than what I was used to. I definitely preferred beans that were refried the traditional way, but I didn't voice any complaints. Living with Ramona was nourishment enough to my heart, so the food I ate didn't matter so much.

On my second day in Mérida, Ramona sent me to the nearby mercado to buy more corn tortillas and beans.

"Anna, I've wrapped these pesos in a handkerchief. Don't take out the money until you need to pay. I don't want you to lose it."

I nodded. I felt confident, having gone to the store dozens of times in Catemaco and Calería.

"Go down the main street until you see the *panadería* (bakery) with a large, pink door. Turn left, and the mercado will be one block down on the right."

I set out for the store feeling lighthearted and enjoying the abundant sunshine. I walked and walked and walked, but I never saw the pink door Ramona had described. After walking what felt like several miles, I came upon a giant grocery store like the ones I remembered seeing in the United States on the rare occasions when we would go inside to shop—much larger, cleaner, better-lit, and more well-stocked than a neighborhood mercado. I knew it wasn't the local, open-air mercado Ramona had described, but

I knew I could find the items I needed there. I searched aisle after aisle and eventually found tortillas and beans.

On the long walk back home, the big bag of dry beans and tortillas, secured within the cloth sack Ramona had given me, banged repeatedly against my leg as I walked. I had to shift the heavy bag from my right hand to my left and back again. By the time I arrived at the apartment, my legs were aching, and my arms felt shaky from the weight of the groceries. She had been worried about me taking so long, but I thought nothing of it.

A couple of days later, Ramona sent me to the store again. This time I noticed a closed door painted bright pink, clearly visible to me for the first time. I turned left and spied the mercado that Ramona had described to me initially—mere blocks from our apartment.

We didn't stay in that apartment long. After dinner one night, my half-sister Lillian and her husband, Mark, came to Ramona's apartment with Celia and Hyrum, who were living with them. They picked us all up and took us to a beach house they had rented for Ramona in Progreso, a port city also in Yucatán. Lillian and Ramona were much older than I was and were close in age to each other. They were friends, having spent time together growing up as step-sisters.

"What's the house like? When will we get there?" Celia and I chattered with excitement. We kids loved being with each other.

Lillian turned around in her seat and flashed a smile at the rest of us jammed into the backseat of the station wagon. "We have a big surprise for Anna too."

I stared at her in stunned silence. I couldn't remember anyone ever giving me a surprise before. "What is it?"

"You get a bedroom all to yourself."

I stared in utter disbelief, unable to speak, as I tried to imagine having a room all to myself. "Really? I can't—I mean, thank you." Celia looked at me, eyes bright with excitement.

Mark pulled into the driveway and parked the station wagon on a large circle made of gravel. He had barely stopped the car before we kids began opening doors and climbing out. I ran past the younger ones into the house and selected the tiny bedroom on the right as my own. I didn't care if I lived in a closet or under the stairs. Here, I was even farther away from Antonia's critical reprimands, the real benefit. A room to myself was icing on the cake.

After I claimed my new room, I ran out onto the back porch. In the moonlight, I could see grassy shrubs, then flat, white beaches beyond. The sound of waves crashing on the shore mesmerized me. I decided to sleep with my window open so I could hear those waves each night as I drifted off. Out of the corner of my eye, I caught a glimpse of something wiggling across the wooden planks. A tarantula! Even though it was huge, I wasn't frightened because we used to hold them when we lived in California, during my toddler and kindergarten years. "Everybody! Come out here and see the tarantula I found," I shouted.

Mark arrived first, peered down, and smashed the creature under his cowboy boots, then kicked it off the edge of the porch just as the others joined us. He leaned over, placed his hands on both knees, and looked each of us kids in the eyes. "That was a scorpion, Anna. They are poisonous, and their sting makes your skin feel like it's on fire. Stay away from them, and never play with them or pick one up."

Suddenly, I wasn't so keen on having my own room. In fact, I didn't sleep in the room I'd claimed "for Anna" mere moments before. Not once. Ramona had a bed and a hammock in her room, and I opted for the hammock. I liked the gentle sway, but mostly

I liked that it was up off the ground, where scorpions couldn't get to me.

Ramona had three children, born one after another, stair-stepped down in age—Heidi, Melissa, and Amanda. Amanda was just a few days old when I came to live with them, and Ramona put me in charge of watching her. I certainly had enough time, since I never went to school during the time I lived in Mexico. I spent hours lying in the hammock, rocking back and forth with Amanda on my chest. I felt quite proud of myself that I could get Amanda to sleep. I felt like such a good mama! I adored Ramona's children and would do anything for them.

Melissa had a book, *The Cat in the Hat Comes Back*, which she carried with her everywhere in that house. I read it to her countless times each day, so often that we both memorized it. I tired of it more quickly than Melissa, but she insisted that I read the entire book, word for word. If I tried to skip ahead to finish the book faster, she protested and turned back the pages. I found it hard to say no to her giant, pleading eyes.

One morning while we prepared breakfast, I mentioned an idea to Ramona. "We should camp out and live on the beach. Wouldn't that be fun?"

"That wouldn't be much fun to me with three little girls who get sand in their eyes, ears, mouth, and hair." She pantomimed a shiver at the thought. "But if we don't sweep the house for a week, the beach will come to us. Then you could get your wish." The wind blew in the sand faster than we could keep it swept up. Ramona patted my head, and then kissed it for good measure.

I laughed, although my longing for the adventure of living on the beach in the salty air never went away.

Mark and Lillian brought their kids, along with Celia and Hyrum, to the beach house almost every weekend. Celia, Hyrum, and I not only played on the beach, but we also explored the entire area. We loved playing hide-and-seek around that house. One of my favorite places to hide was in an old, weathered wooden boat on a dry dock in the front yard. The boat became a playhouse for us. We cleaned it out as best we could and played house in it for hours on end. It certainly wasn't seaworthy, but we loved it.

Coconut trees dotted the lawn. We had fun shaking the trunks because every now and then a coconut broke loose and fell to the ground. One afternoon, I proudly carried one of the larger coconuts into the kitchen to split open and share with everyone. I used a sharp knife to remove the "meat" from the shell of the coconut and accidentally pushed the knife all the way through the thick coconut shell deep into my palm. I screamed as blood began to ooze where I had cleanly sliced my hand. "Ramona, help me!"

Ramona rushed into the kitchen, holding Amanda. When she saw the blood, Ramona handed Amanda to Celia. "Anna, you poor thing."

Not having any proper medical supplies, she washed the wound and wrapped it with a piece of cloth, cuddling me and speaking in soothing tones the entire time. I couldn't help but contrast it to the time I'd cut my leg at Antonia's house, where no one had seemed to care.

After Ramona finished wrapping the cut, she brought the back of my hand to her mouth and kissed it. "Is that better?"

I nodded and leaned into her, where I picked up the comforting smell of sweet breastmilk on her blouse.

"You'll have to hold your hand closed to keep the cut from reopening. Do you think you can do that?"

In spite of the throbbing pain, I smiled up at her. "Yes."

A few weeks later, a scar about the width of the tip of the knife blade that had cut into my hand was all that remained, but

I carried with me the caution of working with sharp objects of any kind.

x x x x x

Not long after my cut healed, Ramona hollered for me from the back of the house. "Anna, come in here, please. I need help getting the girls ready before Mark and Lillian get here."

I hurried to the bedroom to help her finish dressing her girls. We all bubbled with excitement that beautiful morning.

"I was thinking about asking Celia to read *The Cat in the Hat Comes Back* to Melissa for a change," Ramona said as she smoothed the thin blanket on the girls' bed.

Melissa held up the worn book for me to see again.

I laughed to myself as I thought of Celia getting stuck reading it instead of me. I'd make sure that Celia knew that when Melissa said "Be-at," in her little toddler way, what she was really saying was "Read it," which she repeated countless times each day.

"Hyrum and I are going to build a huge sand castle," I told Ramona. I gestured with my hands to show the size of our proposed palace. "We talked about it the last time he was here. I've been collecting sticks and leaves for the princess and her family who will live there."

A little smile tugged at the sides of Ramona's mouth. I imagined she was happy everyone was coming today too. "All done. Thank you, Anna."

I hurried out the front door to wait on the steps that led to the long gravel driveway out to the gate that opened to the street. If Celia didn't arrive soon, I might burst! To my surprise, an orange pickup pulled through the gate. Whoever was driving the vehicle—probably Lorna, my dad's fifth wife—was making her way slowly and cautiously. The truck bounced up and down and back and forth as the driver tried to avoid potholes and larger rocks. Suddenly, before the truck could make it completely up the driveway, the passenger door opened and out jumped my mom from the still-moving vehicle. She ran toward me, her arms outstretched.

I stood rooted to the porch, trembling with the shock of seeing her rushing toward me. I couldn't believe my eyes. No one had told me she was coming. How could they? We had no phone service in the house, and the mail was unreliable and slow. As much as my heart longed for my mom, I certainly hadn't expected she would show up that day, after such a long drought of uncertainty, of not knowing if I'd ever see her again.

I willed my feet to move, which they finally did. I sprinted toward her, and we enveloped one another in a tight embrace that lasted several minutes. My heart couldn't contain the joy, and I began sobbing uncontrollably.

"Mom," I cried, my voice muffled from my face being pressed up against her.

"Anna, let me look at you, honey." She held me at arm's length and surveyed me from head to toe. "Who cut off all of your beautiful hair?" Mom's high-pitched voice as she questioned me let me know she was displeased. Several times, she ran her fingers through the cropped remains of my strawberry-blonde locks.

"Carmen cut it because she said it was always a tangled mess." The memory of the day Carmen, the sister of a recent convert, had butchered my long hair came flooding back. This time it was my mom who burst into tears. We both were crying now, me with my face once again buried in my mom's chest. Mom seemed to mourn the loss of my hair as much as I did.

Eventually, she leaned over and whispered in my ear, "I think you look pretty. You always do."

I felt like my heart would break open into a million pieces. I simply could not process the shock and joy of having my mother's arms around me again. Peace and security flooded my soul and brought me much-needed comfort.

"So take me inside. I hear you have your own room!"

I grabbed her hand in mine and led her toward the house. "Not really, but I do have my own hammock."

Mom gave me a quizzical look.

"It's a long story."

x x x x x

I clung to Mom all weekend, chattering constantly about all the things that had happened to me in Mexico. I asked about my other siblings and the sister-wives who still lived in the United States. Mom and I walked down to the beach together on Saturday morning. I showed her all the good places to find the seashells that weren't broken. I told her how much I missed her, and she told me the same.

"Are you going to stay here with us?"

"I wish I could." Mom leaned over to pick a strand of seaweed off her foot. She tossed it toward the water, but the wind blew it back behind us. She turned toward me. "But I can't. I have to go back to work."

"When?" My body tensed up involuntarily. When she didn't answer me right away, I pleaded with her. "Take me with you, Mom. Please." I put all of my energy into the most pitiful begging face I could muster.

"I can't, honey. Not right now. It's not safe for you in the United States. The reason you were sent here is because your father had a revelation that my children were in danger. He believed all of you would be safer in Mexico. But we will be together again soon."

I slowly closed my eyes and hung my head as I felt the weight of another separation. A part of me couldn't help but wonder if my dad had sent us to Mexico to protect himself.

She lifted my chin. "Anna, I would stay if I could. But I need to do God's work, and so do you. And right now, God needs you to help Ramona take care of her girls. Can you imagine if she didn't have you here? She would never have time to feed and bathe and diaper them all."

"She could manage . . ."

"Maybe so." Mom looked out at the wide expanse of the ocean.

I stared at her face, noticing how drawn and pale her skin looked. If anyone needed to be living on a beach, it was my mom. Suddenly she smiled and the space around her eyes crinkled. She turned her face toward me again.

"And Anna, if you weren't here, who would read *The Cat in the Hat Comes Back* to Melissa?"

We both laughed, deep laughs that expelled worry and uncertainty even better than my tears had. Mom grabbed my hand, and we continued collecting seashells along the beach. I held her hand every moment I wasn't picking up shells.

The weekend passed all too quickly, and I was forced to say good-bye to Mom once again. Though I shed many tears after she left, I knew that seeing her—for however brief a time—had soothed my weary little heart.

TEN

WHILE IN MÉRIDA, Ramona and I lived a façade. Residents of the Mexican coast and tourists to the area considered beach houses as dwelling places for the wealthy. Poor people lived on the other side of the highway—or much further inland. Except for us. I'm sure everyone thought we were rich, simply because we were Americans and because of where we lived. What they didn't know was that we had only the bare essentials to keep body, soul, and spirit together.

Thankfully, we celebrated what we did have—love and affection. Ever since my mom had first left me in Dallas, and then later when I was living with Rafael and Antonia, I'd felt alone. Ramona was like a second mom to me. Her presence, care, and unconditional love were a great comfort to me and helped heal some of my wounds.

But she wasn't perfect. And some of the traits she exhibited impacted me and stuck with me more than I knew. While living with Ramona, I first experienced a "feast or famine" mind-set about dieting. Like women all over the world, Ramona struggled with getting back into shape after having a baby.

Still, she splurged and overate at the most random times. On one occasion, she sent me to the store with twenty pesos. "Buy anything that has chocolate in it, Anna. We will enjoy it together."

I didn't question her directive, mainly because I rarely got to enjoy chocolate in any form. I craved the rare treat as much as Ramona, who never splurged on nonessentials. I crisscrossed the mercado, priced out items, and kept a running total in my head. When I checked out, everything came to just under twenty pesos.

When I got home, I burst through the door, nearly waking Ramona's daughters, who were taking their afternoon naps. "Look at all I bought!" Ramona and I feasted on those chocolates, relishing every single bite with exaggerated moans, finally bursting out laughing. Ramona told me that she was starting a strict diet the next day. It didn't matter to me what she was planning; I was just glad to have the sweet taste of chocolate to savor now.

x x x x

One morning I awoke with a sense of anticipation, though I couldn't pinpoint why. I dressed quickly and hurried to join Ramona and the girls in the tiny kitchen. Right before I entered, I caught a whiff of something wonderful, something I hadn't smelled in a long, long time. I rounded the corner, and there was Ramona, standing beside the kitchen table, with Heidi and Melissa on either side of her. Ramona held a plate in her outstretched hands. On it was a stack of ten pancakes, drizzled in so much homemade syrup that it pooled around the edges of the bottom pancake.

"Happy birthday to you, happy birthday to you. Happy birthday, dear Anna. Happy birthday to you!" Their unison voices stretched out the final lines of the song to make it last as long as possible.

"You're ten!" shouted Heidi. "And Mom made you a pancake cake."

"I know. I can't believe it!"

The girls led me to the kitchen table, where Ramona cut the stack of pancakes in half one way and then the other. She placed one-fourth of the "cake" on each of our plates. While we enjoyed the sweet goodness, the girls peppered me with questions about what I wanted to do on my birthday. Though I was tempted to say that we didn't have money to celebrate in a big way, I said enthusiastically, "After we finish my birthday cake, let's go to the beach. We can look for shells and build a sand castle and maybe take a nap out there. When we get back home, we can play hide-and-seek. Won't that be fun?"

Heidi and Melissa liked my plan, and Ramona worked tirelessly to make it happen. She didn't require any work from me that day, except for helping with her girls, which felt more like play to me.

That night as I lay in the hammock, I reflected on turning ten in Mexico, far from my mother and my home. I didn't have many possessions, but I had many things to be thankful for, such as the love of my sister and her kids. Ramona had sacrificed and planned ahead to pull off a special birthday celebration, despite our poverty. Though I worked hard every day, I didn't live in fear or shame. I didn't worry about some evil person kidnapping me as I trudged from house to house selling painted rocks or cakes. I didn't worry about Rafael's sexual advances and what might lie in my future, such as being married off to one of my dad's followers. I didn't have to put up with Antonia's cruelty. By contrast, Ramona lovingly taught and nurtured me. It had been a good day. I knew this year would bring greater joy.

x x x x x

"Be-at," Melissa said again as she held up a different book, as though she could entice me by suggesting something besides *The Cat in the Hat Comes Back.*

"I will in a few minutes, but I need to finish this first."

Her bottom lip quivered, though I couldn't tell if she felt true sorrow or was working extra hard to manipulate me.

"Here," I pushed a chair away from the table so she could climb onto it. "Want to watch me? I only have one page to go."

"What are you doing?" Heidi asked.

"I'm copying the *Teachings of the Prophet Joseph Smith*."

"What's that?"

"It's a book by Joseph Smith. He was a prophet, just like your grandpa. Joseph Smith led God's chosen people and taught them all about God."

"Why are you copying it?"

I stared at the page, half scribbled with my childish writing. Somehow, despite moving so frequently, I had managed to keep with me my notebook, pen, and the *Teachings of the Prophet Joseph Smith* book I had started copying. Ramona's praise for my work encouraged me to keep doing it regularly and studiously.

"It helps me learn more about God and His kingdom." That answer seemed to satisfy Heidi, and she sat quietly while I continued copying the remainder of that page. But her questions kept replaying in my mind. *Was I doing this to become a better disciple, or was I just craving the praise that I received?*

As if on cue, Ramona entered the kitchen and surveyed the scene. "Ah, I see you're hard at work copying again. Heidi, you can learn a lot from Aunt Anna. She's a good girl; she's working hard for God."

I pressed my lips into a tight smile and tried to block out the conversation while I finished. Finally, I held up my notebook. "All done."

"Let me see." Ramona compared the book to my scribbles. "Very nice. Want me to put these away for you?"

I nodded. Ramona always hid my book, notebook, and pen under her mattress, along with her other Mormon books and my dad's writings. She worried about the landlord stopping in unexpectedly and seeing the religious books and Dad's writings. Sadly, when we eventually moved from the beach house, we forgot to take those items. We were miles from Mérida, being whisked to a safer place, when we realized we had forgotten them. I mourned the loss of those priceless treasures. From time to time, I wondered what the next residents thought when they discovered everything tucked away underneath the mattress.

Living with Ramona and her girls in a safe and loving environment was a gift to me. In addition to her kind words and encouragement, she made me feel like I was needed and contributing to her family by helping in whatever way I could. I took seriously my responsibilities of shopping and running other errands. Each time I ran errands for her, Ramona paid me a single peso. Though not significant in terms of actual money, her gesture meant a lot to me. She recognized and rewarded my hard work. I saved as many of those pesos as I could during the several months I was there, and when Mark told us one weekend that it was time to move again, I realized I had saved up about seventy pesos.

As moving day drew closer, Ramona decided to take everyone shopping. We all dressed up and took the bus to the market in the larger town nearby. I took my pesos with me to buy a hammock. I had enjoyed sleeping in one during my beach stay, and I wanted one to call my own. I carefully compared all the colorful hammocks on display in the market, and a purple hammock with white vertical stripes on each end caught my eye.

"I'd like the purple one, please." I grinned at the vendor.

Ramona stepped up and asked the man, *"¿Cuánto?"* ("How much?")

"Fifty pesos, *señora.*"

I glanced up at Ramona, thankful that my savings would be enough.

Before I could hand him my pesos, Ramona took out her small leather change purse and counted out fifty pesos.

I stared at her, mouth wide open. "But Mona . . ."

"I want to pay for it, Anna. It's the least I can do—for all you've done for me, and especially for my girls, since you moved in with us." She gestured toward the hammock. "Even this is not enough for all the help you've been to me."

The vendor rolled up the hammock and placed it into a cardboard tube for me to carry. I couldn't believe it. Not only did I have the exact hammock I wanted, but I felt like a rich kid with all those pesos still in my pocket. That abundance helped lessen the blow of having to move yet again.

x x x x x

Not too long after our shopping excursion, Hyrum was dropped off at the beach house with his belongings. Lorna showed up again in her orange pickup truck with a camper shell on the back of it. Her children rode up front with her, which meant my brother and I rode in the camper. Most of the sister-wives gave preferential treatment to their own children, understandably so. Lorna was no exception. We traveled like that all the way from Mérida, Yucatán, to Houston, Texas, a three-day journey.

We couldn't open any windows in our enclosure, and the lack of fresh air made it difficult to breathe in the stifling heat. I found it impossible to get comfortable sitting or lying on the uneven bed of the truck. There were a few boxes in the back, along with some large garbage bags filled with everyone's belongings. I wished a thousand times that I had thought to grab a pillow or two to bring along. We leaned up against the garbage bags in an effort to get comfortable.

Several hours into the trip, one of Lorna's kids slid open the tiny glass window between the cab of the pickup and the camper. "We're going to stop soon for a potty break. Make sure Hyrum is awake."

A few minutes later, Lorna pulled to the side of the highway and we all got out. She and Natasha, one of Lorna's daughters who was close to my age, held up ratty towels to give me a little privacy while I peed. Still, I felt extremely exposed as cars sped by. A few drivers honked their horns at us, which made me jump. We took turns holding up towels for each other on the side of the road as one by one we relieved ourselves. After everyone finished, Lorna asked, "Is anybody hungry?"

Our chorus of yeses was loud and unanimous.

"Follow me." She carefully held apart sections of barbed wire for us to climb through, and we made our way to the farm at the side of the highway. We crossed several rows of plants before she knelt down and picked up a watermelon. We all sat in a circle around her as she took a pocketknife and began cutting into the massive fruit. After breaking open the watermelon, she carved off chunks of the red fruit and handed pieces to us. Half starved, we attacked our juicy treat and spit seeds at one another. The juice trickled down my arms and dripped off my elbows into the dirt.

I was grateful when I got to wash my sticky hands and arms at the next gas station restroom, because so much dirt clung to the sticky residue from the watermelon juice. The pit stops to forage for fruit quickly became my favorite part of the long journey.

At night, Lorna pulled off onto a dirt road, and we simply slept wherever we were. Thankfully, Lorna opened the back of the camper. Though we didn't get a breeze, we did get to breathe fresh air for a change.

On the third day, Natasha opened the sliding window and said, "We're coming to the US border checkpoint. Mom is going to pull over and explain to us what to do."

Lorna stopped the orange pickup near a small park, and she opened the back of the camper. "Okay, kids, time to get out."

Hyrum and I hopped out quickly.

"Here's what's going to happen. I'm going to drive across the border with my kids, because I have their papers. I'll park the truck on the US side and leave my children with it. Then I'll walk back, get the two of you, and we'll cross back over together."

"But we don't have any papers." I regretted the words as soon as they left my mouth. I knew better than to question one of the sister-wives.

"I'll use my kids' papers for you. That's why we have to go in two groups. And we'll have a different border agent when we walk across than I will when I drive across."

I marveled at the brilliance and simplicity of the plan.

"If you do as I ask and stay put, I'll buy you ice cream after we get across the border."

Hyrum and I sat on the park bench and watched the orange truck disappear into Mexican traffic. We waited patiently for Lorna to return. I enjoyed sitting outdoors instead of lying down in a closed camper, and I eagerly anticipated eating ice cream.

Lorna eventually showed up, looking every bit like a tourist just out to see Mexico for the day. "Come on, kids. Let's go back to America."

We crossed the border without incident and soon were in line at the McDonald's in Brownsville, Texas. Lorna ordered three chocolate shakes and gave one to Hyrum and me to split between us. The rich chocolate tasted incredible, especially after months of tortillas and smashed black beans!

We still had several hours to go before we reached Houston, but after the chocolate shake, the drive didn't seem as hot or difficult. I smiled at Hyrum, who still had a tiny, brown mustache from trying to get the last couple of drops out of the cup we shared.

Lorna took us to Mark and Lillian's house in Houston, where I was reunited with Celia. We hugged and talked a mile a minute, catching up after months apart. We only spent a night there. The next morning Mark and Lillian put Celia, Hyrum, and me on a plane to Denver, my first plane ride ever.

Hyrum and I were buckled in our seats when one of the stewardesses came over to check on us. "Y'all doing okay?"

"Yes, ma'am. When will the airplane take off?" I asked.

She laughed in a sweet way at my question. "The airplane took off about five minutes ago, honey. We're already flying."

I stared at her in shock.

The same stewardess later brought us each a pair of airplane wings to pin on our shirts for being first-time travelers.

When we landed, Mom was there to meet us at the gate. I hugged her so hard I didn't want to ever let go.

ELEVEN

LIVING IN THE BEACH HOUSE had been such a high point in my life that I was overdue for things to start going downhill. And they did, with our move to a tiny three-bedroom, two-bathroom, dilapidated house on Ogden Circle in Denver. All told, three sister-wives and twenty children were crammed together in a 1,900-square-foot living space. My mom had little time to spend with me, but I'd grown used to that. Her nearness and presence was enough.

Once again, I was ushered into a new era of discomfort, fear, and insecurity any time I wasn't in the new school with my younger siblings. I loved being at school. It was a haven and a respite from the realities of my home life. I saw my mom only in the morning before I left because all of the sister-wives and the older teenagers in the family worked at Michael's Appliance—named after the archangel Michael—while the younger kids were in school. They typically stayed at the warehouse until nine o'clock. So all afternoon and evening, we younger ones were home alone, unsupervised. One of the older—barely older—girls would be left behind to tend all the little kids. A twelve- or thirteen-year-old kid would be left in charge of a mass of ten or more children.

I still had my secret stash of pesos that I had earned in Mexico.

Only a few people knew about the money. I was afraid the pesos might disappear if I didn't watch them carefully. I finally confided in my mom's sister-wife Linda, who handled finances and did the bank runs for the family business. She offered to exchange the Mexican money for US dollars. The total came to more than twenty dollars. Never having had—or even held—more than a few pennies at one time, I felt rich. I spent the money buying treats and other goodies at the store.

Linda lived in a small, roach-infested apartment located on the second floor of the appliance business. A kindhearted woman, she always treated my siblings and me with respect. Her daughter, Darlene, was my age, and we enjoyed playing together. When we were younger, our moms had given us matching dresses with a colorful apple print on them. Linda's two sons, Tony and Robert, were also my playmates. Since she had a sweet tooth, Linda frequently bought a ten-pack of Snickers bars for herself and hid them in various places in her apartment. We quickly found her favorite hiding places and tried not to get caught enjoying the chocolaty goodness.

When—or more likely, if—anyone actually paid us for the work we did in the appliance warehouse, we kids quickly learned how to manipulate the soda machine in the break room. After inserting the quarter that Linda gave us, we could reach up into the space where the cans come out of the machine and grab multiple cans. With a really deft hand, we could empty out the entire row of soda cans. We drank so much soda we made ourselves sick.

During the summer of 1979, authorities finally found my father in Mexico and arrested him for ordering the hit on Rulon Allred. Dad was extradited to Salt Lake City, Utah, where he languished in prison awaiting his trial. I don't recall how I found out about his arrest, other than seeing pictures of him in newspaper clippings. One photo of him in handcuffs that appeared in the

National Enquirer after the Mexican police finally caught up with him haunted me every time I looked at it. Though I recall thinking, *Wow, my dad's in jail,* his arrest didn't affect our day-to-day lives—except I did notice that my mom and the other sister-wives seemed more fearful for their own safety and were more protective of their children.

Mom explained to us that Dad was persecuted for doing God's will, and every night she made us kids kneel down together in a tight circle to pray for his release. But neither our father being a prophet nor our prayers stopped authorities from trying, convicting, and sentencing him to a life sentence in a Utah prison for the death of Rulon Allred. Years later, I would learn much more about his evil actions and the many mob-style hits he ordered for anyone who attempted to leave his church.

x x x x x

The days dragged by, and one particularly boring afternoon when we kids were home alone, someone suggested we watch *The Exorcist* on TV. I managed to make it through about half of the movie before fleeing, terrified, to a back bedroom. I knelt beside the bed, shaking uncontrollably, as I sought relief from the torment of satanic scenes and begged God to keep demons from possessing me. Moments later, I heard footsteps. Celia and Hyrum had followed me and now stood there with ashen faces. Seeing the look of panic in my eyes, Celia rushed to my side.

"My poor Anna!" She wrapped me in her arms and stroked my hair. "We never should have watched that awful movie."

I closed my eyes as she soothed me, but as soon as I did, horrific images from the movie flooded back into my brain. I bolted upright. Hyrum stood there, hands in both pockets, with hair disheveled and panic in his eyes.

I stared at them. "Why in the world did we watch that? I'll never be able to sleep tonight. Maybe ever again."

Hyrum nodded.

"I'm sure we'll be fine, but I know what we can do to take away the spirit of the devil. Let's read the Bible out loud together," Celia said.

I saw through Celia's attempt at bravery on our behalf. "How do you know that will work?" I pressed my lips into a tight line.

We continued to debate whether the devil could also possess us, just like the young girl in the movie. I desperately wanted to close my eyes to shut out everything around me, but when I did I ended up battling the onslaught of horrible images. I grabbed fists full of hair and plopped backward on the floor.

Finally, Celia stood up. "Hang on. I'll be right back."

I looked quizzically at my brother.

When Hyrum shrugged, I buried my face in my hands.

Seconds later, Celia returned with a Joseph Smith translation of the Bible, the only Bible we were allowed to read because it was translated "correctly." She held it out to us like a peace offering. "I think this will help."

We looked doubtful.

"Well, it couldn't hurt," Celia said, smiling.

She sat down cross-legged in front of us and began reading from the book of Psalms. The words had a calming effect on us all. After we each read a chapter or two of the Bible, I finally started to believe the devil wasn't going to try to enter my body and possess my soul. At least not that night.

x x x x x

Not long after school started, the restriction of being cooped up together at home began to wear on my siblings and me. We began to get on each other's nerves. We fought over silly things and one-upped each other every chance we got. Card games sometimes ended prematurely because there were arguments about the rules. I think our discontent was partially due to being around other normal kids who lived in homes with a mom and dad and brothers and sisters. I had no trouble making friends at school, but I knew better than to talk about them at home. We weren't allowed to make friends with outsiders.

Roller-skating was big at the time, and many of our classmates went to the roller rink on Friday or Saturday nights. We never went because it cost too much and the music they played was worldly. But one Friday at school, my friends invited my step-sister June and me to go with them to the rink. I was thrilled to be asked, but I didn't want to admit that we didn't have enough money to pay our own way, so I didn't commit either way.

At lunchtime, I caught up with June in the cafeteria. "Some of my friends are going roller-skating tonight and invited us to go with them. I want to go so bad. But how can we go without any money?"

June shook her head, but she gazed beyond me as if lost in her own thoughts. "You know what, though? I have an idea. Tell them we'll figure it out so we can go."

"Really? But how?"

"We'll work something out." With that, she turned and carried her tray to the other side of the cafeteria to eat with kids in her class.

That afternoon when we got home, June and I formulated our plan. We needed $2.25 each for admission and to rent skates, but when we pooled our resources we came up with only fifty cents between us.

"Where are we going to get the other four dollars?" I didn't want to be negative, but I knew Mom wouldn't give us the money, and she wouldn't give us permission to go if we asked.

"Let's ask people in the neighborhood," June suggested.

"You mean beg for the money?" I stared at her, frowning. "No, thanks. I had enough of that when I lived in Mexico."

"We're not begging. We're just asking if they can help us out. You never know. Someone might want to help us." June stuck out her bottom lip and looked at me with puppy-dog eyes.

"Okay, but we can't tell anyone what we're doing. I don't think Mom would approve."

We bundled up against the winter cold and started going door to door. The awkwardness of flat-out asking for money was quickly overcome by our eagerness to go roller-skating. June and I took turns with our opening pitch. "We want to go roller-skating tonight, but we don't have enough money. Can you help?"

Several neighbors in a row said no. But our boldness and persistence paid off—literally—when a neighbor across the street answered the door, disappeared for a moment, and came back with four one-dollar bills and three quarters.

I was surprised at this stranger's generosity, and we thanked him profusely. We wouldn't even need to use any of our own money! To this day, I can picture the front porch of that house and the kindness in the man's face.

June and I skipped back home, and I called my friend. Later, we sneaked out and walked to my friend's house. Her mom drove us to the rink, dropped us off, and picked us up several hours later. I reveled in the fun of the entire evening, a night my mom never found out about.

x x x x x

In Denver, all of us girls slept downstairs in the basement, along with my fifteen-year-old brother Heber, who had some privacy behind a walled-in space. June and Megan, two of Beverly's children, lived more typical teenage lives. They knew all the Top 40 hits, falling asleep to the rock 'n' roll countdowns on the small transistor radios they kept under their pillows at night. They wore makeup and fixed their hair in the popular feathered style. I tried to feather my hair on numerous occasions, but the thickness and texture didn't cooperate. Both girls had boyfriends and hung out with the popular kids at school. My mom was mostly unaware of their activities.

I longed for my older step-sisters' acceptance and tried to be as cool as they were. But I felt like a tagalong most of the time. They would leave the house to roam the neighborhood with their boyfriends, sometimes ending up at the boys' homes when their parents weren't there. June and Megan would disappear into bedrooms with their boyfriends while I waited in the living room. My longing and desperate need for acceptance put me in uncomfortable situations that no grade-schooler should be in.

On Sunday nights, the "big people" went to a church meeting at someone's house, and when the meeting wasn't at ours, we kids fended for ourselves with one older sibling in charge of the multitude of younger kids. One evening Heber was the designated babysitter, although when everyone left, he immediately sequestered himself in his room. When I went to the basement, I heard sounds coming from his bedroom and knocked on his door.

"Come in," he shouted, rather impatiently.

I eased open the door and saw Heber's face illuminated by a small black-and-white TV sitting on his dresser. I didn't know he had his own TV! *He must have gotten it for free on an appliance pickup or bought it at a thrift store with the money he'd found inside the dryers he had fixed.*

"What are you watching?"

"*Battlestar Galactica.*" The picture was fuzzy since the reception with the "rabbit ears" antenna wasn't the best.

"What's it about?"

"Space. And interplanetary battles," he said, never taking his eyes off the screen.

"Sounds cool."

He sighed. "Wanna watch it with me for a few minutes?"

I nodded and rushed to sit on the floor at the foot of his bed. I had to crane my neck, but I didn't care. I was fascinated by the program and fell in love with the show that night.

When I stood up, I decided to take a chance. "Um, Heber, can I ask you something?"

Smiling, he pointed his forefinger at me, like a gun. "Shoot."

"I was wondering if I could watch *Battlestar Galactica* with you every Sunday night." I tried to give him just the right combination of pathetic look paired with eager anticipation.

"What do I get out of it?"

"What do you mean?"

"Well, you want to watch my TV in my room and disturb my privacy. What's in it for me?" He ran his fingers through his hair and then laced them behind his head.

"What do you want?" As soon as the words popped out, I regretted them. I should have given him my thoughts on a potential trade-off first. Anything he came up with would undoubtedly be worse.

"I want you to clean my room."

"What? How often?"

"Once a week. If you clean up my room every week, I'll let you watch with me. That seems fair."

I noticed he didn't ask me if I thought his proposal sounded fair. But I didn't care. "You've got yourself a deal." I walked over to his bed, and we shook on it.

x x x x x

While we lived in Denver, Child Protective Services stopped by occasionally to ask Mom questions. We knew that when CPS was there, all of us kids had to be on our best behavior and not say or do anything that would alert anyone that things weren't okay. Mom always made a point to call Beverly's kids to come out and say hello to the visitors.

Sister-wife Beverly hadn't been around in a long time. All we knew was that she was in prison, probably for the rest of her life. Mom and the other sister-wives told us kids the same things they always said when family members were arrested—Beverly, like others before her, was being persecuted for her beliefs. In truth, she was in prison for killing one of my dad's followers who had been rumored to be going to the FBI with information on the cult. Still, all of my memories of her from earlier years were good.

A creative and spontaneous person, Beverly sometimes taught our Sunday school lessons, and they weren't boring like everyone else's. She taught us about Joseph Smith's vision in the woods, where he was saved from an evil presence by two personages hovering above him. This eventually led Joseph Smith to establishing himself as the founding prophet of the Latter-day Saints. When we memorized and recited one of the Ten Commandments for Beverly, we'd get a rare treat—a large, puffy marshmallow. At this point, we were too young to learn much about the principles of polygamy or blood atonement, both of which would later have a huge impact on my life.

Beverly took us to Lake Dallas (now Lake Lewisville) to swim.

With so many of us to look after, though, she couldn't keep an eye on us all at once. I remember one time when several of my siblings and I swam under a dock and I nearly drowned. The water reached up to the bottom of the dock, and I couldn't find my way out, despite frantically trying. Eventually I found a way to safety.

I felt horrible about Beverly being locked away, so I faithfully wrote her letters about whatever was happening at home or school. Beverly always answered my letters with sweet, encouraging words and always included something creative—a drawing, a poem she'd written, or a joke she'd made up. I eagerly anticipated her letters because I wanted to see the special thing she had enclosed. I prayed often for her safety and her release, which finally happened decades later, after she had served more than thirty years of her life sentence. Her parole instructions prevented—and still prevent—her from having contact with anyone from the cult, except her own children.

"Why do those government people come by our house all the time?" I asked Mom one evening while she was preparing dinner.

"By law, they have to check on Beverly's kids."

"Why do they have to do that?"

"It's a long story, Anna, and I don't really want to get into it. You know how it is. Others always want to persecute us for being God's chosen people."

I nodded, even though I didn't understand how the world could be so mean to those of us who had been specially selected by God Himself.

x x x x x

That house contained one gift available for anyone to use—a piano. I have no idea how it got there—whether the previous tenants left it or someone in the family bought it—but Beverly's son, Sean, played it all the time. Though I loved all the music he played, I especially enjoyed "The Entertainer."

One Saturday afternoon I was bored, so I opened the piano bench and found a *Michael Aaron Piano Course* book for beginners. I read it, studied the illustrations on the pages, and began teaching myself the basics. Mom noticed my interest and decided to arrange for several of us kids to take piano lessons. She found a teacher who taught in his apartment nearby and agreed to give affordable group lessons. Mr. Peter Katz was an eccentric, large man who had a floor-to-ceiling computer he called Cecil that took up most of his living room.

In the space that was left, he placed several chairs for us to sit on and wait for our turn to play, across from the piano and bench, with Mr. Katz's chair beside it.

Mr. Katz also distributed Amway products. As I waited for my lesson one afternoon, I leafed through his Amway catalog and spotted a sleek camera. I read the description, which made it sound like the best camera ever made. Then I noticed the price in bold print just below: $12.00. When Mr. Katz finished Celia's lesson, I mustered the courage to ask him about what I saw in the catalog.

"Mr. Katz, I really like this camera."

"Yes, it's quite a nice item. Would you like to buy it?"

"I—I don't have twelve dollars."

"That's okay. You can make payments on it. Just bring me your money every week, and I'll keep it safe until you save enough to buy the camera. How does that sound?"

It sounded fine to me, so I told him so. "But it might take me a while. I don't make very much money."

"As long as it takes," he said with a smile.

I began giving Mr. Katz any money I earned cleaning appliances, if and when we actually got paid, which was intermittent at best. Mr. Katz made a notation in a little book he kept by his stack of Amway products. It did take me a while, but eventually I paid Mr. Katz the final installment, and he proudly gave me the camera at my piano lesson.

My birthday came soon after I got that camera, and my sister Kathleen gave me a photo album. Any money I earned or received as a gift went toward buying film and developing photos. It cost about three dollars for a roll of film, plus extra for flashbulbs that snapped on top of the camera. Even though I had to spend about $3.50 to develop a roll of film, I didn't care about the cost. Nothing would stop me from taking pictures. I loved that camera, and I loved taking pictures of people and putting them into my birthday photo album. I never threw away a single picture, even the blurry or grainy ones, because each photo was an investment.

Between watching TV with Heber, learning to play the piano, and taking pictures with my very own camera, I felt like a normal kid for the first time in my entire life.

TWELVE

THE NEW SCHOOL YEAR meant changes once again. At the end of the summer, the twenty of us who had occupied the Ogden Circle house moved into a new, slightly larger house on Elmer Drive, just a few blocks away from our previous address.

Because of the yearlong gap in my education when I was living in Mexico and sporadic school attendance in the States, I started at Stukey Elementary School as a third grader. Even though I was about a year older than everyone in my class, I didn't mind that when I met Mrs. Klitsner.

Mrs. Klitsner was tall and slender. She walked gracefully with smooth and careful steps, and her voice was soft and gentle. She had long, dark auburn hair, which contrasted beautifully with her fair skin and freckles.

I adored my teacher and obsessed over everything about her— how she dressed, how she styled her hair, and even how she smelled. I had always craved attention and approval from all of my teachers, but Mrs. Klitsner soared far above the rest. She was patient with me and motivated me when the work seemed overwhelming and I wanted to quit. Somehow she knew when I needed a hug and kind words of encouragement.

Though I could always read well above my grade level, I was behind in math, science, and history. My education with its starts and stops was like a tangled pile of yarn that stuck out every which way, instead of being a tightly wrapped ball. Being a strong reader with excellent comprehension saved me, allowing me to manage fairly well in subjects I wasn't familiar with. Mrs. Klitsner helped me when I didn't understand things—sometimes very basic concepts—that I should have known. She brought out strengths and abilities in me I never knew I had. And because of that, I worked harder in her class than I ever had in any other. I was determined to earn her approval.

I loved books, especially the ones by Beverly Cleary and The Boxcar Children series. Another favorite was *Where the Red Fern Grows* by Wilson Rawls. It was difficult to read the last chapter of that book because I was bawling my eyes out. At times, I'd open it up and reread the last few chapters just so I would cry. I believe I was grieving things in my personal life that I didn't realize needed grieving. The act felt therapeutic. The days when the "Reading Is Fundamental" cart came to our room were my favorites—I got to return the book I'd been reading and borrow a new one!

Construction paper cutouts of the planets dotted our classroom wall. Every time a student finished reading a book, Mrs. Klitsner moved his or her name to the next planet closest to the sun—the ultimate goal. One boy, a fast reader, always had his name ahead of mine. I wanted to pass him because I wanted to be the first one to reach the sun to please my teacher. I never did get ahead of my competitor, but this little game helped me learn about the planets.

When we studied Colorado state history and read about the Indians who lived in the southwest corner of the state, we got to make biscuits like the Indians did. Since I was constantly hungry, I grabbed the biggest biscuit, much to the dismay of my classmates.

At recess, I loved to play tetherball—and I was good at it. Being taller than the other kids gave me an advantage, and I won a lot. On the swings, we would go really high and then jump off, trying to outdo one another. The monkey bars presented a challenge: If your hand slipped and you fell, your turn was over. I was so determined to swing from bar to bar that I practiced over and over until my hands became blistered and raw. I always made it across without falling.

There was a boy who liked me and showed his affection by drawing me a picture of a Denver Broncos helmet. Then we started "going together," and he occasionally walked me home from school.

The highlight of my need for approval came during a school assembly when I received the Stukey Elementary Student of the Month award. I knew Mrs. Klitsner had nominated me and possibly even argued my merits to her fellow teachers. Just thinking about her confidence in me made me want to try even harder in her class. I couldn't get over seeing my name on the fancy-looking certificate.

After school, I ran ahead of my siblings and the rest of the kids to get home as fast as I could. I burst through the door and shouted, "Celia! Celia! You'll never guess what happened today!"

She hurried into the living room from the kitchen. "You got a hundred on your spelling test?"

"No. Better."

I held up the cream-colored certificate and shouted, "I'm the Student of the Month! Mrs. Klitsner nominated me. Can you believe it?"

She beamed with pride.

Later that night when Mom came home from work, I showed her my certificate. Her jaw dropped in mock disbelief and then her lips slowly curled into a huge smile. She pulled me close to her in a giant hug. "It doesn't surprise me at all. You're a wonderful student—so kind and obedient and hardworking." She stood back, pushed up her glasses that had slipped down her nose, and read the certificate. "I'm so proud of you, Anna. Here, this honor deserves another hug."

I buried my face in her chest, smelling the Oil of Olay cream she used, the only luxury she allowed herself. I smiled and sighed, contented and secure.

x x x x x

Another reason I loved going to school was for the food. All of the kids in our family qualified for free lunches. While other students may have turned up their noses at the cafeteria food, it seemed like a gourmet meal to me, much better than I ever got at home. I especially loved the pint cartons of whole milk. At home, we had only powdered milk, which Mom would overly dilute to make it go further. The whole milk I got at school was rich and creamy, so I thought I could replicate it at home with powdered milk by adding less water. But instead of being rich and creamy, my concoction was thick and lumpy and made me gag.

One lunchtime I had finished my milk, and when a girl I was sitting with was about to throw her unopened carton away, I asked her if we could swap cartons. I couldn't bear the thought of that perfectly good milk going to waste. The cafeteria monitor saw me trading food with another student, which was against the rules, and sent me to a table with the other "troublemakers."

I was horrified and humiliated at having to eat there. That was the one and only time I got into trouble at school.

At one point during the year, the cafeteria kitchen was being remodeled, so Mrs. Klitsner sent me home with a note to my mom, saying I needed to bring a lunch to school for a few weeks. It was extremely embarrassing to take two cooked, mashed pinto bean sandwiches or two peanut-butter-and-jelly sandwiches wrapped in an old bread bag or reused tinfoil to school, instead of the normal sack lunches that other students brought. And sadly, there was no milk to wash the sandwiches down.

That school year passed far too quickly. On the last day of school, most of my classmates couldn't wait for the bell to ring at three o'clock to signal their freedom for the summer. I had been dreading this day because it would usher in another depressing three months of labor at the appliance store. School had become my safe haven. So when everyone ran out the door, with Mrs. Klitsner making sure no one got run over, I lingered in the classroom, picking up candy wrappers and other bits of trash.

Mrs. Klitsner returned, surprised to find me still there. "Anna, it's officially summertime. Why don't you join your friends outside and celebrate?"

My stomach churned and my mouth went instantly dry. I longed to pour out my heart to my favorite teacher, to share my burdens with her. How could I explain that I didn't want to say good-bye to her, to the school building, to the yummy cafeteria food and the playground equipment? I wished I could stay there year-round, in this safe place where I could learn so many things.

But I kept my mouth shut and simply approached her desk and shyly hugged her. "I'll miss you. You're the best teacher I ever had."

Mrs. Klitsner hugged me tighter, then squatted down in front of me so she could look into my eyes. "I enjoyed having you in my class, Anna. I enjoyed school growing up too. I wanted to be at school more than anyplace else because I felt loved and challenged. Is that the way you feel?"

I didn't trust my voice not to crack, so I merely nodded.

"Listen, you are a wonderful girl, but it's time for you to go enjoy your summer. I'll see you in the fall, okay?"

What if I'm not here next fall? What if we move yet again?

THIRTEEN

SUMMER MEANT WORKING ALL DAY, six days a week, at the appliance store warehouse, instead of just on Saturday. The sister-wives and the kids old enough to work woke up early each morning. It took a long time for a dozen or more people to get dressed and eat a "tasty" breakfast—hot mush with watered-down powdered milk and toast broiled in the oven and slathered with margarine.

Before we left the house, we formed an assembly line to prepare our lunches for the day. The women would set loaves of bread on the table—bread that had been bought at the bakery thrift store, so far beyond the expiration date that it was intended as animal feed. Anyone who spotted any mold on the bread just pinched that part off. Then we kids coated a side of one piece of bread with a thin layer of mayonnaise and another piece with a generous dollop of refried beans. We alternated between that combination and peanut-butter-and-jelly sandwiches. One of the older children stacked the sandwiches back inside the bread bags to take to the warehouse.

When everyone was ready, we would scramble into several vehicles, with most of us kids riding in open truck beds. It took about a half hour to drive to the store, so we would leave the house by eight o'clock to get there and be ready to open the store at nine. We worked until nine at night, with a few breaks throughout the day for a sandwich or to play. If we were caught playing when we should have been working, the adults yelled at us for wasting time.

About the same time we moved to Elmer Drive, I underwent another transition. One day while I was working at the store, Mom called me into the break room, where she and Ramona, who now lived in Denver too, were having a cup of coffee. Both of them had enormous grins on their faces.

"What's going on?" I didn't think I was in trouble. *Did something good happen to someone in the family for a change?*

"Anna, come sit by me." Mom patted the seat of a faded blue plastic chair. "I have something to tell you."

Mom glanced at Ramona and then looked back at me. "On Monday, you start helping with the younger children."

"I get to help watch the kids?" This may sound like work, which it technically was, but to me at age ten, it meant that I had graduated from being one of the annoying little kids to contributing to the family. I would alternate between being a mother's helper and cleaning the appliances.

Mom knew I understood the gravity of this rite of passage, and she nodded solemnly.

With all of the women working, each sister-wife who had a nursing baby assigned her infant to an older girl between the ages of eight and ten, who served as a second pair of hands. Our job was to do whatever the mothers asked us to do to keep the babies happy while they worked nearby. I was thrilled to be promoted from a liability to an asset, just like that.

I had always hoped that I would be assigned to watch the children of Ramona or Faye. I felt closest to them because they were my half-sisters from my mom's first marriage. Sadly, that proved too much to hope for. Dan Jordan had given two of his older wives, Sheila and Jody, complete authority over the girls who tended the younger children. They discouraged any form of favoritism and deliberately placed in our care preschoolers and babies we weren't closely related to. Determined to break up family loyalties, the sister-wives used this self-imposed authority as another way to control us. After being reprimanded and shamed for showing favoritism to my sisters' children and accused of ignoring the children of Dan's other wives, I learned not to question who was assigned to my care each day.

Every day brought new excitement, as several of us girls would get together and play moms. We diapered and clothed "our" babies and carried them on our hips around the vicinity of the appliance store. When the babies got hungry, we took them to their moms to be nursed. We often did odd jobs, like cleaning house and doing dishes for the moms, especially the ones who had living quarters on the warehouse property.

The warehouse was located off Federal Boulevard, surrounded by a chain-link fence woven through with plastic slats for privacy. The driveway to the warehouse was beside Taco House. The living quarters of some of my extended family was a tiny, rundown house on the side of the drive. At the end of the driveway was an L-shaped building that contained two areas of warehouse space, the storefront showroom, an office, and Linda's upstairs apartment, accessed by a dark stairwell. The high ceilings in the warehouse made it hard to regulate the temperature, so in the winter we nearly froze and during the summer it was deathly hot. The big industrial fans hanging from the ceiling did little more than move warm air around. Thankfully, someone usually opened the oversized garage doors leading into the warehouse areas to allow fresh air in.

One afternoon, my step-sister June, my half-sisters Darlene

(Linda's daughter) and Eva (my dad's seventh wife Rosemary's daughter), and I took our babies out for a walk in the neighborhood. We passed the white house just inside the gates of the property, turned right, and headed toward Taco House, the restaurant right outside of the property gates. The owner just happened to be changing his menu on the sign out front when we passed.

"My, my. You girls have quite a parade going, don't you?" he said, with his arms folded over his ample belly.

"No, we're just taking the babies for a walk," Darlene said.

"Is that so? Very nice." He smiled and nodded at each of us. Suddenly, he raised his eyebrows and held up his right index finger. "Hey, wait here. I have something for you. I'll be back in a minute." He disappeared into the restaurant.

June's brow furrowed. "That's suspicious."

Eva chimed in. "Yeah, I think we should go. Our moms wouldn't like it if they knew we were talking to him."

"I think he's nice. We should see what he wants." I rarely turned down the opportunity to get anything free.

"It would be rude to leave now." Darlene, the voice of reason, finalized our decision, and we waited.

Moments later, the restaurant owner emerged, holding four colorful lollipops in his left hand. "Here you go—something sweet for some sweet girls." He handed each of us a different flavor.

We thanked him, pulled off the wrappers, and began licking our tasty treats. I made mine last the entire walk. When we returned to the warehouse, our tongues were bright blue, red, green, and orange.

x x x x x

When I was not assigned to a mom and her baby, I was working in the warehouse cleaning used appliances. We never got to pick what appliances we scoured. Instead, each morning, we lined up to attack row after row of never-ending, filthy old appliances. Washers and dryers were always our first choice since they required less work to get them in sellable condition. But once we were done with these machines, we had to move on to the other appliances.

I detested working on stoves the most. Probably attracted by food remnants, there were often dead mice or rats or layers of their droppings inside, as well as dead—or more often, live—roaches scurrying out of reach, and years' worth of charred, encrusted food and grease that had to be removed.

We used razor blades and Easy-Off to scrape the gunk off everything. The girls cleaned while the boys and some of the women made repairs. Next to the cleaning area was the washer and dryer repair department, then there was a big sliding metal door that separated the warehouse from the showroom.

The showroom floor was old, discolored tile that had to be mopped and waxed regularly. In the middle of the showroom there were rows of stoves, dishwashers, single washers and dryers, and matching sets of washers and dryers. Freezers and refrigerators lined the perimeter of the room near wall outlets, since customers often requested that someone plug in the appliance to show that it worked. The bathroom on the showroom floor had to be kept clean for customers, so sometimes we were assigned the task of cleaning it, too.

Whenever we kids were given permission to take a break, all of us headed for the yard behind the warehouse, where hundreds of discarded refrigerators and freezers were kept for parts. The appliances closest to the warehouse were lined up in neat rows, but those further out on the property were scattered willy-nilly. This huge area was our playground, where we enjoyed games of hide-and-seek, climbed on top of and inside the scrap appliances, and created forts and hideouts. Although I didn't like them at first, I quickly grew used to the furry mold and the gross smells from the array of machines.

This is why I always dreaded the end of the school year. I would gladly have opted for listening to the world's most boring teacher or taking tests or doing countless sit-ups in gym class rather than slaving from morning to night at the warehouse.

After work, we would drive home and eat a meager dinner before heading to bed, only to repeat the same grueling schedule the next day. One night I stayed later than usual with my mom so she could finish some paperwork. On the way home, Mom made a surprise stop at Wendy's and bought two hamburgers, with an order of French fries and a chocolate Frosty to split between us. I was so happy sitting in the car with Mom, enjoying this rare treat with her.

FOURTEEN

We were on our way home from another long workday. I sat in the middle seat of the station wagon next to Celia and closed my eyes while I rested my head on her shoulder. My job had changed from babysitter to appliance scrubber, and I was exhausted. It seemed like I had used every muscle in my body that day.

Mom's voice interrupted my brief respite. "Who wants to go gardening?"

"We do!"

The mood in the car shifted immediately from sheer exhaustion to energized excitement.

Mom drove the few blocks to the Safeway grocery store, making her way to the rear parking lot and finally behind the building where the giant blue dumpster was located. I breathed a sigh of relief when I saw that only two spotlights were shining above the service entrance of the store. *The other two bulbs must be burned out.* My brother Hyrum and I were the designated "gardeners," and the dimmer light would lessen our danger of being caught.

Mom swung a wide path in front of the dumpster next to the double doors where deliveries were received. With great precision, she backed up and stopped close to the dumpster. Heber jumped out of the passenger seat and opened the station wagon's rear window, and we kids climbed out silently.

We knew the drill from previous excursions to various grocery stores. As stealthily as a SWAT team, we took our pre-appointed positions. Heber helped Hyrum and me up onto the tailgate of the station wagon. Then Heber and Sean lifted the heavy, metal lids of the dumpster. A stench immediately filled the air. Out of the corner of my eye, I saw Celia covering her nose and mouth with her hand, and I flashed her a big grin. She rolled her eyes in return. Celia hated "gardening," my family's code name for dumpster diving. She couldn't stand the smell or even the thought of rifling through garbage. But more than anything, she feared getting caught. I found everything about the experience exhilarating, but mostly I couldn't wait to savor the spoils.

Before I knew it, Hyrum had hoisted himself up and over the top of the dumpster and disappeared from sight.

"You're next," Heber whispered. He squatted in front of the tailgate and hoisted me up until I could reach the edge of the dumpster opening. I swung my legs over and dropped inside.

My eyes adjusted quickly to the shadowy darkness inside the dumpster, and Hyrum and I got to work. We knew the rest of our family would serve as lookouts and signal if someone walked or drove by, or far worse, if someone from the store came out the service entrance. The exit plan was always the same—find a place to hide either inside or outside the dumpster.

I found a wide, flat box of overripe oranges. I leaned in for a quick whiff of the sweet-smelling fruit before I hefted the box over my head to Heber, who was standing next to the container. Hyrum and I worked quickly, sifting through packaging, old newspapers, boxes, and bins to find anything salvageable to eat.

"Anna!" Hyrum hissed with excitement.

"Shhh!" I reprimanded him for being too loud.

"I found a crate you're going to want to see." He held it proudly at waist level, his eyes beckoning me to take a peek.

"This had better be worth it," I muttered, as I picked my way over a couple of mounds of garbage.

"It is."

I peered into the box. *Ice cream.* I placed my hand on one of the two cartons. Not exactly freezing, but still cold. I grinned at Hyrum. "I hope one of them is chocolate."

Hyrum stacked up some boxes from the crate and carefully leaned over the top of the dumpster and handed them to Heber.

I found a couple of gallon containers of milk in a corner. They were past the expiration dates, but so was most everything in the dumpster. As Mom said, those labels were guidelines the government required; they didn't mean the food was bad—just that the store couldn't legally sell them anymore. Why should we let it go to waste? We didn't mind eating around the bruised spots in a banana or downing yogurt that tasted a little tangier than what most people enjoyed. These buried treasures added variety to our meager and mundane diet. Scraping my legs on the corroded metal and getting rust on my hands while going in and out of the dumpster was a small sacrifice for usually a big payoff.

I continued my search. Suddenly I stepped on something squishy and knew I'd found something good. I backed up a step, squatted, and peered into the darkness. Bananas! I loved the sweet smell and taste of overripe bananas, though truthfully, I'd never eaten a perfectly ripe one in my life. I tossed aside the two that I'd accidentally squashed when I stepped on them, but then I picked up the rest of the bananas to pass over the opening to Heber.

Right at that moment, I heard a hushed warning. Someone was coming! Hyrum and I hunkered down. I hoped whoever had interrupted our mission wouldn't catch us stealing. I was looking forward to the bananas and the half-melted ice cream.

"It's okay," Heber whispered. "It was just a car going by. No one saw us." *Thank goodness.* Although it had never happened yet, I knew that Mom would have to drive off and temporarily leave us in the dumpster if someone surprised her.

All in all, it was a good night of gardening. Hyrum and I had harvested two large boxes of apples, oranges, and bananas, two six-packs of yogurt, three gallons of milk, several cartons of sour cream and cottage cheese, and—of course—the coveted box that contained two half-gallons of ice cream.

Hyrum hoisted me to the top of the dumpster, and I grabbed Heber's hands to be guided back onto the tailgate of the station wagon. The ten of us squeezed back into the car, holding large boxes on our laps for the drive home. A variety of smells permeated the car, and we chattered about what we would eat first.

Because we had found the ice cream, Hyrum and I were heroes. Although it was strawberry instead of chocolate, it was delicious. We passed the containers around in the car and took turns drinking the half-melted treat, finishing it all before we got home.

Once there, we each carried boxes into the tiny kitchen. Mom and Teresa quickly doled out the containers of yogurt, and Celia handed out spoons. During the handoff, my spoon clattered to the dirty floor. I didn't care. I picked it up, wiped it on my even filthier jeans, and waited for my yogurt.

My family and I devoured everything that night, except for a couple of cartons of sour cream and cottage cheese. Both would be great on sandwiches the following day, enhancing the bean and mayonnaise combination. We didn't go gardening as much as I would have liked, only a couple of times a week, but when the opportunity came, I always rose to the occasion.

FIFTEEN

THE SUMMER DRAGGED ON, with each week the same. Although it was wonderful not to have to go to the warehouse on Sunday, there were plenty of regular chores to do around the house. Wednesdays always seemed the longest to me, maybe because they marked the halfway point of the week. On one particular Wednesday, my muscles were especially sore from chipping gunk off a disgusting trade-in stove for hours. All I wanted to do was go home and fall into bed. I followed Celia to the station wagon and squeezed between her and Hyrum. With Yolanda and Teresa and their children, there were twelve passengers.

As she exited the parking lot, Mom announced, "Who wants to go 'gift boxing' tonight?"

The response was both immediate and enthusiastic. "Yes!" Next to gardening, "gift boxing" at a Goodwill collection bin was our favorite after-work pastime. Digging through bags of clothing was definitely less smelly and cleaner than rummaging in a dumpster. For efficiency, the strategy was to grab as many bags of clothing as we could transport home, where we would sort through the bags to see what fit. Odds were, we would all have "new" clothes by the end of the night. And what didn't fit would be returned to the donation bin.

"Quiet down, please." Mom raised her voice to be heard. "We're almost there, and we don't want to announce our arrival." The station wagon bounced along through Northglenn, a suburb of Denver, before Mom pulled over to the side of the road a couple of blocks from the Kmart parking lot, our destination. She adjusted the rearview mirror so she could see me. "Let's go through everything again, Anna."

I swallowed and nodded dutifully. I was the "designated diver" because I was the only one in the car who could fit through the small opening in the receptacle.

"When we get there, I'll back up right to the front of the bin. And what do you do?"

I felt all eyes on me in that moment and stammered, "I, uh—well, Heber will lift me to the opening. I look in to see how many bags of clothes there are. If there are enough, I climb in. If not, we'll go to a different one."

"And why is that?"

"I have to have enough bags to stack on top of each other to be able to reach the opening to climb back out."

"Yeah, you don't want to get stuck in there," Heber laughed.

Mom glared at him, so I didn't have to. "Then what?"

"Then I start handing bags to you and Yolanda."

"How many?"

"As many as I can—still leaving enough to stack into a pile."

Mom smiled her approval. "What happens if somebody comes into the parking lot?"

"You'll drive away, but you'll come back to get me." Though I made the statement without hesitation, I must have sounded as though I questioned her.

"Of course I will. But what do *you* do?"

"I stay as quiet as possible so the people won't hear me."

"Good, Anna. It's important that you don't get caught in there." She readjusted the mirror and drove toward the parking lot. "Okay, kids, it's time to 'shop.'" She got out of the car and opened the side door for me.

I crawled over Celia and Kathleen and followed Heber to the back of the station wagon. He opened the rear door, and I climbed up on the tailgate. As my brother hoisted me up to the opening, he whispered, "How do things look?"

"I see lots and lots of bags. This bin is really a good one."

"The clothes are probably already in bags, but let me know if you need a couple of paper sacks. And don't try to sort through anything. We don't have enough time for that."

Heber lifted me even higher so I could climb in. I rested my forearms on the thin metal opening, which felt like it would slice my arms open. I took a deep breath. There was no turning back because my family was counting on me. I squeezed my eyes shut, hoisted myself, and dived through the narrow slit. I landed on a couple of plastic bags filled with soft clothes.

When I opened my eyes, I couldn't see much more than I could with them shut. I waited a few moments for my eyes to adjust to the dim light streaming from the streetlight through the narrow opening. I rubbed the sore spots on my forearms where bolts from the bin had left indentations.

"Everything okay in there?" Heber's voice sounded far away.

I stood up quickly, trying to keep my balance on the shifting bags underneath me. "Yes, I'm about to start handing you stuff." My soft voice echoed off the metal walls and sounded kind of cool. Under other circumstances, my siblings and I could have had fun playing in such a place. But not under these conditions. I just wanted to select bags and get out of there. Before the police came. Or someone dropped off a donation.

I hefted a few bags through the opening to Heber, who whispered, "Got it" with each handoff.

I touched one bag and felt something wet and sticky. Since I couldn't see what it was, I quickly tossed it aside and wiped my hands on my pants before I moved on to another.

I worked quickly, talking to Heber only when absolutely necessary. By now I could see pretty well. I tried to keep my mind on the task, but my heart tugged it in different directions. I remembered asking Mom one time why we couldn't buy clothes in a store like other kids did. What I didn't ask was why we had to scrounge through shirts and pants and jackets that people didn't want anymore. She told me that we have to sacrifice for God's kingdom and that the money had to go for much more important things than something as superficial as fancy clothes. I should just be grateful.

I recalled our class pictures that year at school. I had selected a pair of faded jeans and a tan shirt with multi-colored, horizontal stripes, the nicest one I had. I watched as other girls walked into the classroom. Two styles ruled the day—flowing Bohemian blouses paired with cute appliquéd jeans, or jewel-toned velour tops and designer jeans. Most girls had their hair feathered Farrah Fawcett–style.

While I waited in line with my classmates to be photographed, the girl in front of me turned and asked, "Didn't you know it was picture day today?"

I nodded.

"Then why would you wear that?"

I crossed my arms over the front of my hand-me-down shirt and bowed my head in shame.

Tonight I hoped I'd find something good in this bin.

I lifted sack after sack of clothing over my head, flattening some of the bags to squeeze them through the opening. I could hear Heber catching them on the other side. Finally, I heard him say, "Anna, that's enough."

I stacked several bags to create a squishy pyramid, climbed to the top, and peered out of the opening at Heber standing below.

"Can you pull yourself up?"

"I think so." I placed a worn sweatshirt I found at the bottom of the collection bin over the base of the thin metal opening so I wouldn't cut my forearms and hoisted myself up once more. I wriggled through the opening into Heber's waiting arms.

"Great job, sis! This is a really good haul for one stop. We have a lot to go through when we get home."

Mission accomplished. And maybe I'd find a pretty shirt and a pair of designer jeans that fit me.

We each held a bag of clothes in our laps for the drive home. Gift boxing was like Christmas to us. Actually, it was better, since our family rarely celebrated that pagan holiday.

When we arrived home, we placed the bags into a large pile on the living room floor.

Mom, Yolanda, and Teresa began opening the bags one by one and holding up items for everyone to see. We were always told to stay calm during this process, but what usually happened is we'd all see a potentially nice article of clothing, like a cute shirt or denim skirt, and we'd begin clamoring for it. The adults always got the final say about who got what, and they gave the better items to the most-favored kids.

Sometimes I would see something I thought was really cute, but because there were so many girls who were the same size, I hardly dared to hope I might actually end up getting to keep that item. Most of the time, we got things by sheer luck, depending on which of the women held up the article of clothing and which girl was in good favor with her. After the sister-wives had divided up all the clothing among the kids, we were allowed to trade with each other, as long as the items fit. If I really liked something someone else had, I might have to trade two or three items to get it.

That particular night, Mom sifted through the next-to-last bag and pulled out a bright red piece of fabric. She held up a scarlet, polyester, bell-bottomed jumpsuit that zipped up the front. I just had to have it. *Please say Anna*, I repeated silently over and over, until I heard my mom say, "Anna, this looks like it might fit you."

I beamed at her and caught the jumpsuit as she tossed it my way. I hurried from my spot on the floor to go try it on. It fit perfectly.

Everyone congratulated me on such a great haul of clothes that night. I thanked them, but I was most excited about my red jumpsuit.

I nearly wore it out the first month. After wearing it to school a dozen times, I realized how risky that was. What if some girl recognized my "new" jumpsuit as one of her castoffs? I would never have lived that down!

I figured out why I liked the outfit so much. Heber had an Olivia Newton-John record album with a striking photograph of the singer sitting on a wooden rocking horse on the back cover. She was wearing a bright red, zippered jumpsuit like mine. I always imagined I looked like her when I wore my red jumpsuit. It was an odd dichotomy, given that we were supposed to be such super-spiritual people. Heber had bought that album—one of many things he kept hidden from my mother—with its worldly cover photo, which put the idea of such fashion in my head.

My excitement took me back to a similar night before I was old enough to go gift boxing. When the bags of clothes were divided up at home, I ended up with a cute pink-and-gray plaid dress with a tie at the neck, which I remember begging my mom to let me wear for school pictures the next day. She refused because the dress had a V-neck and needed to be modified with a triangle of white fabric at the neckline since modesty was paramount in the polygamist culture. (I am wearing that dress in my photograph on the cover of this book!) Our clothes certainly weren't fancy, but I could usually find something I liked.

Two days after the gift boxing, Mom picked me up from school so we could go by the Goodwill donation bin to drop off our "donation" of clothes that didn't work for anyone in the family. It seemed strange seeing the bin in the daytime. The hypocrisy of piously making donations of our stolen goods was lost on me.

According to my father, lawbreaking and lawlessness were justified because the US government and culture were both corrupt. The disciples who followed him were God's chosen people, which meant we could go outside the normal bounds of rules and regulations. The ends justified the means. Although at times I was worried about getting caught stealing, I kept my concerns to myself.

SIXTEEN

INTERACTING WITH SO MANY FAMILY MEMBERS was alternatingly fascinating and maddening. My sisters (including step- and half-siblings) and I learned much about the culture of polygamy by observing the interaction among the sister-wives. We absorbed things by listening to conversations conducted in hushed tones. Over time, we discovered which sister-wives to avoid—some were simply mean or downright cruel, and others used their status to dominate. In polygamy, the hierarchical ranking rules everything. The first wife is not only revered by her husband, but also feared by the second and third (and additional) sister-wives married to the same man.

Another rather odd phenomenon occurred with regard to disciplining children. The sister-wives felt free and empowered to discipline the children of other members of the group, with one exception: No one dared discipline the children of wives who were higher than they were in the pecking order. In our family unit, that meant Sheila Jordan's children had immunity from any correction. Another sister-wife would not lift a hand or speak a harsh word to them without fear of retribution.

I began to view our time in Denver as a form of slavery. Every child labor law was violated indiscriminately. We lived our own sort of indentured nightmare under the rule of Dan Jordan, my father's right-hand man. Dan controlled everything while my father was in prison.

I struggled most whenever Dan's children worked in the warehouse. Everyone gave his kids preferential treatment. My siblings and I were the hired help receiving either low or no pay. Of course, we had no choice in the matter.

Ervil's children dutifully followed two unspoken rules when it came to the Jordan children: Don't discuss the injustices, and don't dwell on the unfairness. God wouldn't like that kind of selfish attitude because it wouldn't help grow His kingdom. We just did what we were told, and nobody said anything. You most certainly didn't complain to Dan Jordan or anyone in the family about it.

Dawn Jordan was exactly three days older than I was. Though we belonged to the same religious group and spent the vast majority of our time at the same places around the same people, our lives differed greatly. Dawn and I wore different clothes. Mine were from Goodwill collection bins or an occasional more stylish hand-me-down from an older sibling. Dawn's clothes came from the local department stores, and her new outfits matched, right down to her shoes.

From time to time, Dawn invited me to spend time at her house and her sister, Joyce, would invite Celia over. We never reciprocated. Truth was, I wouldn't have dreamed of inviting her into our home. I couldn't imagine the humiliation of having her see the squalor we lived in. But I always enjoyed going to the Jordans' house. Their sprawling home was situated on lots of land in Bennett, Colorado. Their children were involved in Future Farmers of America, an after-school pursuit that took time and cost money—things we didn't have.

Their house had a central vacuum system and an intercom, which Sheila used to call her kids downstairs to dinner. Their house was beautifully furnished, while ours contained garage sale and thrift store finds or something we picked from curbside trash. Their beds had matching comforters and were always made up neatly. We played in a huge field by their house, but the house itself made more of an impression on me than anything we did. Dawn didn't realize how extravagant her environment was compared to mine, and I marveled at the luxury of her family's everyday life.

Dawn and her mom and siblings worked at Michael's Appliance, but they put in far fewer hours than any of the LeBarons. The Jordans typically sauntered in between eleven and twelve noon, many times carrying fast-food cups and bags of leftovers from their meal. We knew their mom or dad had taken them to a drive-through for cheeseburgers and fries. When Dawn passed by me, I got a whiff of that mouthwatering hamburger smell. I tried not to breathe in so deeply, but I knew it was the closest I was likely to get to a fast-food burger.

Dawn's family members didn't work much or for very long, leaving around 5:00 p.m. I imagined them sitting down for dinner at an actual table, instead of trying to balance a sandwich and glass of tap water while standing in the grimy warehouse.

In time, I learned to swallow my disappointment and envy. The situation was what it was. Internalizing my feelings didn't hurt anyone but me. Dawn never knew a thing about how I felt.

x x x x x

On the first day of my last summer break in Denver—which was actually no break at all—Dan called all the employees together in the repair shop area of the warehouse. Celia, Hyrum, and I speculated about his agenda.

"I wonder if he has news about Dad," Hyrum said, sounding hopeful.

"I wonder if we're in trouble," Celia said.

I didn't have any more likely suggestions, so I just waited for Dan to speak.

"Michael's Appliance is paying Ervil's legal expenses, and lawyers cost a lot of money. We need to work even harder to help him get out of jail. I'm going to offer each of you an incentive for the summer. If you will work harder than ever, I'll give each of you a fifty-dollar bonus to spend on new school clothes." His arms were outstretched, and he had a big smile on his face when he finished.

We all clapped and cheered. For the first time ever, Dan had offered hope in the form of something tangible. Celia leaned over and whispered in my ear, "Can you imagine how many clothes we could buy with fifty dollars?"

I grinned broadly and embraced her. "I'd love to have some new jeans."

At twelve years old, I'd come to notice how much clothing mattered at school. Our donated clothes and hand-me-down items looked ratty compared to what our fellow students wore.

"I know. Me, too. And maybe some new shoes. Both of my pairs have gotten so dirty from working in this place."

On the way home that evening, Mom brought up Dan's incentive. "What do you kids think?"

We chattered about what we would buy with the money. She listened to each of us describe what we'd previously only wished for but now saw within our grasp.

My siblings and I worked extra hard all summer, often staying until after nine at night, if needed. We scrubbed appliances until our necks were stiff and our backs and feet ached. Since we didn't wear gloves, our hands were red, dry, and chapped. But we worked with smiles on our faces.

Using a razor scraper, I removed layers of dead, dried-up roaches from the traps below the stoves and refrigerators. We scraped mold off of everything and used muriatic acid to remove the hard-water stains off the washing machine lids. I gagged more times than I could count at the foul odors that assaulted me when I opened a refrigerator or freezer that had been sitting for weeks on end, a giant petri dish for bacteria and who knows what else. Through it all, the promise of a reward at the end kept us going and lightened the mood when we grew tired or missed having free time to play.

Rosemary was sometimes put in charge of inspecting our work. Each time one of us finished cleaning a dryer or range, we called out her name and asked her to inspect the appliance. If we missed something, Rosemary would point it out with her long, bony index finger, or if we did a good job, she would give us a thumbs-up. Refurbished appliances were put on dollies and moved into the showroom adjacent to the warehouse area. The "preferred" sister-wives, dressed in nice clothing, worked in this sought-after area. Occasionally other sister-wives, including my mom, were allowed to work in the showroom, particularly if they were good at sales.

As summer drew to a close, our anticipation had reached a fever pitch. About five o'clock on the Saturday before school started, Dan called all the sister-wives into the showroom. We kids tried to temper our enthusiasm but couldn't hide our excitement. The warehouse had a festive feeling like never before.

A few minutes later, the sister-wives returned, faces downcast. Mom didn't look directly at any of us, but just said as she passed, "Let's go. Load up in the car, please."

Celia grabbed our mother's arm. "Mom, what happ—"

Mom turned and repeated curtly, "Did you hear me? Get in the car, now."

We followed her out in single file and crammed into the station wagon. No one spoke until we had turned out of the warehouse parking lot and headed for the house. Kathleen finally broke the silence. "Mom, what's wrong? Didn't Dan give you our fifty dollars?"

"Sort of."

Celia and I exchanged glances, and I shrugged.

Kathleen opened her mouth to ask another question, but Mom spoke first. "I have the money." Then, in a low voice, as though she didn't trust herself to speak more loudly, Mom related what had happened in their meeting. "Dan gave me fifty dollars, but *only* fifty dollars. Apparently the business didn't do as well as he had hoped, which meant he didn't have enough to give each child fifty dollars as promised. He was only able to give out that amount per family."

Since Mom also cared for Mary Lou's and Beverly's children, that meant we had to split our meager bonus with seven other kids besides the seven of us. Someone did the math and announced that the individual share was about $3.57. Murmurs erupted from front to back throughout the car, and they grew in intensity and volume. Heber finally said out loud what we were all thinking. "That's not fair."

"Maybe not," Mom replied. "But Dan's in charge. And we have to trust that he's doing God's work, and that he knows what's best for all of us."

At that moment, I didn't want to hear about Dan Jordan's excellent leadership skills. I didn't want Mom to make excuses for such a mean, unfair man. I didn't want to be envious that the other sister-wives didn't have as many children in their care, which meant their children each got more to spend on their back-to-school clothes. I didn't want to deal with the crushing disappointment of working all summer for something that could so easily and swiftly be taken away. Instead, I just sat there and listened to Mom try to be cheery about going shopping the next day.

"We'll go to the thrift store. Won't that be fun?"

x x x x x

I'll admit that we did enjoy picking out a few shirts and jeans from an actual clothing rack in a store rather than sifting through a Goodwill collection bin. I chose two shirts, one red and one powder blue, both with the word "FOXY" emblazoned across the front. I wore the powder blue one to the first day of school the next morning. In fact, I wore both new shirts twice that week. In addition, I got a pair of jeans and a pair of shoes that had been marked half price. I went slightly over my school clothing allotment, but not by much. I could hardly fathom what I might have been able to get if I'd had the entire fifty dollars to spend.

The following Sunday, we headed to one of the sister-wives' houses for church. Celia, Hyrum, and I sat on the floor of the crowded living room, awaiting Lesley, our Sunday school teacher. The smell of burnt bread lingered in the air from breakfast earlier that morning.

Suddenly, the front door opened, and in walked Dan Jordan's family. Dan and his wife headed to the back room for their class, but the kids crossed the living room to stand in the doorway to the dining room. I watched Dawn walk across the rust-colored shag carpet. She wore a brand-new dress with a big bow tied in the back, matching tights, and a new pair of shoes. Dawn didn't make eye contact with anyone. But everyone stared at her, especially me. Her siblings had new clothes too.

So Dan couldn't afford to give us money for new clothes? He blamed us for not working hard enough. How could twelve hours a day, six days a week not be enough? I felt myself flushing red with rage and disappointment. It seemed evident that Dan took our hard-earned money and spent it on his own children, who didn't even work half as much as we did in that filthy, disgusting warehouse. I knew making a scene wouldn't do any good. I choked down my feelings of resentment, bitterness, and betrayal just like the bean sandwiches we ate every day that summer in the warehouse. But those feelings burrowed deep inside my soul to fester and grow.

SEVENTEEN

I WAS NOW IN FOURTH GRADE, and a few months into the school year, my older half-brother Ed surprised us with a visit. He took all of us kids to Woolworth's and bought each one of us a new outfit with money he'd earned working at one of our family's Reliance Appliance locations in Houston.

A few weeks later, he surprised us again when he came back with a U-Haul truck, and we packed up our things to move near him. Not all of us were heading to the same destination. Teresa and Yolanda moved to Phoenix to work for an appliance business there, but Rosemary accompanied us to Houston, where she opened a new remote location of Reliance Appliance.

We lived in a yellow, two-story house on the Gulf Freeway in Houston. The upstairs level housed the kitchen, dining room, and bedrooms. Another large room up a few steps served as a living area, furnished with a shabby couch and several beds that became one of the makeshift places for the girls to sleep. The lower level felt like a typical basement space with an outside entrance. Mom was going to use this space to sell appliances, too, as another remote location of Reliance.

The men divided the inventory of used appliances among the

various locations. I remember thinking that Dan Jordan and his family must have been devastated by the mass exodus of cheap labor. Maybe now his kids would actually need to work as hard as we had.

With the move to Houston, we enjoyed greater stability than we had ever known. We were reunited with Mark and Lillian, who oversaw the main Reliance Appliance store, and Mom actually made a decent wage working for them out of our home. She had enough money to buy normal food for our school lunches—a bologna-and-cheese sandwich, a few Oreos, and a handful of Doritos—packed in individual plastic baggies that she reused to make them last. Mom put the baggies into paper lunch bags with our names written on them. *We must be rich!* For the first time that I could remember, I didn't dread eating my lunch with my classmates.

I definitely had to adjust to a new school, though. I had started my school year in Denver in the fourth grade, but here in Houston they placed me in sixth grade, based on my age. I was way behind the other students in my class, and I dropped from making mostly As and Bs to making Bs, Cs, and even a D that shamed me to my core.

One day my teacher, Mr. Gentry, asked me to remain in the room while he dismissed the rest of the class for lunch. *What did I do?* I stood by his desk, nervously twirling a lock of hair around my index finger, waiting for him to finish recording something in his notebook.

"Anna, I'm not going to waste any time getting to the point. Are you having trouble seeing the blackboard? Sometimes I notice you squinting."

I blushed and stared at the floor.

"Listen, needing glasses is nothing to be ashamed of. Believe me, when you get the right prescription, it will make all the difference in the world." He smiled and tapped the side of his own glasses. "It will help you learn, and you will do better in school. I'm writing a note for your mother. Will you please give this to her tonight?"

"Yes, Mr. Gentry." I nodded and then fled his classroom, mortified at the thought of having to wear glasses in public. *I don't have to give Mom the note. She'll never know about this conversation with Mr. Gentry.* But my desire to do better in school made me change my mind.

When I got home from school, I took the note from the back pocket of my jeans, unfolded it, and placed it on the table in front of her. "My teacher says I need glasses. I'm having trouble seeing the board. He thinks that might be why my grades are so bad."

She looked the note, moving her lips as she read each word. "Well, I guess I need to make you an appointment with an eye doctor."

A couple of days later, she picked me up from school and drove me to an optometrist's office around the corner from the appliance store. A man with bushy, black eyebrows directed me to a chair in front of a giant machine and began moving different dials. With each new adjustment, I could see much better, until finally I was able to read the tiniest letters on the eye chart with ease.

Mom helped me pick out frames we could afford. I thought they made me look hideous, so I refused to wear them at school. I confided to Lillian how much I hated wearing my glasses, and she urged me to tell Mom, but I felt bad that my mother had spent so much money on me. Sometimes, out of desperation, I'd pull my glasses out of the case tucked into my desk, slip them on, quickly read the board, and then put them back, hoping no one saw me.

I took advantage of the Park Place Public Library, stopping there on my way home from school each day to check out books.

It became a refuge for me and broadened my world. I had never lost my interest in photography, and from the wages I received from working at the store on weekends, I quickly upgraded my first camera to a Kodak 110 Instamatic. After finding the cheapest place within walking distance to buy film and get my pictures developed, I began regularly adding more photos of my classmates and siblings to the album Kathleen had given me for my birthday.

One morning, as I ate my corn bran cereal, I read to Mom an offer on the back of the box for a Polaroid camera. I knew that kind of camera was way out of my price range, but I longed for it anyway. Mom secretly began saving proofs of purchase from the cereal boxes, mailed in the form, and surprised me with the camera on my thirteenth birthday. I couldn't believe I had received such an expensive gift, one that someone knew I wanted so badly. I felt as if it magically appeared because we had never been able to afford such luxuries before.

Because Mom operated the appliance business out of our house, I occasionally answered the phone to take down information from people who wanted us to come pick up their used appliances. I'd been listening to others take these calls for years, so I knew exactly what to do. On one of our preprinted cards, I wrote down the person's name, address, phone number, and details about the appliance, including the type, make, and model number.

After I hung up the phone, I looked up the address in a big Mapsco book and located the corresponding square on the giant grid map of Houston that hung on the wall. Once I had taken several calls and pinpointed the pick-up locations, I could plot out a route for the driver that would take him to all of the houses without any backtracking. I became skilled with maps and directions, both giving them and getting to places with directions someone had given me. I quickly memorized the Houston highways and streets.

One afternoon, Mom had to run an errand and left me in charge. Minutes later, the doorbell rang, and when I opened the door, a middle-aged man was standing there.

"Welcome to Reliance Appliance," I said.

"Hi there, little lady. I'm looking for a clothes dryer. Is there someone who could help me?"

"Sure, come on in. I'm Anna, and I can help you."

He studied me curiously. "You can, huh?"

"Yes, sir. We have several dryers I can show you." I led him downstairs to that section of the house and pointed out the features of the dryers we had in stock at the time. I knew exactly what to say, including the pros and cons of different makes and models, and the guarantee we offered on every appliance sold. Before Mom got back, I had sold my first appliance. I was busy writing up the receipt when she returned from her errand. I'll never forget the shocked but pleased look on her face when she walked into the office. I had such fun that day.

x x x x x

Lillian and Mark cared about us and wanted good things for us, and they did everything they could to make that happen. Lillian was the daughter of Delfina, who was Mexican and my father's first wife. Though I didn't have many encounters with Delfina when I was a young child, I distinctly remember that when she was around, she used to wield her power over us by saying, "I'm the first wife. I can spank you if you don't obey." In actuality, Delfina never really had any power. My mom was the one with power. Delfina tried to exercise control, but when we learned the truth, we knew we didn't have to obey her.

My half-sister and her husband also cared deeply about educating my siblings and me, since Lillian had experienced firsthand many of the same educational deficits we had from being moved so many times when she was growing up. She resolved to see her younger siblings have a better education than she had. Mark and Lillian read an article about Accelerated Christian Education (ACE) in either *U.S. News & World Report* or *Time*. Intrigued and impressed by the description of the Christian-based, church-run school curriculum, they attended the training in Lewisville, Texas, with the intention of starting a school for us kids.

At this time, the two of them were fringe members of my dad's group, but they wouldn't separate themselves completely because they were afraid for their lives if they left the group. In order to have an ACE school, you needed to have a church established first. Mark and Lillian obtained a 501(c)(3) status for their church. When that step was done, Mark and Lillian remodeled their garage and converted it into a classroom, complete with individual cubicles for us, offices, scoring stations, and other furnishings based on the instructions they'd received. We worked together enthusiastically as a family to make this exciting project happen.

When the schoolroom was ready, they pulled a dozen or so of us teenagers out of public school to begin this curriculum. Each school day would begin with opening exercises, a Bible "sword drill," and prayer before we would go to our cubicles and learn at our own pace. That was part of what had attracted Mark and Lillian to this curriculum. Because all of us had gaps in our education, it was impossible to have a one-room schoolhouse approach. But with a self-taught, self-paced curriculum, each of us could pick up at the level we needed to. Lillian was always there if any of us had questions.

On Sundays, the church service mostly followed the Mormon format established by the group I had grown up with, with one interesting twist. Mark assigned each of us kids a different denomination to research, which involved interviewing a local clergy member. Each week, one of us gave a report during the church service on our particular "religion." I had the Seventh-day Adventists, who intrigued me because they worshiped on Saturday instead of Sunday.

The night before starting our new home-based schooling plan, I had sat on Mom's bed and rubbed her aching feet. She asked, "What do you think about this new approach to school?"

"I'm so excited!" My mind flitted briefly to the teasing and bullying I'd experienced at nearly every public school I'd ever attended. "I think I'll do better, because I'll be able to work at my own pace in each subject."

"I also think you'll do better if you start wearing your glasses."

I hung my head. Lillian must have spoken to Mom about my refusal to wear my glasses.

"Anna," Mom lifted my chin. "You are so smart, and I know you can do really well in school. But you have to be able to see to learn."

"But I hate those glasses. My eyes look gigantic in them. No one else has to wear them, so they don't understand."

"I understand about not loving how you look. Do you think I'm one hundred percent happy with my appearance?"

I shrugged.

"Well, I'm not. For starters, I'd like to be about five or six inches taller. And I'd like to have thinner hips and thighs. I've been doing well at Weight Watchers, but I still have a way to go before I reach my goal weight."

I smiled as I thought about Mom faithfully attending her Weight Watchers meetings—the only thing she did outside the group. She ate a lot of fish to help her weight-loss efforts, and none of us could stand the smell when she cooked it.

"But we can't help things like our eyesight," Mom continued. "That's how God made you. And you have a choice tomorrow. You can refuse to wear glasses and suffer the consequences in your grades. Or you can choose to wear them and see just how well you can do academically." She brushed a loose strand of hair off my forehead and kissed it lightly.

The next morning at school, as I joined the dozen or so other students, I sat down at my school desk in Mark and Lillian's garage, reached into my bag, and pulled out my glasses. I gazed at the shiny, new classroom. I could see across the room now. After that, I wore my glasses every day.

EIGHTEEN

DRESSED IN MY SUNDAY BEST—a wrinkled plaid skirt and dingy white blouse—I padded across the concrete floor in the appliance showroom to the phone that rang so loudly it echoed off the bare walls. I could smell that something had been burned in the kitchen upstairs. The person in charge of making the toast had probably been distracted and forgotten about the bread under the broiler in the oven.

It was August 16, 1981, a memorable Sunday for me because Mark and Lillian had recently promoted me from appliance cleaner at the warehouse to receptionist at the Gulf Freeway location of Reliance Appliance, aka our house.

"Anna can answer phones. She has a pleasant demeanor. And she thinks quickly," Mark told Lillian.

I couldn't believe any of the adults in my family noticed me, let alone would say such nice things about me. I assumed the adults around me thought about me the same way I felt about myself, as nothing but a nuisance and a bother. But apparently Mark and Lillian had enough faith in me for this new responsibility. After I thanked them, I silently thanked a God I didn't actually have a relationship with. We still didn't talk about Jesus or reference

Him in conversation, but I was definitely becoming more aware of spiritual things and the basis of the Christian faith. Slowly, I was beginning to put the pieces together.

A couple of times a week, Mark ran ads in a local newspaper called the *Greensheet*. My favorite ad pictured a pirate with the headline "Wanted Dead or Alive! Reliance Appliance will pick up your unused appliances, working or not."

So when the phone rang that morning, it was perfectly natural for me to answer the call. We had only one phone line for both business matters and personal calls, but we always answered it as a business phone until we knew who was on the other end. I picked up the phone and was about to begin my usual friendly greeting, "Reliance Appliance, how may I help you?" but before I could utter a word, I heard a familiar deep voice. An involuntary shiver snaked its way up my spine. *Dan Jordan!* Although I hadn't thought of him for quite a long time, his voice immediately brought back my intense loathing for this man. In that split second, I realized that Mom had picked up one of the phones upstairs the moment I had and was on the line too.

I knew I should hang up. Or identify myself. After all, Dan Jordan hadn't called to talk to me. In the span of a millisecond, my curiosity and obedient nature began wrestling. *Why was Dan calling on a Sunday morning? Shouldn't he be getting ready to go to church?* Usually he was all business. Or all religion, depending on what the situation warranted.

What would Mom say to him? I couldn't imagine she really liked this man who mistreated and verbally abused the wives and children of Ervil LeBaron, but he was in a position of authority over us so she dutifully gave him the attention he demanded.

My curiosity won out, and I stayed on the extension to listen to the conversation. I covered the mouthpiece of the phone with my hand so that neither of them would hear me breathing. Still, I could feel guilt and fear rising in my gut. I wondered what horrible punishment Dan would order if he found out I was eavesdropping.

"Anna Mae, you're my first call to a member of the family. Ervil was found dead in his prison cell." Dan relayed the news without any emotion, as though he'd called to tell my mom about the weather in Denver that day.

I suppressed a gasp. *My father's dead.* Even though I scarcely knew him and had seen him only a few times in my life, I was sad. With Dan's matter-of-fact declaration, any opportunity for a relationship with my father was gone forever. Not that I had actually believed he might be capable of that. After all, many dads with only two or three children struggle to make time for their families. Imagine trying to maintain relationships with more than fifty kids, scattered all over Texas, Colorado, California, and Mexico.

The silence on the phone hung heavy, to the point I could hear the blood pounding in my ears. I tightened my grip over the mouthpiece for fear Dan might hear my short, panicked breaths.

Finally, Mom spoke. "What? Are you sure?" Her voice sounded far away. I wondered if she had dropped the receiver.

"Yes, I'm sure. His attorney called me a few minutes ago."

I was still mulling over what this news would mean for our family when Mom's voice interrupted my thoughts. "How can this be? He was 'The One Mighty and Strong' who was supposed to usher in the Millennium."

"It's true, Anna Mae. The assistant warden called Ervil's attorney as soon as they found the body. The attorney didn't want the family to hear about it on the news."

Mom let out a heavy sigh from deep within. "What happened? Was he killed?"

"Well, it's not outside the realm of possibility," Dan said. "But they say he suffered a massive heart attack. He died instantly. A cell block guard discovered him during roll call. There's some talk that it could've been an orchestrated murder at the hands of someone hired by the LDS church. But we'll never be able to prove anything, even if that is what happened."

Her next words were barely above a whisper. "I just can't believe it. He's just so . . . Ervil . . . dead."

She coughed, then cleared her throat. "What do I need to do?"

Though I continued listening as she and Dan discussed arrangements, I can't recall another word they said.

After the two of them finished talking and hung up, I quietly hung up the phone. I stared at a blank wall, thinking, *How will the rest of the family react to this startling news?*

Mom's voice rang throughout the house. "It's time for church. I need everyone in the cars now." I could hear the strain and urgency in her voice.

I broke out of my trance and headed out the door. My siblings and I got into two vehicles to drive to Lillian and Mark's house, about thirty minutes away. Even though I was bursting inside, I knew better than to say anything. My lips were zipped, but I felt anxious, wondering what would happen to us. I knew that Mom was waiting to tell everyone when we were all together. She was somber, never taking her eyes off the road, obviously sorting through all the implications of Dad's unexpected death.

When we arrived and walked into the converted garage that transformed from a schoolroom to a church on Sundays, it was filled with the usual volume of talking and laughing. I looked down the hallway from the garage to the kitchen, and I could see Mom deep in conversation with Mark and Lillian. Mom held Lillian's hands in hers, and Mark kept nodding his head as Mom spoke, all three of them stone-faced. Then Mark and Mom took turns hugging Lillian before the three of them headed into the garage and took their seats in front.

Moments later, after the last few stragglers had arrived, Mark, the leader of our Houston faction of the cult, announced to the group, "Anna Mae just received word that Ervil died during the night. Prison guards found him in his cell this morning. They believe he had a heart attack." After a few initial gasps, people began whispering to others seated near them.

Since I didn't know exactly how I should respond, I figured I could take my cue from other family members. I glanced around the room to gauge people's reactions. There were some tears, sobs, perhaps even wailing. I was still in such shock from overhearing the news just a half hour earlier that I was swirling in my own anxious world. I bit my fingernails and if I did shed a tear, it was out of empathy for my mother rather than grief.

Though my mom was Dad's fourth wife, she was the one listed on his death certificate. The state of Utah needed someone to take possession of the body, someone who had enough money to pay for something other than a pauper's grave.

Mom had somehow managed to save money through the years, so she paid for Dad's body to be transported from Utah to Houston. Money was pooled for him to be buried, and a grave marker was ordered bearing the words "Beloved Father" above my dad's name, date of birth, and date of death.

On the day of the funeral, my sisters and I giggled and laughed as we were getting dressed, until Mom sternly admonished us for not showing proper reverence for the occasion.

Reporters showed up for the service in hopes of interviewing family members, but Mom angrily asked them to leave. Although I don't remember seeing him, I'm sure that Dan Jordan was there among the large group of family mourners assembled.

After the service, we drove to the cemetery for the graveside service, led by a police escort on motorcycles. As I stood by the grave, I did my best to stand still and be respectful, but a foreboding question taunted me: *What is going to happen to us?*

I looked around at my family. Mom was in front, crying softly, certainly shell-shocked and sad but remaining stoic, whereas other sister-wives were weeping and wailing loudly. Most of my siblings seemed detached, wanting it all to be over with. Celia was the exception: She sobbed the most, grieving the loss of our father. Kathleen's emotions would catch up with her later when she realized that no one was taking care of us. When the cemetery workers finished filling in the grave, I placed flowers on the small mound of earth, with others following behind me.

Things returned to our version of normal pretty quickly, although I could see that, at times, Mom seemed lost. Dan Jordan was in charge now, and she needed to take instructions from him. How that would affect all of us would become clear over time. For now, we were no longer on our knees praying every night for Dad to be released from jail. Once the initial somberness of his death passed, the collective mood of our family seemed lighter.

Within days of the funeral, I attended my first-ever wedding. While my father was in prison, Rena had visited him and courageously announced she was divorcing him. Because she was never married to him legally, there were no documents to be filed. Rena had fallen in love with John, an outsider. It was a new experience for me to watch a man and woman holding hands and being affectionate to one another, not to mention laughing and flirting. It stirred up longings within me to have that kind of relationship in my life someday.

NINETEEN

IN ADDITION TO WORKING at Reliance Appliance, Megan, June, Virginia, and I were also permitted to babysit for people outside the family. All of us girls were experts in child care. After all, we'd looked after the babies of our older sisters and the many sister-wives since we were in grade school. We knew how to feed, change, clothe, bathe, and, most of all, keep the children entertained.

I especially enjoyed watching the baby of a couple who lived in a mobile home nearby, because the baby was well-behaved, the couple paid me well, and the job also offered perks like watching TV and helping myself to snacks while I was there. The Grants played in a band, so I stayed there until late into the night. Their home wasn't anything like the homes I'd seen and lived in. Mrs. Grant had gone to great lengths to decorate the trailer with cute furnishings and tasteful art and décor.

On many occasions after I put the baby to bed, I'd wander around their house, snooping. Dozens of family photos hung on the walls of the living room and the long hallway to the bedroom. The couple looked so happy in all of them—from their wedding pictures to a photo of them holding their newborn. In my mind, they embodied everything I considered normal, though I'd never experienced normal to have a truly accurate picture. The couple had a waterbed, which they allowed me to sleep on after I put the baby to bed. What a luxurious experience! *They must be rich*, I thought. I ran my hands over the coordinating furniture, took in the bright warm colors, and fantasized about someday having a home and family like this.

x x x x x

December arrived, and the weather in Houston remained relatively mild. One particular Saturday, Mrs. Grant had asked me to come over early in the afternoon to babysit while she and her husband went out for dinner. I took my school notebook with me to take advantage of the peace and quiet while the baby slept. At 7:15, I heard the Grants' car pull into the driveway. I quickly rubbed my eyes and gathered my things as they came in the door.

"How did everything go?" Mrs. Grant asked before she handed me several dollar bills rolled up together.

"Great."

"Are you excited about the upcoming Christmas holiday? And putting up your Christmas tree?" Mr. Grant asked, his deep voice booming in the relative quiet.

"My family doesn't celebrate Christmas. But even if we did, we couldn't afford a tree."

The couple exchanged glances before Mr. Grant cleared his throat. "Um, we're getting a new artificial tree this year. Would you like our old one?"

"You can have our old decorations, too," Mrs. Grant chimed in. "I've decided to get all new ones this year."

I swallowed, letting their words sink in. "Are you sure?" I couldn't believe our good fortune!

"Of course. We'd really like your family to have them." Mrs. Grant hugged me. "Anything for our favorite babysitter."

I smiled and thanked them and then ran all the way home. I stopped for a moment to catch my breath before going into the house.

Hyrum and Manuel were playing cards on the showroom floor. "Where's Mom?"

"She's cooking dinner."

I hustled into the kitchen, my heart pounding both from running and the excitement of possibly having our first Christmas tree. Mom was taking garlic bread out of the oven, and the aroma filled the tiny kitchen. A pot of water was boiling on the stove for pasta. Suddenly I remembered my mission. "Mom, can we get a Christmas tree?"

"No, they cost too much."

I'd started with that question simply to trap her. I knew if she went with the excuse that a tree cost money, she wouldn't have a defense when I posed the next question. "What if I told you we can have one for free?"

"I'd say, 'How can we do that?'"

"You know the Grants, the couple I babysit for?"

Mom nodded as she poured the cooked noodles into the plastic strainer in the sink.

"Well, they're throwing away their old Christmas tree, and they said we could have it. So we get a tree, and it's free. Oh, and their old decorations, too."

"Are we going to celebrate Christmas?" said Celia from the doorway. I had no idea that Christmas marked the celebration of the birth of Jesus. Acknowledging Him never entered into the equation. I did know about Santa Claus, though.

I turned and grinned at her. "What do you think, Mom? Can we get it and put it up in the house?" I paused for effect. "Pleeeze."

Mom wiped her hands on her apron, leaned her head to one side, and sighed. "I don't know what I'm going to do with you, Anna. But, yes, you may go get the tree after dinner. We may as well take it, if it's free."

Celia, Hyrum, and I rushed through dinner. Then the three of us dragged the tree and carried the box of decorations from the Grants' house to ours and set it up in an upstairs room. We spent the rest of the evening making popcorn and stringing it onto thread for the tree. The next afternoon, Mom brought home a couple of strands of lights. We laughed and sang Christmas carols while we wrapped the lights around the branches and painstakingly placed the decorations—silver tinsel and red and green balls—on the tree.

Once we finished, Mom found an extension cord to plug in the lights. "Here, Anna, since you found us the tree, you get to do the honors."

As I inserted the plug into the extension cord, Mom turned out the overhead lights. The room was transformed with the soft glow from the Christmas lights. The beauty and calm of the scene took my breath away. I didn't care that my dad was dead. I didn't care that we still had Beverly's and Mary Lou's kids living with us. I didn't care that I had to wear hideous glasses to read the board at school. Everything paled in comparison to the serenity of that moment.

x x x x x

That first Christmas celebration was memorable for other reasons, too. We actually had money to buy real presents for each other; we had saved from the money we earned at the warehouse, helping the sister-wives, and outside babysitting jobs. All of us siblings planned and schemed, both together and separately, about all the things we wanted to buy each other. I specifically remember all of us girls pooling our money to buy Beverly's son, Sean, a navy blue velour robe that we had seen in an ad from Palais Royal. I think it cost twenty-nine dollars on sale. With so many of us living under the same roof, the mound of presents under the tree grew higher and wider during the weeks before Christmas.

I also got to witness true love in action. My eighteen-year-old sister Kathleen was deeply in love with her boyfriend, Jim, who lived in Denver. He was not a member of our church, which made Mom and others in leadership determined to make Kathleen break it off. Despite everyone's attempts to separate them, Kathleen had secretly kept in touch with him by paying her friends to let her use their family's phone to call him. Ever since we'd moved to Houston, she and Jim had written faithfully to each other. If Kathleen knew she wouldn't be home in time to pick up the mail before Mom, she asked me to check it, in case there was a letter from Jim. If there was, I picked it out of the pile and left the rest for Mom to retrieve. I obliged because I thought the idea of their love was so romantic.

I was impressed when Kathleen boldly invited Jim to join our family for Christmas. Even more unbelievable? Jim accepted the invitation. He arrived two days before Christmas to stay for a long weekend. Mom didn't want him to come—at all. Mom and the other sister-wives were afraid of Kathleen and Jim being together. They didn't want anyone from the outside to come in because they feared losing control of us kids and our closed family. She and Kathleen argued about it, but my sister stood her ground.

Seeing the two of them together impressed on me what young love looked like. Other than Rena's recent marriage, the other marriages in our family had all been arranged. So getting to witness the affection and closeness of two young people truly in love broadened my outlook. Their relationship, along with Rena and John's, gave me hope that one day I might have the same thing.

By Christmas Eve, all of the presents were wrapped and the pile took up more than half of the large room! We girls thoroughly enjoyed the look on Sean's face when he opened his gift. He tried on the robe immediately and raved about how comfortable it was. In fact, he wore it all morning as he played carols on the piano, and for most of the rest of the day.

Amid the chaos of opening presents, I watched Jim quietly give Kathleen her Christmas gift, a silver necklace with an eagle pendant. After he closed the clasp around her neck, she never took off that necklace, not even to bathe.

As we spent time giving and sharing that joyous Christmas morning, I felt a deep sense of contentment—an unfamiliar feeling, to be sure. That day was probably the happiest I'd ever experienced during my entire life. My eyes were opening up wider to the outside world that had been hidden from my view.

TWENTY

WE MOVED FROM THE HOUSE on Gulf Freeway located on the south side of Houston to another place on the north side of town. The squat, white, one-story house on West Little York was closer to the main Reliance store, which made life much easier for family members who worked there.

Our move wasn't the only change that happened. As 1982 began, my siblings and I were enrolled in public school again. Some of the others were happy about going to public school, but I liked the structure and security of the ACE school. Later, when we got pulled out of the ACE school, we no longer went to church at Mark and Lillian's either. Over time, I began catching snippets of conversations between Mom, Lillian, and Mark that began to make me nervous. *Mom's thinking of moving us back to Denver!* I feared she would succumb to the gravitational pull toward Dan Jordan and his manipulative wooing.

On numerous occasions, Mom and others in the family had mentioned that Dan Jordan needed helpers to run Michael's Appliance. So it wasn't much of a surprise when we learned that the business had gone under. I wondered if Dawn and Joyce had been forced to work longer hours and actually had to scrub appliances as thoroughly as we had. The LeBaron children and Dad's wives were the labor force that had made the business a success.

One Saturday evening, my older sister Marilyn and I, along with several other siblings, returned home from working at the warehouse. As I got out of the station wagon, Marilyn was standing rigidly in the driveway, staring at the house.

"What is it?"

"Shhh!" She put her finger to her lips and with her other hand pointed to the car in the driveway.

I recognized it instantly. *What was Dan Jordan doing here?*

"What should we do?" I whispered.

"Well, we kind of have to go in." She threw back her shoulders defiantly and marched straight toward the front door.

I followed a few steps behind, a little less defiant.

We entered the house and saw Dan Jordan seated on our couch, deep in conversation with Mom. We remained silent, afraid to address him. We knew our place; we were too far below him for him to acknowledge our existence.

Mom broke the awkward silence. "Girls, Dan has had a long drive, and we need to discuss some business. Please go to your rooms and keep quiet."

I couldn't wait to get out of there, so Marilyn and I hurried to our back bedroom. Our other siblings followed suit, heading to their respective rooms. Marilyn placed her purse on the dresser and turned on the radio. I stared at her in disbelief.

"What are you doing? Mom said to be quiet! Don't you want to listen to what they're saying?"

"Not really." She plopped down on her bed, closed her eyes, and rested one arm across her face.

"Well, I do." I carefully opened the door just enough for me to squeeze through and sat down in the dark hallway. Still, I had to strain to hear the muffled voices coming from the living room.

Dan droned on and on. "We're very concerned about you, Anna Mae. And about Ervil's kids, too. I think it would be best if you moved back to Denver."

I held my breath for Mom's response.

"I'm concerned too. That's why I took my children out of the ACE school. But I still worry about the worldly influences they face. I wonder if living here will cause them to make choices that will get them in trouble."

Dan mumbled something I couldn't hear.

"You're right. If I don't put a stop to this soon, things could get far worse. Sometimes I wonder if we would all be better off back in Denver, surrounded by people who can help keep the kids in line."

Nooo! I screamed inside. *I love it here. I feel so much safer. And we get to eat normal food and make money for a lot less work.*

Dan's voice trailed down the long hallway. "This is what Ervil would have wanted. And as his successor, I'm telling you, Anna Mae, I think it would be best if you and your children came back to Denver."

I shivered, despite the sticky, humid Houston air. Here we were, once again—Dan Jordan trying to force us to do his bidding. It all made sense. He undoubtedly missed the free child labor that he and his family had benefitted from. And until my dad died, Dan didn't have the authority to make us do his bidding. Apparently he felt like he did now.

Surely Mom wouldn't listen to him. Surely she would recall the deplorable living conditions, the verbal abuse, and the long, backbreaking days spent working in the shop. Surely she would remember what a tyrant Dan had been. Surely she wouldn't subject her children to that again.

But Dan could be very persuasive and intimidating. He was a man who was used to getting his way. And Mom never wanted to rock the boat. She always seemed eager to keep the peace, especially when it came to men of influence in her life. Whenever she made decisions that didn't benefit her children, she reminded us that it was for our own good. "We have to make sacrifices for the kingdom because we're God's chosen people."

I sat there and listened as the man I hated most in the world deliberately and methodically backed my mom into a corner. Mom proved to be no match for his deft arguments. From my post at the end of the hallway, I could hear the defeat in her voice. Finally, after what seemed like hours, Dan prepared to leave. Once they reached the front door, I couldn't hear any more. So I got up and hobbled back into the bedroom, my muscles stiff and aching from sitting in that position for so long.

Marilyn still lay on the bed with her face covered, but she looked up when I came in. "Well?"

I struggled to find the right words, to tell Marilyn that our happy life—going to a school that we enjoyed, making decent wages, and eating store-bought food—was going to end. The thought of returning to that horrible indentured life was unspeakable. I opened my mouth to say something, but nothing came out.

"We're moving back to Denver, aren't we?"

I flung myself on my bed and numbly nodded my head.

x x x x x

A few days later, June and I headed to her new boyfriend's house when school let out. He lived in a trailer park just down the road from us. When we arrived, June and her boyfriend disappeared and I sat on the living room couch with his friend Andrew, unsure of what to say.

All of a sudden, there was a loud knock on the door. Andrew opened it, and there stood Mom, catching her breath.

I stood and stared at her in disbelief. How did she know where to find us? Had she gone house to house asking for us? Perhaps she saw us walking past our own house after school and became worried when we didn't come home. Regardless, there she was, standing at the door using the most authoritarian voice and posture that she could. "It's time to come home, girls."

"I'll get June."

Mom sent June home ahead of us so she and I could talk privately. Before she could say anything, the feeling I had bottled up inside spilled out. "I really like living here, Mom." I couldn't help myself, nearly giving away that I had overheard her conversation with Dan.

"Let's sit for a few minutes, Anna." She headed to a thin strip of grass that ran alongside the ditch by the side of the road, and I sat down beside her.

"Anna, I need to talk to you about something. Actually, I need you to trust me on something. As your mother, I expect you to follow my guidance and accept whatever decision I make about your future." She stared straight ahead while she lightly stroked my arm.

A sickening feeling welled up inside of me. I didn't like where this conversation was going. I felt a knot in my stomach, knowing that her decision to take me back to the hell in Denver was not for my benefit. Her face gave away her worry, despair, and resignation. Her voice was higher pitched than usual, screaming her uncertainty. And yet, I knew she was determined to be a dutiful follower and would do whatever Dan Jordan commanded.

My mind raced in terror. *She has made up her mind.* But I had made up my mind too. I could not go along with her decision.

I nodded my head in compliance and mumbled, "Whatever you say." I knew better than to share my true feelings with her. More than anything, I just wanted to get away from my mother. I was convinced that she was not herself, but under Dan Jordan's control. I walked slowly the rest of the way home because my legs were trembling.

When we got there, I fled to my room, my heart pounding. *What am I going to do?* I knew I needed to come up with a plan quickly. My only hope was to call Lillian.

I stepped out of my room and tiptoed to the cream-colored phone that rested on a little ledge in the hallway. I carried it into the bathroom and dialed Lillian's number with shaking hands. I knew I was taking a huge risk defying Mom's decision. We were not raised to voice our opinions or speak of our desires, needs, and longings. We were trained to simply do as we were told.

My heart beat wildly, and the blood pulsed in my ears. Fight-or-flight reactions battled one another, and the adrenaline rush was overwhelming. I felt my face, neck, and chest flush, and I knew if I looked in the mirror, I would find my skin red and splotchy.

"Reliance Appliance, how may I help you?" Lillian's friendly greeting made my throat begin to close. "Hello?"

I couldn't get my mouth to formulate words.

"Hello, is anyone there?"

In a strained voice, I finally spoke. "Lillian, this is Anna. I'm really scared. Dan came by and was talking to Mom. She wants us all to go back. But I can't! I don't want to move back to Denver."

I don't remember much else about our short conversation—as my emotions tugged at me, raw and fierce—but I recall the last two words Lillian uttered.

"Start walking."

TWENTY-ONE

LILLIAN DIDN'T HAVE TO TELL ME TWICE. I hung up the phone, feeling renewed hope and a courage I had never experienced before. Suddenly, I had the power to make a choice and change my life. I crept out into the hall and gently placed the phone back on the ledge.

I was thankful that I was already wearing my favorite pair of Gloria Vanderbilt jeans and my two-tone brown Nike tennis shoes, both of which I had paid for with my own hard-earned money. I wouldn't have to take valuable time to change clothes. After all, I didn't want to take a chance that Mom or anyone else would try to stop me. I knew in my head and my heart that if I didn't leave today, if I didn't flee right at that moment, I might never be able to get away.

A wave of nostalgia washed over me as I glanced around the kitchen one last time. Several fresh loaves of bread on the counter sat ready to be toasted. I swallowed hard and purposefully didn't let myself get caught up in the emotion of my decision. I crossed the living room knowing I was leaving the home that had given me the most positive memories of my life thus far.

I opened the front door, then the screen door. I hoped Mom

or Sean wouldn't hear the loud creak of the hinge on the screen door. I passed by the used appliances we had for sale under the carport and made my way to the road. Once there, I glanced back only briefly to make sure I wasn't being followed. I walked down the sidewalk without hesitation. I didn't know what Lillian's plan was, but I knew how to get to her house, and I knew I could make it on foot, even if it were a hundred miles away. Though tears threatened, I choked them back, turned left, and started walking in the direction of Mark and Lillian's home on Campbell Road.

My whole body was electrified and alert. Still, I couldn't help but glance over my shoulder every few moments, wondering if someone was coming after me. I stayed on a constant lookout for someplace along the road that I could quickly dart to and hide, in case I saw a car I recognized—one of my family members driving to pick up an appliance or, worse, Mom searching for me. I was deathly afraid that I might not make it to Lillian's house before someone intercepted me.

We had traveled this route so many times that I knew I was going the right way. I recognized familiar landmarks and buildings that were helpful, but they also worked against me. This was the same route that many other drivers in our family used daily for the appliance business. Someone could easily spot me and report my whereabouts to my mother. Or worse, pick me up and drag me home against my will.

I pictured Mom at home, looking for me. I could hear her asking, "Have you seen Anna?" I imagined her conversation with Celia when they figured out I wasn't there. How would Mom react? *She'll probably be shocked or bewildered at first, which will quickly give way to worry.* Her anxiety would soon shift to action, and Mom would probably hop in the station wagon and crisscross Houston to find me. I could imagine her gripping the steering wheel, driving to my friends' houses searching for me. My breath caught in my throat at the thought. I didn't want to put her through that; I really didn't.

I considered all these feelings, all the variables, and felt the weight of them in my gut. But I simply could not face working in that dingy warehouse and being under Dan Jordan's control for one more day. I'd worked for the benefit of others my entire life. I'd never experienced a day without oppression. Even though I was only thirteen, something deep inside me knew that was wrong and had to change.

I felt like I might get whiplash from my zealous efforts to make sure nobody was following me. I battled brief moments of hesitation, but the will to live on my own terms compelled me onward. Part of me fled the horrible fate that awaited me in Denver, but the other part ran toward something better. Part of me knew escaping Dan's clutches would bring other problems, potentially far greater than those I'd experienced thus far. But with every step I took toward Lillian's house, I felt a greater sense of freedom.

The lifting of that emotional burden buoyed my spirits, giving me hope where I'd had none. Though I didn't have a clue about what the future held, I felt certain I had better prospects with Mark and Lillian than with Dan Jordan, and that compelled me to keep walking. I passed dilapidated buildings with pawnshops and check-cashing stores. I passed by a donut shop and a taqueria and other fast-food joints, wishing I had brought some money with me. My tummy growled unhappily.

The smells of Houston—mainly gasoline and oil—filled my nostrils. I noticed how filthy the streets were; cigarette butts, fast-food wrappers and containers, receipts, flyers, dead insects, and gum littered the gutters and sidewalks. A few store owners emerged to sweep sidewalks in front of their shops. One heavyset man with a giant handlebar mustache greeted me. I simply nodded and kept going.

After walking nearly an hour and covering a little over three miles, I finally spotted Lillian's car coming toward me on the busy street. She honked and then pulled into the parking lot of a car repair place right in front of me. I jogged toward her beige station wagon and watched as she reached across the seat to unlock the passenger-side door. I scrambled into the car as quickly as I could, and when I buckled myself in, the fear and tension that had gripped me began to subside.

I offered Lillian the best smile I could muster. "Thanks for coming to pick me up." Then I took a deep breath in and let it out slowly, feeling relief flood over me. *I'm safe.* The magnitude of what I'd chosen to do suddenly weighed heavy on my heart.

Lillian reached across the seat and patted me tenderly on my leg. "How are you? You doing okay?" Her brow furrowed and her eyebrows knotted tightly. "I'm sorry you're having to go through this—having to make this choice. But you are very brave, Anna. You'll make it. I know you will."

I stared at her. *How can she know that? Mom could be coming after me right at this moment.* I shuddered at the thought.

As if she could read my thoughts, Lillian pulled out of the parking lot and got back on the road. "We need to go. You're not safe out here in the open."

"Are we going back to your house?"

"Oh, no! That's the first place they'll look for you."

TWENTY-TWO

LILLIAN STOPPED AT A DONUT SHOP and bought me glazed donuts and a carton of milk. I gulped them down, the food satisfying more than just my physical hunger. Lillian smiled at me as we continued toward her house. When she turned into the entrance of a La Quinta Inn, I looked at her. *Why are we stopping here?* Lillian pulled into a parking space, turned off the car, leaned her head on her arms resting on the steering wheel, and sighed deeply.

Finally, she lifted her head and turned to face me. "You're going to have to stay here for a couple of days. Can you do that?"

"I—I guess so." I glanced around at a few run-down cars in the parking lot. A man with long, stringy hair and an unkempt beard emerged from one of the ground-floor rooms. He fumbled with the door, locking it behind him before weaving his way to his bright yellow Volkswagen Bug. I didn't relish the idea of running into him any time soon. "Why can't you take me to your house?"

"I told you. My house is too obvious. I need to be able to look your mom or anyone else in the eyes and honestly tell them you're not there."

"Okay, I understand." *If only I had grabbed my camera or one of my stuffed animals to bring with me.*

I hated the thought of being in a strange place. "But what if I get hungry?" I wanted to add "or lonely," but I held my tongue.

"I'll come up with some excuse to get out of the store later, and I'll bring you something to eat." Lillian opened the car door and slid out.

I followed her silently into the lobby, and we walked to the front desk, where Lillian dinged a little bell to summon the desk clerk. Moments later, a heavyset woman waddled through a door behind the counter. "Need a room? Just the two of you?"

"Yes, please." Lillian glanced at me, reminding me to keep silent.

I understood. *She doesn't want this woman to know I will be staying in the room by myself.*

Lillian paid in cash, and the clerk slid a key toward her. "Room 207. It's up the stairs at the far end of the building." Then she placed several towels on the counter. "Fewer of them disappear when we do it this way." She smiled.

I scooped up the towels, and Lillian picked up the key. "What time is checkout?"

"Noon. And if you decide to stay another night, make sure you come back to the front desk and pay for it by then. Otherwise, housekeeping will come knocking on your door."

Lillian nodded. "I will."

I followed my sister as she turned and pushed open the door we had just come through. Lillian wasn't heading to the car but to the far outside stairwell of the motel. When we got to room 207, she handed me the key. "Here, you open it."

I slid the key into the doorknob and turned it. Thankfully, the door opened easily. The room was clean, although the décor was somewhat dated. I sat on the bed, picked up the remote control, and clicked on the TV, instantly transported to *Gilligan's Island*.

"Where did you put the key?" Lillian asked.

I fished into the right front pocket of my jeans and felt the hard plastic key chain.

"Always put the key on the nightstand when you come into the room. That way you won't lose it."

Lillian took the towels into the bathroom, which passed her inspection. She walked to the window that overlooked the parking lot, pulled back the drapes enough to see outside, then closed them even tighter. "Don't open these," she warned.

"Okay. I promise." Suddenly, the room seemed stiflingly hot. "Can I turn on the air-conditioning?"

Lillian lifted the metal covering on the control panel for the air-conditioning and heat. She turned the knob a couple of clicks to the right, and the stuffy space began to cool down.

I lay down on the bed, exhausted from everything that had transpired in the last few hours.

My sister sat down next to me and squeezed my shoulder. "You gonna be okay?"

Did I have a choice? "Yes. Just come back soon . . . please."

"I will." Lillian kissed my forehead, then stood and headed for the door. "I'll see you in a couple of hours. I promise."

The door clicked shut, and my heart sank. *What have I done?* I didn't have enough energy to cry, and I didn't want to think too much or I'd get scared. Sleep seemed the best option, so I snuggled up under the covers, the TV still droning softly in the background, and tried to turn off my brain.

x x x x x

Hours later, I woke up groggily. *What is that? Is someone knocking?*

"Anna?" The knocking paused, then began more frantically. "*Anna!*"

I quickly got up, went to the door, and looked through the peephole into the hallway. Lillian was just about ready to bang on the door again. I opened it immediately.

Lillian rushed in and hugged me. "Why didn't you answer the door sooner?"

"I was taking a nap, and I didn't hear you, I guess. Sorry."

"You scared me." She offered a warm, matronly smile. "Hey, I brought you some dinner." She held up a McDonald's bag.

I grabbed it from her hands and pulled out a burger and fries. I gobbled several fries, then offered some to my sister.

"No, thanks. I already ate. That's all for you." Lillian pulled the armchair in the room to the side of the bed.

While I devoured the meal, Lillian said, "Your mom came to the house looking for you."

"You didn't tell her where I was, did you?"

"Of course not. If I had, she would already have come to get you. Mark played it really cool. He said you probably ran off to one of your friends' houses."

"What did Mom say?"

"She was worried about you."

Part of me longed to hear that my mother had changed her mind about moving to Denver, that she'd come to her senses and realized she didn't want to put her kids in the horrible situation that awaited us there. But I knew that just wasn't possible. "What did she do?"

"She left. I guess she went back home."

I wish I could go there and comfort her, tell her I hadn't meant to hurt her by leaving, tell her I wanted to be with her and Celia, just not working for Dan Jordan. I couldn't hold back a yawn. "I can't believe I'm so tired. I slept for most of the day."

"Yes, but you've gone through a lot." Lillian checked her watch.

"Listen, I need to get back home. Are you sure you're going to be all right?"

"You'll pick me up tomorrow, right?"

"Yes. I'll be here by 9:00 a.m."

"Then I'll be fine. It's just one night."

Lillian hugged me tight and left.

Exhaustion took over, and I barely moved all night.

x x x x x

I woke early the next morning and watched reruns of *Sesame Street* until Lillian arrived. She knocked lightly on the door, and when I opened it, Lillian was talking to someone behind her. My eyes widened in shock when I saw my sister Marilyn, who was three years older than I was. Lillian gave me a paper bag with a couple of pieces of cold toast inside. "Sorry I couldn't get you donuts again, but I'm in a hurry to go open the shop."

I kept staring at Marilyn, waiting for an explanation. "What? How?"

Lillian glanced from me to Marilyn and back again. "Oh, sorry. I guess I didn't tell you. Marilyn is going to stay with you for the next few days until things settle down."

Marilyn offered me a weak smile. Though I'd seen her just before I left our house the previous day, it seemed like weeks ago. She looked tired. I understood completely. Leaving family, leaving everything you're used to, everything you hold dear, takes a toll on you.

Lillian reached inside her purse and took out a few bills and coins. "Here's some cash for the vending machine. Stay inside the room unless absolutely necessary. I'll stop back by soon to bring you food and check on you." With that, Lillian left.

"I-I didn't know you were leaving too," I said.

"Yeah, same here. I had no idea until Lillian told me on the way over here."

I sat down on the bed I had been using. "So how are you doing?"

Marilyn plopped down on the other bed with a big sigh. "I'm scared."

I nodded. "I know how you feel."

She burst out laughing. "That's so true. If anyone can understand how I feel, it's you."

I joined her in laughter, despite the gravity of our situation.

Over the next few days, Marilyn and I had many such talks as we bared our souls to one another and faced our fears. I found comfort in having her there, someone who was going through the same thing I was. TV and Lillian's visits with fast food were all we had to break up the long days in hiding.

After we had been confined for three days, Lillian showed up one evening without food. "Girls, I have some news that I will tell you at dinner. We're going out to eat tonight."

"What?" My heart leapt at the thought of leaving the self-imposed prison, but I worried about being spotted.

"That's right. You're leaving. It's time to go home."

Marilyn and I cast panicked glances at one another.

"Well, it's time to go to my home. It's finally safe for you to leave the motel."

Lillian, Marilyn, and I hugged each other, gathered a couple of toiletry items, and left the room. The three of us walked to the front desk to check out and return the key. A different clerk— a thin man with red hair and freckles—gave Lillian the printed receipt.

We got into Lillian's car and headed out of the La Quinta Inn parking lot and onto the crowded Houston streets.

We drove most of the way in silence. At first, my eyes were

half-closed, but when we passed some familiar landmarks, I sat up. We were close to *my* house. "What are you doing? What if they haven't left yet?"

"They have. Someone checked on the house, and it's deserted. Your things are still there, though, so we're stopping by to get them."

I pictured my siblings and half-siblings, forced to move yet again. "Did the kids know where they were going?"

"No, your mom just told everyone they had to leave again, that Houston was no longer safe."

I cringed when I heard that. *Houston was safer than any other place we'd ever lived.* Mark and Lillian loved us and really wanted what was best for us. They provided us with a good education and a nice place to live, and when we worked for them, we were actually paid—more than we ever made in Denver. *What was Mom thinking?*

Lillian pulled into the driveway of the recently abandoned house. Marilyn and I slowly got out of the car, still skittish that Mom or Dan would appear around the corner and haul us back to Denver. Lillian used her extra key to get inside. It felt dark and ominous, but I was determined to collect my belongings, something I'd never been able to do before. I packed up all my clothes and the little odds and ends that held meaning for me, filling three small boxes and two paper bags. Marilyn quietly packed her things as well. The house felt empty and eerie, so we worked quickly. Lillian helped us carry our boxes and bags to the car.

Marilyn and I rode in silence, our belongings piled on our laps. I struggled to process everything that had just happened, but the stillness and quiet felt peaceful.

Lillian broke the silence. "Marilyn, you'll be staying with Ramona for a while."

Marilyn's face brightened. "Thank you," she said, her voice barely above a whisper.

Lillian drove to Ramona's house and pulled into the driveway. I got out of the car and hugged Marilyn good-bye. I knew I'd see her soon, but we had lived through such a powerful event, having only one another for support. Lillian helped Marilyn carry her bags of clothes to the front door, but she returned quickly.

Before Lillian backed out of the driveway, she turned toward me. "Ready to go to your new home?"

TWENTY-THREE

WITH THE DEPARTURE OF THE OTHERS back to Denver, the home-based ACE school was disbanded. Lillian and Mark, only in their twenties, were now in charge of my education. They enrolled me in a Christian school just down the street from their home. They considered Spring Branch Church of God Academy to be the lesser of two evils, the worse option being public school.

I woke up late the first day of school, probably because I'd had such a hard time falling asleep, imagining every possible bad scenario that could happen to me in the cafeteria at lunchtime. When I tried to get ready, my frazzled nerves kept me from doing anything right. I dropped lotion on the bathroom floor, and it splattered everywhere. Then I struggled to get a brush through my thick mane, eventually giving up trying to tame it into submission.

I hurried into the kitchen, ready to choke down a bowl of cereal. To my surprise, Lillian was standing behind a chair at the kitchen table and motioned for me to take a seat. She had prepared sausage-and-egg breakfast burritos, one of my favorites. As if sensing my anguish, she said, "Don't worry. You have plenty of time. I can drive you to school this morning."

I ate every bite of that delicious breakfast. It helped calm me as well as fuel me for the coming day.

Fifteen minutes later, Lillian dropped me off at school. As I reluctantly approached the school entrance, I realized how alone I was. I had no one—not Celia, not my mom. I wouldn't even have the familiar comfort of passing Hyrum in the halls between classes. Thinking of everything that Lillian and Mark had done for me to be here, I resolved to find the adventure in this new chapter.

Thankfully, several students embraced me, the new girl—so much so that they became the first real friends I'd ever had outside the cult. I would come to treasure their genuine love and acceptance.

x x x x x

One sunny day in November, I arrived home from school to an empty house. *Lillian and her girls must still be at Reliance Appliance.* I plopped my backpack onto the floor and went to make myself some peanut butter crackers. When I reentered the living room, I saw two figures outside the window. I put my plate on the coffee table and stealthily crept closer to the window, careful to stay out of sight. I got there in time to see my mother walk around the corner and up to the back door.

My throat constricted, and I broke into a sweat. *What was Mom doing back here?* My hands began to shake, and the motion spread until my entire body shook uncontrollably. I couldn't move. Thank goodness, Lillian had a phone sitting on the built-in bookcase next to the window where I stood rooted in fear. I called Lillian as fast as my shaking fingers could dial the numbers.

"Reliance Appliance, how may I—"

"Lillian, it's Anna. I need your help!"

"You're scaring me. What's going on?"

"My mom is here." My breath came in shallow pants.

"What? What is she doing there?"

I could hear rustling on her end of the line, then a door closing. *There must be someone in the store.* Lillian knew the importance of keeping our conversation private.

"I have no idea. I was hoping you might know something."

"No, no one told me she was coming."

"What should I do? I'm afraid to let her in."

"She's still outside?"

"Yes, I locked the front door behind me as soon as I came in. I don't even think she knows I'm here."

"Okay, here's what I want you to do. Stay where you are. Don't answer the door, regardless of what she says or does. I'll be right over."

I placed the phone receiver back in its cradle and stayed where I was, squatting between the bookcase and Mark's easy chair. My legs, which had been falling asleep, tingled. A few moments later, I saw Mom's shadow pass by the front window that was covered with gauzy drapes that Lillian kept closed. I heard the *click-click* of Mom trying the front doorknob.

When she peered in the sidelight, I tucked my legs back up underneath me. I didn't know if she could see well enough from that angle to notice them sticking out from behind the chair, but I couldn't take that chance. I remained frozen. I waited for what seemed like hours, although it couldn't have been much more than ten minutes.

I finally heard the truck come screeching to a halt on the street out front. Both doors opened, then closed. Voices—one especially deep—called out from the street. Mark had come with Lillian. Relief flooded through me. I knew they would protect me. I knew they respected my decision to leave, and they'd do everything in their power to keep me with them in Houston.

I stood up, went to the front door, and opened it. "Hi, Mom."

Shock, then hurt and disappointment crossed her face in a matter of seconds. I knew she felt betrayed. I'd been in the house the entire time but hadn't let her in. I would have been hurt too. Still, I hugged her—an awkward, rather one-sided hug.

"Why didn't you open the door? Surely you heard me knocking." Mom followed me into the house, with Mark and Lillian right behind her. Lillian turned on the lights, and the four of us sat in the living room.

"She's scared, Anna Mae. She's afraid you're going to try to talk her into going back to Denver with—."

"I want to hear it from Anna." Mom's eyes bored into me.

"Lillian's right. I don't want to go back to Denver. I don't want to work for Dan Jordan again." Just the thought of it brought a bad taste to my mouth. I swallowed it down and sat up straighter.

It was Mom's turn. "But that's where your family is. We miss you. Celia misses you, more than I can even tell you."

"I miss her and you, too, Mom, but I'm not going back. I like it here with Mark and Lillian. I like my new school, all the teachers and the friends I've made. I want to stay here."

"Do you think I don't love you?" Mom dropped her gaze, then wiped a tear from the corner of her eye.

"Not at all. I know you love me, and you do the best you can. But Dan is so mean. He doesn't care about us. He didn't while Dad was alive, and I can't imagine how much worse things will be now that Dad is gone . . ." My voice trailed off as I recalled that last summer in the warehouse when we slaved away. Dan had yelled at us to work harder and faster, his face turning beet red and the spit flying from his mouth as he called us every ungodly name in the book. We knew then that the children of Ervil LeBaron were less than worthless in his opinion, except for his own gain. *How did Mom convince Dan to let her take time off and spend so much money on gas to drive to Houston just to see me? She must have used her own money.*

"Anna, you have to trust me. Things are going to be different this time. You'll see."

Sure thing, Mom. Though Mom kept talking—all afternoon and into the evening—I stopped listening. Truth is, I'd grown tired of her defense of the indefensible. She fully embraced the life I was determined to escape. It was the only thing she knew. But I'd glimpsed something different, something I liked much better. I now craved affirmation, encouragement, and freedom because I experienced them all on a regular basis in my new life. My old life in the polygamist cult was oppressive, and I knew things would never be different, unless they got worse. Eventually, Mom gave up trying to convince me to come back with her and left.

x x x x x

The next day at school, I was called out of class by my classroom supervisor and told to go to the main office. The school secretary, a lovely brunette with a kind smile, asked me to have a seat in her office. I noticed a few other staff members present, all with serious looks on their faces.

"Anna, I just got off the phone with your sister Lillian."

My mind raced. *Has something bad happened? What's wrong? Please tell me.*

"She told me your mother came to town looking for you. Apparently she wants you to live with her in Denver."

I nodded, then chewed my bottom lip.

"Lillian said you don't want to move to Denver, though."

"Actually, if I went, I would be moving *back* to Denver. We moved to Houston from Denver. And no, ma'am, I don't want to move back. I like it a lot better here."

The giant smile, with those beautiful white teeth, flashed at me again. "I'm glad you feel so comfortable here. Um, unfortunately, we have a little problem."

Oh no! They're going to have to send me back because that's what my mom wants. I laced my fingers together and bounced my hands up and down in my lap.

The secretary continued. "It's our job here at Spring Branch Church of God Academy to protect all of our students. That includes you. So our administrative staff will have to ensure that our doors are always locked when you're here. Just for the next few days until your mom leaves town. Your mom or someone else could come to the school to try to take you to Denver. So for your protection, as well as the other students and our faculty, we need to take this precaution."

I sighed in relief. They weren't kicking me out. They were trying to keep me safe. They wanted me to stay. I beamed back at her. "Sounds good to me." I had no idea how good it was.

Later that night, Lillian clued me in on what had happened to Marilyn. Mom and another person from the cult had driven from Denver, resolved to take Marilyn and me back with them—by force, if necessary. They found Marilyn first, and she made it clear she wasn't about to go with them. Not only was she a strong-willed teenager, but she was also fit enough to physically fight them off. I'm so glad that didn't happen to me. Based on my weak-kneed reaction and the crippling fear I'd experienced just seeing Mom outside Lillian's house, I wasn't sure that I would have had the strength to stop them from abducting me.

TWENTY-FOUR

AFTER MOM RETURNED to Denver without either Marilyn or me, life settled into a nice routine of school, work, homework, and taking care of Mark and Lillian's kids. For the first time in my life, I felt normal. I could hardly believe the difference as I walked into Spring Branch Church of God Academy each weekday. Following the incident with Mom, all the teachers knew my story, but they didn't treat me as odd because of it. Instead, they treated me with kindness—an intentional outpouring of thoughtfulness and care—from the first moment. I'd never been on the receiving end of such love. Their eyes showed they cared, and their words were understanding and compassionate.

The same was true of my fellow students. They made me feel welcome at school and invited me into their circle of friends. The small school had fewer than a hundred students in K–12, so we all got to know each other well. Plus, the families all attended the same tiny Church of God, a requirement for a having a student enrolled in the school. In this tight-knit community, everybody knew everybody, but more important, we had each other's backs. I became fast friends with siblings Madlin and Alex Campbell, as well as Michelle Carpus and David Heyen.

My new girlfriends invited me to go with them to the youth retreat planned for Thanksgiving weekend, just a few weeks away. As Lillian drove us home from the appliance store that evening, I began to think through how to ask her if I could go to the retreat. *I just needed to find the right moment.* Even though my free time was limited because of school and work, I still longed to join my new friends.

Lillian looked more fatigued than usual as she tried to finish dinner and deal with the babies. After dinner, I took the kids off her hands, put them in a bath—which always settled them—and helped get them ready for bed. I knew it was now or never to make my request. Lillian was in the living room, where a laundry basket full of clean clothes waited for me. As I picked a shirt out of the basket and began folding it, I seized the opportunity. My heart was beating fast as I tried to find the words to ask Lillian about the retreat, knowing it would be a sacrifice on her part if she agreed.

"I like my new school a lot. The teachers and kids are really nice to me."

Lillian looked at me. "I'm so glad to hear that. Mark and I both think it will be a good situation for you."

"I do too." I paused and cleared my throat, which had suddenly gone dry. "Can I talk to you about something?"

"Sure. What's going on?"

"Well, there's a youth retreat coming up . . ."

"I heard about that at church on Sunday," she said.

I grabbed a pair of jeans and quickly folded them. "I'd kind of like to go."

I was afraid to see Lillian's expression, so I averted my eyes and began to sort the socks. My head and heart willed Lillian to say yes, or at least say she'd think about it and talk to Mark. I viewed the long weekend away as an opportunity to get away from the endless work at the store and at home with all the children. I desperately needed the break, but I also knew this would be a privilege.

When Lillian didn't say anything, I glanced up. A faint smile was tugging at the corners of her mouth. "I think that would be okay. Do you have any more information about it?"

I told Lillian how much the retreat cost, but quickly added, "I don't have the full amount right now, but if you would loan me the money, I'll pay it back with my earnings."

"Let me talk to Mark, and I'll let you know one way or the other."

The next morning at breakfast, I tried to be as helpful as possible—again, hoping my efforts might be worthy of some time off.

Lillian pulled me into the laundry room. "Anna, Mark and I talked about it, and we are not only going to give you permission to go, but we're going to pay your way."

I stared at her, my mouth open, until one of the kids hollered from the dining room. "Thank you so much, Lillian! This means so much to me. I don't even know how to thank you." I hugged her and held on.

Lillian broke away when we heard another squeal. "I hope you have fun with your new friends."

x x x x x

We met at the church right after Thanksgiving dinner, and after we loaded our luggage and sleeping bags into the back of the church's old bus, all of us climbed aboard and found our seats. I waved good-bye to Lillian and the kids through the window, then settled in for the hour-long ride to J Bar J Ranch, in Sealy, Texas. En route, I learned many of the Christian camp songs popular in the eighties, which we sang at the top of our lungs. Before I knew it, we had arrived. The ranch sprawled over several acres, and even though the grass was brown and many of the trees had shed their leaves, I relished the opportunity to spend a few days outside the city.

During the day, we played kickball, tetherball, Wiffle ball, and tag for hours, then gathered in the chapel in the evening to sing and listen to the youth pastor's sermon. I got to know my new friends better in the carefree, lighthearted environment. I especially liked the camp food—particularly that there was plenty of it.

Though I hadn't envisioned anything other than a break from the mountain of work back home, God had something different in mind for me. On Sunday night, after Pastor James finished his sermon, he stood at the front of the small chapel with arms extended and said softly, "Is the Lord calling you tonight? He is, if you don't already have a relationship with Him. So ask yourself, 'Do I know *about* Jesus, or do I know Jesus Himself?'"

As the pianist played quietly in the background, I felt something pressing on my chest, as though someone had placed a sack of potatoes on it. My heart beat faster and I gasped for breath.

Pastor James continued. "In just a moment, we're going to dismiss for the evening. But if you feel God calling you, if you want to pray, just stay in your seat. Let everyone else leave. Don't worry about what they're doing. You have an appointment with Jesus tonight."

All around me, kids started getting up silently and walking out of the chapel. But I stayed. I don't think I could have willed my feet to move even if I'd wanted to. Honestly, I didn't fully understand what I was doing. But a spectrum of emotions—peace, hope, joy—washed over me. For the first time ever, I felt settled and accepted for who I was. I wanted in on this amazing life that I could see everyone there had. I certainly didn't understand everything, but I knew enough to know these people had something real, something special. The love in their lives was evident to me. How they lived out their faith was palpable. So when Pastor James offered me the opportunity to be a part of it, I wanted to accept.

Eventually, only the two of us remained. Pastor James walked over to me, turned a chair around, and sat down in front of me. "Anna?" His voice was filled with compassion.

I lifted my head to look at him.

He greeted me with a wide smile. "Would you like to pray to invite Jesus into your heart?"

I nodded, not trusting my voice.

He asked gently, "Are you comfortable praying out loud?"

My voice was barely above a whisper. "No."

"That's fine. No problem. You can pray silently. Just repeat after me, okay?"

I nodded again.

Pastor James took my hands in his and began to pray, and when he paused, I repeated the words in my mind.

Dear God, I believe that Jesus died on the cross to pay the penalty for my sin. Thank You for loving me so much that You have forgiven me and offer me eternal life. Amen.

I clutched his hands as my heart beat wildly in my chest. I meant every word I prayed that day.

I felt conspicuous as I walked out of the chapel and joined my friends in the game room. I thought all eyes would be on me as I walked in, but the other kids pulled me into the banter and fun as though nothing unusual had happened. The smile on my face told the whole story. I was loved and accepted by God, and I was bursting inside with the wonderfulness of it all.

x x x x x

When I got back home, I felt different—renewed and full of hope. I knew I had a lot to learn about the Bible and my relationship with Jesus, but I understood that I was saved. If I died, I would go to heaven, and that assurance gave me security and peace. Still, I struggled with actually saying the name *Jesus*. His name had been spoken with such scorn and derision in my family that whenever I did say it, even to myself, I had to fight off negative thoughts and feelings, imagining my family's judgment.

Although I shared most of what happened during the retreat with Lillian and Mark, I didn't say anything about my conversion for fear that they might enroll me in public school. I knew they hadn't sent me to a Christian school to become a Christian; I was there because the culture there would keep me safe from the "sex, drugs, and rock and roll" so prevalent in the public schools.

I knew Mark and Lillian were being exposed to the gospel themselves. In order for me to go to the academy, my "parents" had to attend at least one church service a week. So they dutifully got up on Sunday mornings and took the entire family to church. They began serving the church before they became believers.

Mark, an incredible musician, sometimes played piano during the worship service, and Lillian would sing with him. Mark also volunteered to drive for the bus ministry. Their involvement gave me a sense of relief.

I'm not entirely sure how and when their conversions occurred, but one Sunday night at church during testimony time, they each stood up and shared that they had come to trust Jesus and gave glory to the Lord. I felt even more relieved. I had purposefully chosen to let them come to know God in their own way and in their own time. After I had made my decision to follow Jesus, I was a quiet believer at home. But at church and youth group, I spoke freely about my faith and love for Jesus. Once I heard Mark and Lillian testify, I told them what had happened to me on that weekend retreat and felt free to talk about spiritual things at home, too.

Mark and Lillian still had the daily pressures of juggling work, school, and kids, and we always feared repercussions from Dan Jordan or my mom, but the atmosphere in their home eventually began to change. The undercurrent of stress and fear gradually abated for me. After years of being Lillian's right-hand girl who worked hard for her approval and made sure my consistent efforts secured my place in her home, I now realized I had become indispensable to her and Mark.

In the spring of 1983, at the age of fourteen, I starting "going with" David Heyen. I fell hard for his sweet smile and somewhat shy personality. My mind quickly turned to thoughts of marriage; after all, most of the females in the culture I'd grown up in were married by age fifteen. I began to wonder what it would be like to marry David—and more important, to be his only wife. Though it was a foreign concept from what I'd grown up with, and far outside the realm of my reality, I liked to imagine myself being special to someone, instead of just one of many wives. I let myself fantasize about a monogamous marriage—like Mark and Lillian had, or Jim and Kathleen, who had eloped when they couldn't get permission from my mother and leaders within the cult to marry. I wanted the kind of love they shared.

TWENTY-FIVE

THE MONTHS MOVED BY at an accelerated pace, perhaps because home, school, and work were comfortable places for me. Or perhaps it was because I had escaped the oppression of the cult. Now I got to make some decisions for myself, and my opinion mattered.

When I first moved in with Mark and Lillian, they had just welcomed their fifth child, Hannah, into their family. I enjoyed tending her and became a second pair of hands and eyes when Lillian needed to get things done, which was all the time. My older sister rarely lounged around. She busied herself constantly, accomplishing tasks on her to-do list or making sure others did. I developed my strong work ethic from being around her, watching her check off items as she completed them.

I certainly didn't have a task-oriented personality. Instead, I enjoyed being around people. Still, my chameleonlike nature allowed me to blend in with those around me, so I mimicked Lillian when necessary to garner her acceptance and praise.

I didn't like watching TV when she was around because we could never just sit and watch an entire TV show. Lillian used commercial breaks to get all of us kids to tidy up the living room or fold and put away the never-ending loads of laundry. I felt compelled to help, though I would have preferred to stay planted on the comfortable couch doing nothing but watching *Little House on the Prairie*, the only show Lillian approved of us watching. But with two adults, one teenager (me), and—after baby Calvin came along—six younger children, chores beckoned constantly. I quickly came to understand and embrace the phrase "No rest for the weary," as it characterized my existence.

The tenuous nature of my situation plagued me. I felt tremendous, self-imposed pressure to graduate from high school as quickly as possible. Given the rapidly changing culture I lived in, I never knew if the proverbial rug might get yanked from underneath me, forcing me to live elsewhere. Someplace where I wouldn't have it so good; someplace I wouldn't be allowed to attend a private Christian school; someplace I'd have to work longer hours for far fewer dollars; someplace I wouldn't feel as accepted, nurtured, and loved.

I constantly pondered what life might look like anywhere other than with Mark and Lillian. I never felt secure. I did everything they asked me to do without complaining, without exhibiting a single negative attitude. Mark and Lillian didn't tolerate bad attitudes in their house, no matter the reason or excuse for them. Lillian was the one who would say something to me if I didn't comply with her expectations.

Lillian took this so far as to question every expression on my face that wasn't "pleasant."

"What's wrong?" Lillian would ask me regularly.

Even if something was wrong, I denied it. "Nothing."

We repeated this conversation numerous times while I lived with them because Lillian did not tolerate ingratitude in anyone, least of all someone she was helping. Eventually, I learned to keep a pleasant expression on my face, no matter how I felt inside. Doing so made life easier. It meant I didn't have to answer uncomfortable questions about negative feelings I might have—some of which I couldn't understand myself, let alone explain to someone else. I accepted that Lillian had the right to require anything she wanted of me because it was her home.

When I first came to their house, I slept in the room just off of the dining room with Lillian's girls, which afforded me little peace and quiet. I dressed in the main bathroom that we all shared, which meant I had to carry everything back and forth. During the time I was with them, some of my siblings who were teenagers, too, came to live with us, but most of them left when they couldn't adjust to Mark and Lillian's high standards. Lillian strictly enforced the rules, but my other siblings found ways to get around them—and eventually left or were asked to leave. Marilyn was one of them, eventually followed by Lillian's full siblings, Pablo and Delia.

I toed the line without wavering. From the beginning, Lillian told me that any time I wanted to go back to Denver, they would buy me a plane ticket. I always had the option of going back to live with my mom. That ticket back to Denver became a double-edged sword of sorts, as they used it as a veiled threat to keep me from breaking their rules. The fear of messing up badly enough to be sent back would haunt me for years.

I didn't know Lillian's brother Isaac before he came to live with us. He was bipolar, so he would be depressed for a period of time, followed by manic highs. I got used to his mental instability and wasn't afraid; he just seemed odd to me. He helped around the house and ate meals with the rest of the family, except when he was experiencing depression.

At one point, Lillian and Mark decided to send Isaac to an inpatient facility for treatment. I don't recall how long he was gone, but when he returned home, he seemed okay for a while. And then tragedy struck. Isaac put a gun to his temple and pulled the trigger, committing suicide in his room. Because the room wasn't in the main house, but rather an add-on at the back of the garage, next to the washer, dryer, and utility sink, no one knew what had happened until Mark and Lillian's thirteen-year-old son, Brandon, found him. We were all shocked, but Lillian took Isaac's death particularly hard. I'm sure she felt responsible for him.

A few weeks later, Mark and Lillian asked me if I wanted to move into Isaac's old room. Since I was the oldest, it made sense that I would be the one to move. It would give me more privacy, and Lillian would get to have the main part of the house for herself and her family, so I agreed. Mark helped me move my limited belongings into the space. At first it was weird to be there, but I soon found it to be a reprieve from the noise and activity in the house. I still had to traipse back and forth to the bathroom, which was even farther now, but that wasn't a problem.

To get from my new room to the house, I had to walk through the laundry room, then the garage, then the business office space, which led to the kitchen. Each time I made this trek, I would pause before opening the door that led from the garage to the office in order to stretch my face muscles into a contrived smile, much wider than my normal smile. Once that was done, my face would then relax into a pleasant-looking expression. Since I never knew from day to day—sometimes even hour to hour—what frame of mind Lillian would be in, I found that this preparation kept her questions to a minimum.

Masking my true feelings, unless they were positive, became a way of life for me. Positivity became my self-preservation as I placated my sister.

It seemed to me that Lillian couldn't help herself. She faced emotional issues, no doubt triggered by the fact that she was born into a family that lacked the guidance and discipline, love and protection that a monogamous marriage would have provided. Many of us left in the wake of Ervil LeBaron's influence suffered emotional distress as a result. Given our rough upbringing, Lillian wouldn't entertain the thought of anyone having a bad day.

On many occasions Lillian struggled to hold it together, but she managed, with Mark's help. He provided her with steady strength. To Lillian, life away from the choke hold of the cult needed to be appreciated and lived to the fullest. Sometimes her incredibly high standards had a negative effect on those around her, but she was motivated by love. She wanted those she cared for to rise to her perfectionistic ideal for their own good.

About a month after I moved into the garage bedroom, I heard a knock on my door late one Saturday night. When I opened the door, Mark was standing there, his face serious and weary.

"Would you be able to help me get the children ready for church in the morning?"

"Of course. But what's wrong?"

He cleared his throat and let his gaze drop to the floor. "Lillian and I got into a fight about . . . well, that's not important. Anyway, she left."

"What?" My heart ached for the two of them, but I couldn't help but wonder what a separation between them might mean for my future. "Of course I'll help."

"She checked into a hotel, hopefully just for the night." His breath caught in his throat, and he gave another little cough. "I'm hoping this will all blow over—that it's nothing permanent."

"I hope so too."

He gave me a weak smile and said good night.

Lillian had not come home by morning, so I hurriedly dressed and fed the children before church. Though I didn't relish the circumstances, I got some satisfaction from knowing that Mark was aware he could count on me to be dependable and capable.

Thank goodness, Mark and Lillian worked out their differences. She came back to the house that afternoon.

x x x x x

One of my regular responsibilities was doing the grocery shopping at Weingarten's grocery store across the two-lane street. The manager and checkout clerks came to know me by name, and when I turned sixteen, the manager offered me a job. I begged Mark and Lillian to let me work there. I desperately wanted to have the experience of a normal job, like several of my friends had. Despite my pleading, they wouldn't even consider it. I rarely expressed my displeasure with any of their decisions, including this one, but it was a severe disappointment for me. Clearly, they needed me to help their household and business run smoothly.

Each morning, I was instrumental in getting Lillian and Mark's kids ready for school. After school, I helped with whatever chores needed doing, or I worked for the appliance business—whatever they told me to do. I tried my best to be helpful, regardless of the task. I scrubbed the old tile floor in the kitchen, using a bristle brush to remove dirt and grime from the grout one line at a time. I ironed the kids' school uniforms after they'd been washed and dried. As much as I detested pressing crisp creases in the girls' pleated skirts, there was no getting around it.

Each evening, I made and packed sack lunches for the kids who went to school. Initially, when Pablo, Marilyn, and Delia were living with us, I was making a lot of sandwiches. Marilyn, Delia, and I were on the volleyball team, and we had to show up for practice by seven o'clock each morning. One night I forgot to make lunches ahead of time, so the next morning I grabbed a loaf of bread, a jar of peanut butter, a jar of jelly, and a knife, and took everything with me to school. At lunchtime, I stood at one of the cafeteria tables and made sandwiches for everyone in our family. From that embarrassing experience, I learned my lesson and never forgot to make lunches after that.

x x x x x

Lillian enrolled me in a driver's education class when I was fifteen, agreeing to pay my tuition if I would chauffeur the kids around for them once I got my license. I passed the class easily, and when I turned sixteen I passed my driver's test easily too. The family celebrated my accomplishment at dinner.

"Anna, we're very proud of you." Mark raised his water glass in a mock toast. He glanced at Lillian, who smiled and nodded her head in agreement. He continued, "So proud that we want to propose a deal."

"What kind of deal?" I knew better than to let my excitement get the better of me.

"Since you'll be taking the kids to and from school and to their after-school activities, we'll pay for gas and insurance, and you may drive the station wagon any time you want," Lillian said.

I swallowed hard to choke back tears of joy. No one had ever given me such consideration in my life. Mark and Lillian were all but giving me the station wagon. More than ever before, I realized that they loved me, appreciated my efforts, and considered me a part of their family.

"I don't know what to say. Thank you so much!" Having a car meant I could drive myself to the youth activities at church. I craved that time with my friends, that time of worship and learning. To have the freedom to get myself there and back overwhelmed me. I stood and moved around the table to hug Lillian. I was so happy!

Suddenly it dawned on me why they had recently purchased a new Cadillac Seville for themselves. I smiled at the forethought of their win-win proposal.

In addition to paying my tuition at the Christian school, allowing me to live with them rent-free, and now letting me drive the station wagon, Mark and Lillian paid me seventy-five dollars a week to help them run the appliance business and take care of their children. I wasn't given cash each week. Instead, I kept track of how much they owed me on a calendar hanging in my room. Whenever I needed money, I just asked them for it, explaining what I planned to spend it on. I tried to time my requests when I knew it would be convenient for them to pay me, which meant asking soon after they made cash sales.

After I amassed several hundred dollars on account with them without spending anything, Lillian took me to the bank to open a savings account. I felt so grown up and empowered having a bank account with money in it. I loved watching the balance grow every time I asked Lillian for money and deposited those funds, so much so that I rarely found anything I wanted enough to make a withdrawal.

x x x x x

With Christmas Day approaching, I decided I would send my mom and my siblings some tasty treats as gifts. Lillian had the best popcorn ball recipe, and adding plain M&M's to it only made them better. Lillian helped me get the large, round tin ready for mailing.

"Do you think they'll like them?"

"Of course. And I think they'll be really surprised." Aside from my annual secret birthday phone call from my mom, we did not stay in touch. Cult members were forbidden from having contact with any family members outside the cult.

That thought made me sad, but I tried to hide my emotions from Lillian since I knew she'd lecture me about not being grateful.

Suddenly, the brown paper bag that Lillian was using to wrap the metal tin fell to the floor. She pushed back her chair and said, "Come with me."

I got up and followed dutifully behind her as we headed toward her and Mark's bedroom.

She opened the louvered double doors of her closet, knelt down in front of it, and began rummaging through bags of clothing, boxes, and assorted items.

"What are you looking for?" I couldn't imagine what would be so critical that she'd stop in the middle of a task. That didn't seem like Lillian.

She ignored me and kept digging. Finally, she located a flat, gray box. "Sit down. I want to show you something."

I sat across from her on the floor, my back leaning up against their bed.

Lillian lifted the lid off the box and took out a leather-bound book that was stuffed with papers.

"What is all that?"

"It's stuff from Dad—letters, his sermons, and other writings." She leafed through a few pages until she found what she'd been looking for. Her lips moved ever so slightly as she silently read something handwritten on a yellowing sheet of paper. She wiped away a tear before she thrust the letter at me.

The letter was addressed to Mark, written by my dad while he was in prison. I stared at my dad's handwriting and silently read the letter. This time I couldn't hide my emotions. *My father had promised me in marriage to Mark!* No wonder this letter brought tears to Lillian's eyes.

I felt my own tears begin to flow, but for a far different reason. *Dad knew me. He actually knew my name.* In the letter, he used my first and middle name: Anna Keturah, even though my middle name was spelled incorrectly. This proved to me that my dad didn't just know *of* me—the tenth child of his fourth wife—but he actually *knew* me.

Thankfully, the meaning and intent of the letter had no influence or consequence in our lives. I couldn't have cared less that I'd been promised to Mark. After all, my dad was dead, and the practice of polygamy was no longer significant in our lives. Mark and Lillian had both professed their faith in Jesus Christ. As Christian believers, they would never even entertain the idea of polygamy. Prior to their conversion to Christianity, however, they'd both encountered pressure to participate in polygamy but had resisted.

Finding my one true love was my plan, too, and I believed I had already found him. My relationship with David Heyen from school was definitely secretive, much like Kathleen and Jim's had been. I'd shared many details about my family's background with David and considered him one of my confidants. Still, I was afraid that if Mark and Lillian knew about us, they would consider my behavior "out of control" and send me packing to Denver.

I sighed as I reread Dad's letter, then clutched it to my chest. "Why are you showing this to me now?"

"I'm not sure. Getting the gift ready for your mom got me thinking about our lives up to now. I've thought about letting you see this a dozen times. I just never found the right time."

"Do you mind if I keep this?"

"Sure." Lillian made a distasteful face.

"What? Don't you want me to have it?"

"It's not that. I just don't know why you would want it. It's basically your father pawning you off to someone who's already married, in exchange for their monetary support and faithful obedience."

"I understand." I nodded, then lowered my gaze once again to the letter in my lap. "But this is the only proof I have that Dad knew who I was. I know he wasn't a good man—"

Lillian let out a sudden puff of air through her lips and tried to smile at me.

"I just think this shows that buried deep inside him, underneath the madness of his mind, in his heart of hearts, he must have loved all of his kids. However messed up his expression of that was, he still loved us." I wanted so badly to believe that about him.

x x x x x

The following year, Celia fled Denver and the cult and came to live in Houston with our sister Kathleen and her husband, Jim. Spring Branch Church of God Academy accommodated her challenging work schedule and allowed her to complete the final courses she needed for a diploma. Celia had always been an honor student—sometimes in the top 10 percent of her class. When she left the cult, she was determined not to settle for a GED.

Celia and I graduated together in May 1987. After I crossed the stage, clutching my high school diploma, Mark pulled me into a big bear hug. This man, whose father-in-law had offered me to him as his second wife, had stayed faithful to Lillian and had chosen to act like a father figure to me the entire time I lived with them. That warm embrace encapsulated his gentle fathering, as he whispered words I can still hear today: "I'm so proud of you."

TWENTY-SIX

AFTER GRADUATION, I was excited about what the future held. I wanted to attend the International Institute of Accelerated Christian Education in Lewisville, Texas, but I held off applying when my friends didn't get in. Instead, that fall, I worked as a monitor at the Spring Branch Academy learning center part of the day, and for Mark and Lillian the rest of the day.

Even though I was taking on more responsibility, I still thought the adults in my life treated me like one of the kids most of the time. That was never more evident than when I entered a room and everyone would stop talking. *What are they hiding from me?* I would wonder.

I loathed and feared the secrecy. Removing myself from that toxic environment was one of the primary reasons I had escaped the cult. But keeping secrets was a way of life that wasn't easily changed.

It was mid-October 1987, soon after I turned eighteen. On this particular day, I was more exhausted than usual when I finished my afternoon shift at Reliance Appliance. When I got home, I just wanted to escape to my room so I wouldn't be assigned more chores to do. Moments after I changed into shorts and a T-shirt, Mark called his son Brandon and me into the home office. I studied Mark's face, which seemed lined and worn, making him look much older than his thirty-five years. *Something's wrong.*

Mark rolled the office chair from beside his desk and placed it so the three of us would be sitting in a circle. "I have news." He paused and glanced down at his hands, which he nervously rubbed back and forth on his jeans. "Uh, here's the deal. Dan Jordan has been killed. He was shot while on a camping trip with his family."

What did he just say? I gasped incredulously. Time stopped for a moment as I was mentally transported back to the warehouse at Michael's Appliance in Denver. I hadn't thought about it for years, but the memories came flooding back. The grueling days spent scraping crusty gunk off appliances until my arms ached, cleaning rat excrement out of stoves, collapsing into bed after eleven each night, only to get up and do it all over again at 7:00 a.m. Dan Jordan, the cruel tyrant, was dead? Dan Jordan, who convinced my mother to return to his sweatshop, leaving me without a parent once again? What did I feel in that moment? Not sorrow. Not pain. Not sadness for any of his family members. Honestly, I didn't even feel glad or thankful that justice had finally been served. Instead, I was numb.

Brandon may have asked his dad some questions, but I tuned out everything except my own internal narrative, until Mark broke in.

"Anna! Are you listening?"

"I'm sorry, what were you saying?" I stared at my hands, uncomfortable for being singled out.

"Apparently, there's a list."

"What kind of list?"

"Well, for lack of a better way to put it, a hit list. Apparently

Ervil generated a list while he was in prison. He commanded his followers to carry out the killings of apostates on his behalf."

My stomach roiled with a wave of nausea as I realized what Mark meant. My father was responsible for Dan's death. He hadn't pulled the trigger, but he had given the directive. He ordered someone to kill Dan, and that disciple did as asked. Bile burned in my throat, and I coughed and tried to swallow it back down. I gulped down the glass of water that Lillian had brought in as we started our meeting.

"Are you okay?" Mark's eyes searched my face.

"I will be. It's just a lot to take in." I breathed in deeply and leaned back in the chair.

"Unfortunately, there's more to it."

I picked at a cuticle as Mark continued.

"Ervil wanted anyone who had ever disobeyed one of his orders to be killed—murdered in cold blood. During his later years in prison, he went completely insane. I don't know if it was being in prison, or if the little bit of power he enjoyed went to his head, but he not only believed himself to be a prophet, he also believed he could direct his followers to carry out blood atonement on his behalf."

"What's blood atonement?" Brandon asked, his eyes wide.

Mark explained, "Bottom line, blood atonement is the shedding of blood to pay for someone's sins. It basically cleanses that person for the evil they've perpetrated—or the evil you believe they've perpetrated. Do you remember your mom and I discussing how Ervil and Dan had had a falling out a while back?"

Brandon whispered, "No."

"Ervil asked several of us to come with guns a-blazing and bust him out of prison. But none of us wanted to follow his orders because we knew it would be a suicide mission—an impossible task. Well, you can imagine how angry that would make your father, Anna."

"Who did he ask?" I wasn't sure I even wanted to hear the answer.

"Dan Jordan, your brother Ed, and my brother Duane." Mark lowered his eyes. "And me." He paused to let his words sink in.

"And now Dan is dead . . ." My pulse quickened. I wondered whether my mother and others who weren't on the hit list, but closely connected to those who were, would also be in danger. I could see tears pooling in Brandon's eyes, but he hastily wiped them away with the back of his hand.

"Yes. And because my name is on the list, it means someone could be coming after me. Obviously, we can't know that for sure, and I'm not saying any of this to scare you. Lillian and I just want to take a few necessary precautions. We're going to have to be extra vigilant and watch out for each other. I need you two to help us watch out for the five younger children. Be careful. If you have a strange feeling about something or are wary about going someplace, let us know. If anything seems out of the ordinary, tell us."

It took a few moments for the enormity of what Mark was saying to begin to sink in. Was Mark really next on my dad's hit list? How could that be possible? My father loved Mark. He'd given Lillian to him in marriage because he loved and trusted him. I knew Mark had been one of my dad's most devoted disciples—at one time.

But then Mark and Lillian left the cult, began attending a Christian church, and sent their children to a Christian school. They harbored me when I fled. Would those "sins," coupled with Mark's refusal to break my dad out of prison, be enough to fuel such a horrific fire of retribution?

Brandon broke the silence. "What are you gonna do, Dad?"

Mark rubbed his eyes vigorously and sighed. He took a sip

of water and went on. "Listen, we could uproot and move to Timbuktu. Or we can trust God for His protection. I'd rather do that. I refuse to live in hiding."

Brandon pressed his lips into a firm line and nodded his affirmation.

I wasn't so sure. Having lived under the oppression of Dan Jordan for two years, I knew what kind of tormentor the man was. For Dan's murder to have been orchestrated by my dad and carried out by Dad's fanatic followers seemed to grant my father an awfully far-reaching power beyond the grave. I didn't want that kind of power coming after me—or Mark and Lillian and their children, or anyone else I loved. I shared Brandon's anxiety. "So are we going to do anything?"

"Yes, we're absolutely going to do something. We're going to prepare to defend ourselves, if needed."

"How?" Brandon's jaw clenched.

"I've bought some guns so we can take care of anyone who tries to hurt us." Mark took a key out of his top desk drawer and opened a cabinet in the closet. He pulled out a shotgun for us to see. "I got this shotgun to keep with me at the shop. And I've got a couple of handguns here at the house. Obviously, we need to keep them locked up for the safety of the younger kids, but just know that we have them if they are needed." His eyes began to get misty, and his Adam's apple bobbed up and down as he swallowed.

x x x x x

Before I went to sleep that night, I pulled a wide, flat box from underneath my bed. I lifted a few papers, award certificates from school, and random photos off the top to reveal a book I'd first read three years before. I don't remember how I came to possess *Prophet of Blood*, but I was fascinated that it was about people in my family. The revelations that journalists Ben Bradlee and Dale Van Atta had uncovered startled me.

The authors gave an in-depth account of what they depicted as my father's calculated violence against members of his own family who tried to expose his church and his teachings. According to the book, Ed Marston and Mark—yes, Lillian's Mark—along with Duane and Rena Chynoweth—the same Rena who had so thoughtfully cared for me in Calería, Mexico—had obediently carried out several of those murders, including the elimination of one of my half-sisters, Rebecca. Mentally unstable, probably from years of abuse and mind games at the hands of cult members, Rebecca threatened to flee the church and spouted off about going to the police. Exposing the family's activities, including the practices of underage polygamy and blood atonement, to the police and the FBI would also mean exposing my father for the monster he was.

The first time I saw Mark's name connected with these events was beyond disturbing. As unnerved as I was, and as much as I wanted to ask him questions about what he had done, I had learned long ago in our family that "don't ask, don't tell" was our mantra. So I tried my best to dismiss what I read, believing that at the time Mark couldn't do anything but obey my father.

At times I wanted to burn the book or rip out its pages one by one, and yet I couldn't deny the research behind the journalists' assertions. They had interviewed hundreds of people, including former cult members and law enforcement. Like someone unable to look away from a horrible car accident, I devoured the book, equally mesmerized and terrified, reading it several times. My stomach was always in knots as I read about my dad's violent nature, and yet I felt compelled to continue.

Within its pages, so many things were brought to light. Suddenly, so many mysteries made sense. Questions swirling about our time in Mexico, our repeated moves, the quick exits from houses where we'd barely had time to unpack our meager belongings, the fact that we weren't allowed to make friends with kids outside the group—in context, they now held significance.

The fall and winter at the beach house with Ramona and her girls wasn't a vacation for them. Ramona and the other adults had been in hiding for exacting the blood covenant on the heads of rival cult leaders and others who dared to leave. It was hard for me to imagine that sweet Ramona had been involved in any of that.

I trembled uncontrollably, the adrenaline coursing through my veins as I read about the murders said to have been carried out in cold blood by people I knew and loved dearly, family members I ate dinner with each night. I wondered how my dad could be that evil and exert that kind of dominance over his followers.

Every time I read *Prophet of Blood*, I feared for my life. And now, the blood covenant had come full circle—Mark had a price on his head.

No one ever talked about blood atonement when we were younger. At least they never talked about it with me. When I was young, I do remember one of the sister-wives saying, "If you live by the sword, you die by the sword," which meant nothing to me until now. The phrase "hot lead, cold steel, and a one-way ticket to hell" finally had context.

I closed the book and returned it to its hiding place under my bed. I fought sleep that entire night as visions of Dan Jordan being gunned down replayed again and again. Thoughts of masked gunmen entering our home here and shooting Mark and Lillian and anyone else they felt deserved blood atonement tormented me.

We didn't go to Dan's funeral in Denver, but my mom and some of my siblings who lived there represented our family. Though Mark, Lillian, Brandon, and I tried to act as if things were normal in the aftermath of Dan's murder, for weeks we lived on high alert and, on occasion, borderline panic. But as time passed, things slowly returned to normal. After all, we lived nearly a thousand miles—seventeen or eighteen hours by car—from Denver, where Dan's family resided. Our fear lessened and our anxiety lifted more and more with each passing day, until finally we began to live more relaxed and unguarded lives.

TWENTY-SEVEN

I LOVED MY JOB with the younger students at the school, and I especially relished being recognized in the church as one of the adults. I knew I could handle whatever responsibilities were sent my way.

In early 1988, I developed a cough that wouldn't go away and began to become easily fatigued, but I kept plugging away at both my jobs as best I could. I knew better than to use an inconvenient illness as an excuse to slow down.

After all, Lillian didn't slow down. Ever. When she was pregnant, she worked just as hard as she always did. If she picked up an illness from one of the kids, she powered through with over-the-counter medications. I tried to follow her lead, and usually managed to work almost as hard as she did, until my cough developed into walking pneumonia. When I didn't get better, Lillian suggested I make an appointment to see our family doctor, which I drove myself to.

During my initial visit, the doctor prescribed medications and instructed me to rest—an impossible task with my morning job at the school, my responsibilities with Lillian's children, and my afternoon job with Reliance Appliance. A few weeks later I was still dragging, so I made another doctor's appointment. Once again, he emphasized the need for rest and handed me a prescription for an even stronger antibiotic.

The school year ended and so did my job, but I quickly filled those hours working at Reliance or shuttling the kids to their various activities. A few weeks later, I returned to the doctor and left with more meds. Since I'd never had to purchase prescription medications before, I didn't realize how much they cost. If I hadn't seen my savings account dwindling, I might have kept up the doctor-prescription-wait pattern even longer, until I needed to be hospitalized. But my desperation to hold on to my hard-earned money motivated me to try to get well.

I definitely wasn't improving; in fact, I felt more and more tired as time went on. I did my best to continue functioning at the level I maintained when I was healthy, but it was becoming increasingly difficult. Plus, continually taking time off work to go to doctor's appointments affected my productivity.

One evening, after I finished folding the last load of laundry, I timidly approached my sister. "Will you please go with me to the doctor tomorrow? I'm not getting better, and I don't know what's wrong with me. I'm scared because I'm still so sick."

"Sure, I'll go with you."

I sighed in relief, and she patted my shoulder as I trudged off to bed.

On the way to the doctor's office the following afternoon, I leaned my head back against the headrest and closed my eyes.

Moments later, Lillian patted my leg and cleared her throat. "Anna, there is a sickness unto death, and I don't believe you are going to die. There is a sickness unto salvation; and since you are already saved, that's not it either. There is also a sickness unto the glory of God. You probably have that kind of sickness, but let's see what the doctor says." We had just attended a Bill Gothard seminar, an annual event required by the school, and that was one of the things that we had heard him proclaim.

With my head and chest heavily congested, I had difficulty wrapping my mind around what Lillian was saying. I turned and stared at her blankly for a few seconds. "Just listen, Lillian," I pleaded with her. "He's going to look inside my throat and ears, then listen to my lungs, and then pull out his prescription pad. It's the same thing every time," I moaned. "I just want to get better because these doctor visits and the prescriptions have cost me almost four hundred dollars already." I knew I wasn't resting enough, but I also believed that there should be a medicine that would fix this, if the doctor would just diagnose my illness correctly.

It was Friday afternoon, and when we arrived at the doctor's office, Lillian took over. "Anna has been sick for months, and she isn't getting any better. She really needs you to help her." This was our trusted doctor who had treated the entire family over the years—always on a cash basis, since Mark and Lillian were small-business owners and didn't have health insurance.

He hunched his shoulders as if defeated. "I've been trying, but she doesn't seem capable of slowing down. More than anything, she needs rest."

I glanced sideways at Lillian, whose gaze was focused directly on the doctor.

The appointment went just as I had predicted. He checked my throat and ears, and then listened with his stethoscope to my lungs, front and back. When the doctor reached over to pick up the prescription pad, I burst into uncontrollable tears. Lillian put her arm around me and asked me to wait for her in the reception area.

I nodded, thankful that Lillian saw with her own eyes what I had predicted would happen. *Maybe I really will get better this time.*

Maybe hearing the doctor tell me to rest will make Lillian realize I'm not being lazy or trying to get out of working. The doctor kindly agreed not to charge me for that visit.

Lillian went with me to the drugstore and filled the prescription, and I took the first dose after I ate a few crackers and some cheese when we got home. Soon after, I fell asleep on the living room floor while watching a movie. Lillian told me later that she and Mark had tried to wake me to send me to bed, but I didn't move. I remember fading in and out, feeling loopy, trying to talk but nothing coherent coming out. This strong medicine contained codeine, designed to knock me out cold. Lillian placed a pillow under my head and covered me with a blanket.

Saturday passed in a continued fog of drowsiness, but I still went to work at the appliance store, though I wasn't much help. On Sunday morning, I went to church with the family, then came straight home and went to bed. Late that afternoon, I took my medicine and headed back to the evening church service. During church, I started feeling loopy again. When the service was over, I tried to stand with the rest of the congregation, but I couldn't. My brain told my legs to stand up, but they wouldn't—or couldn't—comply. I grabbed the arm of my friend sitting next to me. "I can't walk. Would you please go get Lillian?"

Several church members put me between them and helped walk me to the car, and when we got home, Mark and Lillian lifted me under each arm to carry me to bed. I slept hard and long.

The next morning, June 27, 1988, I woke early as usual and dressed for work. After I ate breakfast, I took my medicine and rested on the couch, waiting for Lillian to return with the station wagon and pick me up.

"Anna, Anna! Wake up!"

I heard a voice, off in the distance. I woke to Lillian shaking my shoulder. I stared at her but had difficulty keeping my eyes open. I willed myself to sit up, but I kept dozing off again.

"Anna! It's time to go to work."

"Okay, I—let me . . ."

"Anna." Lillian gently took my face in her hands and tilted it up toward hers.

"I'm sorry, I'm just so sleepy."

"I can see that." She laughed. "Well, I don't see how you can possibly work today. Why don't you just stay home and rest?" She finally understood that I really was too sick to work.

Relief flooded through me. She had never spoken those words to me before. No one had ever encouraged me to rest or take care of myself or even consider myself above the obligations in my life. Hearing the doctor's advice in person must have finally convinced Lillian. I curled up on the couch and stayed there, while the children played around me.

At one point when I woke up, I asked one of the kids, "What time is it?"

"Four o'clock."

"It's four already? I need to take my medicine." I pushed myself up to a sitting position on the sofa. No dizziness. I said a silent prayer, thankful that I didn't feel light-headed. I stood up slowly and plodded to the kitchen to pour myself a glass of water. The phone rang before I could take my medicine. I shushed the children as I picked it up. "Hello?"

"Anna?"

"Yes."

"This is Don. Listen to me carefully."

Why would Don be calling me? Years before, Ramona had married Don after she had left Dan Jordan. Was there something wrong with Ramona?

"Are you okay, Anna?"

He must have heard about me being carried out of church yesterday. How thoughtful of him to check on me. "I'm feeling better. Thank you."

"And the kids? Are they all right?"

His voice sounded odd and strangled, as though he had to force out his words—one at a time. "Yeah, we're all doing fine." *Hmmm, odd that he would ask about the children.*

"Melvin is on his way over to the house."

Melvin, who attended our church, worked for Reliance Appliance. "To Mark and Lillian's house?"

"Yes. He should be there any minute."

I noticed the same weird tone in his voice—an urgency, perhaps. My stomach was balled up like a tight fist. "Why is he coming here?"

"Listen, Anna, just gather the kids together and get in the truck with Melvin. Don't ask me any questions. Just do as I say." He hung up before waiting for me to answer.

His last words left me unsettled. Every time I had heard those words before meant we were moving far away in a hurry or something was wrong. This couldn't be good. My mind leapt to a worst-case scenario. Were Mark and Lillian dead? I knew something horrible had happened; I just didn't know what. Seconds later, I heard tires screeching as someone turned off the road into our driveway.

A moment later, Melvin pounded on the front door as he entered. "Anna! You need to get the kids and come with me. Now!"

I reacted much like I had during the FBI and police raids of my childhood—my instincts took over. I never asked what was wrong. I suppose a part of me didn't want to know the truth because I realized that this kind of craziness never happened in my family unless someone had been killed. On autopilot, I raced to find the kids and rushed them out the door ahead of me to Melvin's truck, which he had left running.

We sat in silence as he drove us to the home of Gary and Mary Ann Hammons, trusted members of our church. Other people from church had been waiting on the front lawn for us to arrive and quickly ushered us into the living room, where others were whispering and praying together. A couple of the women dabbed at their eyes with tissues.

I was certain that what I feared was true. *If Mark and Lillian are dead, who will take care of their kids?* I was old enough. My brain began to formulate different scenarios, coming up with arguments I could present in court before a judge, begging him to let me raise the kids. I knew I could handle the task. I'd been like a live-in nanny to the kids for almost six years. The mantle I took on in that moment weighed heavy on my heart and mind, but I knew God would help me do it and do it well.

Hours went by, and no one told us anything. I tried to entertain the children by playing quiet games and telling them stories. A couple of them went into one of the bedrooms to watch TV. Everyone continued to speak in hushed tones. As desperate as I was to know the truth, I dared not ask the question for fear of hearing the words I dreaded were coming.

Finally, the front door opened, and Alma UnRue, the pastor's wife, walked in. "Children . . . Anna," she glanced my way and tightened her lips into a sympathetic smile. "I have some bad news. This afternoon, at about four o'clock, a man entered the appliance store and walked into your dad's office. He had a gun, and he shot your dad."

Her voice faltered, and she choked back sobs. Hannah looked at me, confused. I lifted her up onto my lap.

"I'm so sorry to have to be the one to tell you, but your dad didn't survive the gunshot wound—he died. I am so, so sorry. But I want you to know that God welcomed him into heaven the moment it happened, and your dad is with Jesus right now."

Though I'd been fairly certain something tragic had occurred from the moment Don called, hearing the truth still shocked me. All around the living room, Mark and Lillian's children reacted to the news with everything from muffled sobs to loud crying. My little nieces, sitting on either side of me, burst into tears and covered their faces. I put my arms around them, pulling them both close to me. Emily clutched my arm and began repeating, "Not Daddy. Not my daddy."

My heart pounded in my chest, and my breaths became short, shallow pants. I did my best to hold back my tears, determined to be stoic for the children. I prayed for strength, and God answered by reminding me that Lillian was still alive. I sighed with relief. I wouldn't have to fight a judge for custody of the children. Their mother would be able to raise them. By herself. Because Mark was dead! Gunned down—murdered.

My breath caught in my throat as a wave of grief engulfed me. I choked back my own tears of sadness and kissed the tops of the girls' heads. Other adults hugged sobbing children and whispered things I couldn't hear above the cries.

I closed my eyes and wished I were just having a bad dream, but when I opened them, nothing had changed. The phrase Lillian had mentioned in the car on the way to the doctor's office came to mind: "a sickness unto the glory of God."

At the time she'd said it, I'd had no idea what she meant. How could someone's illness bring God glory? But now, three days later, I had total clarity. Had God planned for me to be so sick that I needed to take medication that would knock me out and make me loopy? Had God intended that I not go to work that day? After all, He's God. He sees all and knows all. He knows what's going to happen before it happens.

Mark's murder hadn't taken God by surprise. If I had gone to Reliance that day, I might have been lying next to Mark in the morgue. Did God spare me because He had bigger plans for my life? The thought pressed hard on my heart.

I have to call Celia! She lived alone in an apartment nearby, and I wanted her safe here with us as quickly as possible. I picked up the phone and dialed her number.

"Hi, Celia, do you have anyone with you?" My throat felt tight, and my voice came out high pitched.

"No. I just got home from work."

"Can you come over to Sister Hammons's house right now?"

"Why do I need to come to her house? Is there something wrong?"

"Just trust me."

"Okay. I'll be right over."

I hung up the phone, relieved that she was on her way.

Ten minutes later, the front door opened and Celia rushed in. I ran to her and held her tightly.

"What's wrong?" She held me at arm's length. "What is it, Anna?" Suddenly, she lowered her voice, looked me in the eye, and gravely demanded, "Anna, you tell me what's wrong!"

Mary Ann quickly gestured at several of us to join her in a back bedroom. Celia reluctantly followed, knowing that was the only way she would get the answers to her questions. I trailed right behind her.

When Sheila, our pastor's daughter, told Celia that Mark had been shot, my sister burst into gut-wrenching sobs. "Is he dead?" she asked weakly, clutching my hands in hers and staring at me, willing me to tell her this wasn't true. Our friend Debbie was stroking her arm, saying, "Keep calm. The kids are in the other room and they can hear you."

I said quietly to Celia, "He's gone."

Celia's wailing began in earnest, and nothing could stop her from expressing her deep well of grief.

Sheila went on calmly. "There's more we need to tell you girls. We've just learned that Mark's brother, Duane, and one of Duane's daughters, Jenny, were also killed here in Houston. And your brother Ed was shot and killed in Dallas." All of the murders had happened right around four o'clock.

I involuntarily clutched my throat as I imagined the last horrific moments in the lives of each of these precious people, all of whom were former members of my father's cult, who had each left The Church of the Lamb of God, determined to get away from the oppression. Look at the price they'd paid. In that instant, another dreadful thought pierced me: *Celia and I had also fled the cult. Would someone come after us, too?*

"What? They're all dead?" Celia wailed, then doubled over. "Who would do that? Jenny's just a little girl! No. Nooo!" She screamed, a guttural cry that forced her to her knees. Celia crouched there for a few seconds and then lifted her head to look at me, her eyes red and swollen. "They can't be dead. They just can't be." She crawled to the bed and pulled herself up on it.

I sat down next to her and put my arms around her, still trying to calm her down for the sake of the children in the other rooms. She clung to me for strength and wailed even louder. "*Nooo!*"

I loved my sister with all my heart, but I couldn't focus on Celia's grief. She would process it and move on, like we always did. Instead, my thoughts turned to Lillian's children in the living room. I didn't want Celia's wails to frighten them. I lightly patted my sister's shoulder in a feeble attempt to comfort her. She rocked back and forth on the bed, her cries slowly becoming low sobs with ragged breaths in between. I continued to rub her back, stroke her hair, and whisper words to console her. "Celia, shhh . . . everything's going to be okay."

I wished I could believe those words myself.

TWENTY-EIGHT

I woke with a start, forgetting for a moment where I was. All the lights in the bedroom were on, but I didn't recognize the room or the bed I was lying on. Celia was asleep next to me, and I shook her. "Hey, wake up."

"No," she moaned and rolled over.

When I sat up and got my bearings, the horror of the recent hours bludgeoned me with full force. Mark was dead. Lillian was a widow. And I had lost the closest thing I had ever known to a real father. Although Mark was only seventeen years older than I was, he had maturity beyond his years. He had led his wife and family well by escaping the LeBaron cult and guiding them toward relationships with Jesus. He owned and ran a successful small business and provided for his children to go to a private Christian school. He even took on the causes of others—fatherless boys and girls like me. He and Lillian had shown me more kindness, generosity, discipline, and guidance than anyone I'd ever known. His murder was senseless!

I just couldn't wrap my mind around the fact that Mark was dead. And not just dead—murdered. Violently killed in his place of business. Who would do such a thing? Rumors among family members were whispered in hushed tones. But for now, I couldn't release my pain through tears. The children needed me. Lillian needed me. I knew I had to be strong to help the others bear their pain. Still, the fear was there as always, knotting up my insides, deep down in my gut. It rose quickly and cut so deep I thought it might split me in two. The fear that they would come back for more of us was a constant threat hanging over our heads.

I heard a faint knock on the bedroom door, and Mary Ann came in. I lifted my right hand and gave her a little wave. She crossed the room, sat on the end of the bed, and whispered, "The police have said it's safe for all of you to go back home."

I propped myself up on both elbows. "Okay, I'll wake up Celia, and we'll get the kids ready to go."

Melvin drove half of Lillian's children and me home. Don followed close behind with Celia and the other children. When we pulled into the driveway, I spotted at least four police officers and SWAT team members in the front yard and by the street. Melvin and one of the officers searched the house before they allowed any of us to get out of the truck and Don's car. We waited in the vehicles until we saw Don wave the all-clear signal from the front door.

Once inside, Celia and I helped the kids get ready for bed. Several never stopped sobbing through the nighttime ritual. We sang the younger ones a couple of songs and kissed them good night. Without fail, children in each room asked us to leave on a lamp or even the overhead light. I doubted they'd get much sleep.

When Celia and I rejoined the adults in the living room, I looked at everyone's face. This room that was usually such a happy place was now filled with grief, tension, and something else I couldn't quite pinpoint at first. Fear? Yes, even the men were afraid. I clutched Celia's arm, and she and I huddled close together on the couch. Celia couldn't stop crying, so I scooted into the kitchen to grab some tissues, but the box was empty. I grabbed a clean dish towel and handed it to Celia as I sat back down on the couch.

The police officer who had escorted us into the house stood near the front door with a little notepad in his hand. He looked over and said, "Lillian is still at the police station, but she should be here shortly. When she arrives, we're going to ask you young ladies to help her identify possible suspects."

"How are we going to do that?" Celia asked. "We weren't there. We didn't see anything."

The officer glanced at Melvin, cleared his throat, and continued. "Good question. Actually, we believe the shooter may be someone you know."

The color drained from Celia's face, and her hand suddenly got clammy. "What? You think we know the person who did this?"

"Yes, we do. Because the attacks were coordinated to occur at the same time in three different locations, we have reason to believe someone orchestrated them—perhaps directed by someone affiliated with your family's religious group."

I closed my eyes and shuddered. Years after my father's death, his legacy of control and killing lived on. It had only been seven months ago that Dan Jordan had been killed in cold blood. Most likely, someone I knew well was responsible—possibly even one of my own brothers.

I dozed off for a while, though I occasionally heard Celia ask the police officer or Melvin a question. Their low voices sounded muffled and far away. Suddenly, there was a commotion outside the house. An engine was whirring loudly, but not in front of the house—it was overhead! The police officer's walkie-talkie crackled, and a voice squawked, "The helicopter is in position." The police officer whispered something to Melvin, and he ran to the window and pulled back a corner of the blinds to look.

Fully awake now, I jostled Celia. She looked at me, her face clouded with confusion. I whispered, "There's a helicopter hovering over the house."

Moments later, the walkie-talkie went off again. "She's here. All units stand by." The officer quickly lowered the volume.

The front door flew open, and another uniformed officer entered with Lillian and a third officer right behind him. Celia and I rushed to embrace our sister. She was shaking. The three of us huddled in a tight circle, whispering words of comfort to one another. Although Lillian was crying, she didn't make a sound. Suddenly, she gulped in air and stepped back from us. "I need your help."

Celia spoke first. "We'll do whatever you need."

I nodded in agreement.

One of the officers stepped forward with what looked like a large photo album. "We need you to look through these mug shots and see if you recognize anyone who could possibly have shot Mark."

At the mention of her husband's name, Lillian winced and began sobbing again. I handed her the dish towel, and she dabbed the corners of her eyes. "Come on, girls, let's do this."

We sat down on the couch and began leafing through the pages, seeing people we all knew. Occasionally, we would stop and linger on a photo, recalling scenes with that person from our past, all of which seemed like distant memories. We remembered loved ones the way we once knew them, not as suspects in the aftermath of the crimes committed. Still, we followed the officer's instructions and indicated a few possibilities before closing the book.

Between the whir of the hovering helicopter and the continuous squawking of the walkie-talkie, sleep was next to impossible that night. The few times I did drift off, I dreamed of men with guns storming the appliance store. I woke up sweating and trembling. Thankfully, as I looked around, most everyone else was sleeping soundly.

The next morning, I got up and put milk and boxes of cereal on the dining table so everyone could help themselves if they were hungry. Celia and I helped dress and feed the younger children. The older ones walked around the house like zombies, their eyes swollen and red. When Lillian eventually emerged from her bedroom, Celia held her arm to steady her, leading her to the table.

No one said much. Other than the drone of the helicopter that intermittently circled the house and the surrounding area, it was eerily quiet.

TWENTY-NINE

THE NEXT DAYS WERE A BLUR. Lillian could barely function, her emotions constantly on edge. I overheard one of the officers talking to her after she had received a menacing, possibly life-threatening phone call. Tension gripped the entire household despite the continued police presence. We were all jumpy, our nerves frayed from fear for our very lives.

A SWAT team continued to surround the house, and occasionally we heard helicopters overhead. Every hour on the hour, a uniformed officer or an FBI agent knocked on the door and asked permission to search the house and check on us. They often met with the adults about any plans for the day. Officers escorted us everywhere we went, even to the grocery store. They had tiny receivers in their ears with wires that ran down the back of their shirt collars, and they occasionally lifted their hands and spoke into equally tiny microphones on their wrists. I decided not to leave the house until the chaos passed.

The night before Mark's funeral, more family members than I could count filled the house. They came into town from all over the United States and Mexico. Mom, Lillian, Kathleen, and I stood in Lillian's closet helping her pick out clothes. I set up an ironing board in the living room and began ironing clothes for Lillian and the children to wear the next day.

In the middle of the task, the house suddenly went completely dark. Even though we were still under police protection, my mind leapt from scene to scene of the few horror movies I'd watched in my life where the unsuspecting victim is ambushed and killed in some gruesome manner. I just knew I'd be next. My knees buckled, and adrenaline coursed through my veins, causing my breath to come in shallow pants. I broke out in a cold sweat, and chills ran up and down my spine.

Feeling my way in the dark, I made it safely to Lillian's bedroom. A large group of us huddled there, whispering to one another about what we should do. Panicked voices questioned where the children were and how everyone was doing. I just wanted to find a safe place to hide.

Lillian hissed, "Everyone, be quiet. Please."

A hush immediately settled over us all. I heard a faint whisper. "What do you want us to do?" I could hear the fear in Celia's voice.

"Let me think for a moment."

I heard whispering again. All of a sudden, I felt someone at my arm. "Who's this?" Lillian asked.

"It's Anna."

"Go hide in the bathroom. Lie down in the tub." I cautiously made my way down the hall, trying not to bump into anyone else.

I tried to regulate my breathing by slowly inhaling and exhaling. I finally felt the thin strip of molding around the bathroom door and went inside and closed the door behind me. Faint moonlight filtered by cloud cover came through the window and dimly lit the tiny bathroom enough for me to see the tub. I climbed in, pulled the shower curtain closed, and hunkered down.

The tub's coldness quickly seeped through my clothes, chilling me to the core. *I wish I had brought something to wrap myself in. I feel so exposed.* My body began to shake, and once again my breaths came fast, each one reverberating off the tile surrounding me, making them seem louder than they were. *I have to get control of myself or they'll find me.* Curled up in the fetal position, I waited.

I fully expected gunmen to enter the house and start shooting us, just like they had Mark, Ed, Duane, and Jenny. Would they kill us all or would some of my family members manage to get away? *Where's the SWAT team? I thought they were supposed to be protecting us.*

Moments later, I heard the hinge on the bathroom door squeak, as someone opened it slowly. I held my breath, panicked. My heart raced as I tried to flatten myself even more in the tub. *Would dying from a gunshot wound hurt? Would I die quickly?* Instinctively, I covered my head with my hands. Footsteps padded across the floor in my direction. I heard the sound of the shower curtain rings sliding on the rod as the curtain was pushed aside, and I braced myself for the worst.

I squeezed my eyes shut. Suddenly, I felt a foot brush up against mine, as someone stepped into the tub. Even though it startled me, I knew better than to scream out, but every nerve in my body was ignited. Whoever had joined me was hunkered down at the other end of the tub. *It's someone I know.* Neither of us spoke. Quietly, we both pulled the shower curtain closed again to conceal ourselves, leaving us in the dark.

After what seemed like a long time, I heard the SWAT team members calling out for us. "All clear. Everything's secure."

I released a heavy sigh and climbed out of the tub. "I'm glad that's over. I was so scared. Who's there?"

"It's me. Celia."

I let out a long breath.

We stepped out of the bathtub, and I led the way back into the living room. Just as we entered, the lights came back on. The large room, now overflowing with SWAT team members and my family, seemed small. I heard murmurings asking what had happened.

"Quiet, please." An officer got our attention. When everyone stopped talking, he continued. "Sorry about that, folks. A circuit breaker flipped and cut all the electricity to the house. Earlier today, an electrician installed motion-detecting floodlights around the house. On a routine pass around the perimeter, two of our SWAT guys on patrol set off the floodlights. That surge was enough to flip the circuits to the whole house."

I didn't care how the outage had happened; I just felt relieved that the crisis had ended without anyone dying.

x x x x x

After a fitful night's sleep, I woke to shouting from the living room. "Everyone please come in here. I have a few announcements."

I hurried out with my other relatives and noticed that like me, everyone had on their same clothes from the night before, all of us too scared to change into pajamas. Who knew if there might be an attack or if we might have to leave suddenly? A different SWAT officer, this one with a dark complexion, probably Mexican, stood near the front door and held a clipboard. He went through travel instructions for each of us, telling us which car we would ride in to the funeral and with whom.

We quickly ate, changed clothes, and got ready to leave. I put on a long black pencil skirt and a loose white cotton top. Celia and I were put in the same group, along with Ramona and a few others, and we left the house by 8:30 a.m. to go to the funeral home. Don drove us and tried to make conversation on the way, although he gave up after several one-word answers. Clearly, no one felt like talking that morning. When we pulled into the driveway entrance to the funeral home, a SWAT member holding a clipboard stopped the vehicle and gestured for Don to roll down the window.

The SWAT member leaned over and peered into the car. "Who do we have in this vehicle?"

Don pointed to each of us, one by one, and said our names.

The man checked us off his list. "Okay, you may proceed. Please drive slowly so I can identify the license number of this vehicle." I turned my head and watched him out the rear window. He made a couple more notes as we drove away.

The funeral home was a red brick building with large white columns. Don dropped us off at the entrance. We were greeted by a male officer just inside the main double doors. "Good morning, everyone. I'm Agent Hansen." He pointed at Celia and me. "Ladies, I need you to follow me. The rest of you, please wait here."

He led us to a side office and seated us at a large wooden desk. He opened a file folder and took out a stack of papers, placing them in front of us. "As I'm sure you can see, these are photos of your family members and other people in your father's church. I need you to go through and put them into two stacks—the 'good' ones and the 'bad' ones." Although there was some overlap with the photos we had already gone through at the house, most of these photos were new.

I stared at Celia, my mouth agape in astonishment. She looked surprised as well.

Agent Hansen placed both hands on the desk and leaned in toward us. "Look, we're not messing around here. We want to keep all of you safe, and we can't do that without your help. I imagine you trust the majority of these people, but we desperately need you to identify anyone who might cause trouble. We'll have plenty of plainclothes officers here today, as well as at the gravesite."

I knew immediately what "might cause trouble" meant. He

might as well have said "might kill someone today." Celia and I spent about fifteen minutes sifting through photos of people from both the LeBaron family and my father's cult following. We identified a couple of people we weren't sure were safe.

When we were done, Agent Hansen smiled and thanked us. As Celia and I got up to leave, he said, "Wait one minute, please. I need to take a photo of both of you to add to the pile of 'good,' safe people." Once that was done, he escorted us back out to the reception area. As others arrived at the funeral home, they were escorted to the back room, too, for the same procedure.

I don't remember much about the funeral itself, but I know my mother sang the hymn "O My Father." I was still taking the medication for my walking pneumonia, which, combined with the trauma of the situation, made things fuzzy. Still, one memory remains crystal clear: I recall seeing Jim Coates, a retired sheriff who was a family friend, standing at the back of the funeral home during the service. Despite all the SWAT and FBI presence, what made me feel most secure was knowing Jim was there, gun in hand, ready to protect us should anything go down.

After the service, the family got into six or seven limos to transport all of us to the cemetery. As we pulled out, I noticed snipers perched in trees around the funeral home. Officials shut down Interstate 10 in Houston for the procession, and policemen—in cars and on motorcycles—dotted the route. Like an event for a dignitary or celebrity, the procession went on for miles. On the way, I looked out the back window of our limo. The line of cars behind us seemed to have no end.

At the cemetery, the men of Spring Branch Church of God stood behind the family, acting as a human shield to the grieving family members of Mark, Ed, Duane, and Jenny, willing to take a bullet for us.

THIRTY

A HEAVINESS SETTLED OVER THE HOUSE in the days following Mark's funeral. With his death, an emptiness enveloped us all. He had been a solid, steadying presence in my life. He had loved gadgets and always wanted to have the latest and greatest technology—he even owned one of the first cell phones, the kind that was so big it came in a bag.

The FBI and police still provided protection for us. We feared for our lives because murder suspects were still on the loose, so officers were stationed in front of and behind the house to offer extra security. The kids, normally lively and boisterous, still played, but overall they were much more subdued. Lillian spent hours and hours alone in her room, emerging only to make sure the kids were fed. When she did come out, her children mobbed her, desperate to hold her hand, sit in her lap, or tell her about their day. Her eyes were hollow and lifeless. Seeing her in such a state unnerved me because she'd always been so busy and energetic.

The days went by in dull activity, with time passing in slow motion. I recovered from my illness, but I had no idea what my future held now. Short visits from my friends, including my school friend, David, offered me some comfort and helped me see beyond the intense pain and heaviness of each day.

Sorrow and fear lingered as well—sorrow permeating mealtime and fear increasing at bedtime. The children begged to sleep with Lillian, and she let them. At least they were able to cuddle together then; during the day, Lillian was consumed by her grief and didn't have much to give them. So the children turned their focus to me, and I tried to keep them occupied. But it took a toll on me at night because I had a difficult time falling asleep.

We didn't leave the house except for emergencies, for fear that someone might be lying in wait to try to kill us. The business was temporarily closed. One day, a banking matter needed to be taken care of at the office, so Lillian sent me. I was thankful that Don accompanied me to the empty and darkened building. The appliances inside were still covered with the black dust the authorities had used to lift fingerprints off them. As I entered the office, I gasped when I saw the bullet holes in the wall.

I also remember going to an eye doctor appointment not too long after the funeral. I was terrified the entire time driving there and back, worried that someone might follow and target me. The FBI had taught us evasive maneuvering tactics and reminded us to vary our routes if we had to drive places we frequented, like church or a relative's house. They drilled into us how critical it was to never follow a distinct pattern with anything and to always keep on the lookout for family members we suspected. It struck me one day that when we were younger, the sister-wives had taught us to fear the authorities, yet now we were cooperating with them for our protection.

At one point, Jim Coates and his wife, Bonnie, invited me to come stay with them for a while. Lillian had plenty of help from other siblings and the women from the church, so I didn't feel guilty leaving her and the kids. Besides, if she needed me, I wasn't that far away. The Coateses' home proved to be a welcome respite for me. I hung on every word Jim said to me, soaking up his wisdom and street smarts as he drew from his law enforcement background to give me advice on how to stay safe. He was rough around the edges, but he provided comfort and security.

One evening, before I headed out to church, Jim asked me to join him on the patio. "I have something for you."

I followed him out the sliding glass door and sat down at the table. "You and Bonnie have done so much for me already. That's really not necessary."

"I think it is." Jim opened a wooden box on the table. He took out something wrapped in a maroon cloth and placed it on the table between us.

"What's this?" I lifted one side of the cloth and pulled it back. Underneath rested a silver .25 caliber gun. "That's . . . I don't know how to shoot—"

"Now don't argue with me. I'm going to teach you everything you need to know, but I firmly believe you need to carry this weapon with you at all times—for your safety and for the safety of your family." His deep blue eyes bored holes into mine.

I agreed. Over the next week, Jim taught me how to hold the gun properly, gave me shooting lessons, and showed me how to clean it safely. The small gun felt odd in my hand. He told me that if I was ever stopped and questioned by the police, I needed to tell them I was "transporting it" from my home to my workplace or the other way around. Jim taught me many other tactical things as well. He said if I ever felt threatened, I should crouch down and make myself as small a target as possible, and if someone came at me, I should stand with my back against a wall and defend myself from that position.

I can still remember the feeling of the gun tucked into the

pocket of my cotton shorts that summer, especially how it banged against my leg when I walked. When I carried it, I was reminded that I could still be a target.

x x x x x

Near the end of the summer, the security presence around the house was lessened, and Lillian used some of the money from Mark's life insurance policy to fly out to California with her children to stay in the home of some friends who were on vacation. The authorities agreed that having Lillian out of the state would be preferable to having her where she would be recognized.

I was left behind to manage the house and business, which we had reopened, helped by a few other family members.

After they'd been gone about a month, Lillian bought me a plane ticket, using an assumed name for me—Amanda Glass. This was before IDs were required for air travel, so all I had to do was show up at the airport with ticket in hand. "I plan to attend some Bill Gothard training seminars here, and you will get a little break from running the shop," Lillian told me on the phone.

I appreciated the invitation, but soon after I arrived in California, I realized the actual reason she wanted me to come: She wanted me to help her start homeschooling the children. She had invested in a teaching curriculum put out by Bill Gothard's Advanced Training Institute of America (ATIA), and she needed my help to implement the program.

"I don't think I can do that, Lillian. I've been talking with a few of my friends, and I really want to finally go to the International Institute of Accelerated Christian Education." Prior to Mark's death, both he and Lillian had wholeheartedly approved of my decision to attend there. I desperately needed the familiarity and support my friends offered.

I struggled with what I should do because I didn't want to disappoint Lillian. I knew she needed help, and she was used to having my help, but I didn't have the emotional wherewithal to continue putting her needs above my own.

"Well, would you at least stay with the children while I go to Chicago to meet Mr. Gothard and attend the training?"

"Of course." I bowed my head, disappointed that Lillian would expect me to continue putting my life on hold for her family. I was nineteen now, and I needed to start making decisions for myself.

When Lillian got back from the training, she bubbled over with idealistic notions of how schooling her children would play out. She begged me once more to stay with them. When I declined, she sent me back to Houston.

x x x x x

A few weeks later, Lillian and the children returned to Houston. Celia, the friends who dropped in to check on us, and I could all see that Lillian's mental state had continued to decline in the months after Mark's passing. Lillian's mood swings were dramatic—from high to low, making it necessary for her to take prescription medication to keep balanced. However, when she returned to Houston, the reality of her situation and Mark's death settled in, causing her to sink into a deep depression.

I was caught in a conundrum. Part of me believed I owed it to her to stay in Houston and help her with the children and Reliance Appliance, after all she had done for me. The other part of me longed to join my friends at college and begin life on my own terms. I knew that if I didn't separate my life from hers at that juncture, it would likely never happen. Lillian depended on me so much that it felt suffocating.

I sought solace from Celia, and counsel from some of the older women at church. They encouraged me to follow my dreams, go to college, and enjoy my young-adult years, if that's what I wanted. I consistently prayed about the decision and sensed the Lord calling me to go to school. Lillian supported my decision to go to college. She still had help from some of her friends and fellow church members, who were bringing meals, taking care of the kids, and doing the grocery shopping.

Jim Coates drove me to Lewisville, Texas, and dropped me off at the ACE campus. I carried in my few possessions and stopped at the admissions office. A kind woman met me and ushered me to her desk. "It's a pleasure to finally meet you. I'm Joan Baker, director of admissions." She smiled constantly, causing wrinkles to form around the corners of both eyes.

"It's nice to finally be here." I twisted my hands in my lap and tried to focus on her face, instead of letting my eyes wander around the room.

"As you know, we're happy to have you as part of our student body. However, as we discussed over the phone, the administration has some concerns. If parents of other students find out about the recent events in your family, especially since one of the murders took place nearby, they might be gravely concerned that their children could be at risk with you going to school here. We don't agree with that. In fact, we would never have admitted you and invited you here if we didn't believe all of our students, including you, would be safe. But it's critical that we keep those events a secret, or we could have parents overreact and withdraw their students from our school." She leaned forward, resting her forearms on the desk. "Do you think you can do that?"

I nodded and said, "Yes."

"There's one more condition." Joan riffled through some papers on her desk, selected one, and pushed it toward me. "We need you to go by a different name while you're here. The LeBaron name carries too much notoriety. Would Keturah Baron be all right with you?"

I stared at the paper in front of me and read it quickly. "Yes, I can do that." I chewed my lower lip and signed my "old" name on the line, agreeing that I would use my "new" name here at school.

For a long time, most students never knew my real name or anything about my history. Then one day, a friend asked if she could look at my high school class ring so she could see the details on it. Without thinking, I slid the ring off my finger and handed it to her.

She read the engraving on the inside. "Hey, why does it say 'Anna K. LeBaron'?"

Blood rushed to my face and neck, and I stammered before answering, "Listen, I can't really discuss it, but would you just keep this between us? Please?" I hoped my eyes begged enough.

My friend agreed and placed the ring in the palm of my hand.

x x x x x

A few weeks later, I lay on the top bunk in the room I shared with a girl named Crissy, when I heard a voice. *That's odd.* The voice came from inside of me, but it seemed different from my other thoughts. The voice said, "When someone dies, you can't go back." *What does that mean?* I finally concluded that I couldn't go back in time and undo things, to make the outcome different. When someone dies, they're dead. They're gone. I accepted the explanation, even though I wondered why such a thought came to me.

The next morning was Saturday, my day to do laundry. I was sorting my clothes when the phone in the room rang. Crissy answered, handed the phone to me, then disappeared down the hall.

"Hello?"

"Anna, is there someone nearby who cares about you?" Celia's words filled me with dread, as I stared out the dorm room window at the cloudy north Texas day.

"Lillian is dead, isn't she?" The words just popped out.

"Anna, go and get someone who cares about you and come back to the phone."

"Lillian committed suicide, didn't she?"

"Please go get someone and come back to the phone."

I hollered down the hall for Crissy. She hurried back from a friend's dorm room.

"I've got someone with me now. What is it?"

"You're right, Anna. Lillian is dead. She committed suicide, and Emily found her body this morning."

"Please contact Jim Coates and ask him to go to the house and not let anyone near the kids who might tell them that Lillian didn't go to heaven because she committed suicide," I said, recalling a tragic memory from when Isaac committed suicide at Lillian's house. Several people at Spring Branch Church of God told me that because he took his own life and didn't have time to ask God for forgiveness, he would go to hell. I didn't want Lillian's children to hear that devastating lie, so I needed someone to run interference until I could get there. I just had to protect them! I wanted them to know their mom and dad were now together in heaven.

"I will." Celia hung up the phone.

I stood there frozen, holding the receiver up to my ear, as if somehow my refusal to put it down would negate the conversation. I turned around and saw the look of horror on Crissy's face. She stumbled toward me and hugged me tightly.

x x x x x

I drove to Houston with Bob and Phyllis Carpus and their kids, friends from Spring Branch Church. Once I arrived, I felt the weight of many decisions. Lillian's sister-in-law Laura and I picked out Lillian's clothes for burial and then drove to the funeral home to identify the body. Despite the fact that Laura was still grieving the death of her daughter, Jenny, and her ex-husband, Duane, she was a big support to me in planning the funeral. I had just turned twenty a month before, and I felt the burden of making decisions that were far beyond my years.

When Laura and I arrived at the funeral home, the director ushered us into the room where Lillian was lying in the casket. We took one look at her and decided that the garish makeup that the mortician had applied wasn't Lillian's style at all. In her final caring act for her sister-in-law, Laura pulled out her own makeup to soften Lillian's look. I was thankful she made her appear more like the Lillian we knew and loved.

Lillian's funeral was a small affair, with mostly local family in attendance. A few of her sisters came into town to pay their respects and figure out what would happen to the kids. Lillian was dressed in the clothes Laura and I had chosen, a pretty white button-down shirt with small pleats down the front and a long mauve skirt with a modest gathering around the waist. She looked like she was ready to go to church.

I don't remember much about the funeral itself. I focused my energy and attention on taking care of the kids and being there for them. At the visitation the night before the funeral, I had made sure I accompanied them into the room for the viewing. I wanted to protect them as best I could, but I also knew they needed to see their mother in order to have closure. At the service, we sang "It

Is Well with My Soul," one of Lillian's favorites. After the funeral, while I was still in Houston, I took care of the kids and stuffed my own feelings down.

Lillian's death pushed all of us—me, her children, Celia, and my other siblings who knew her well—closer to the brink. Mark and Lillian had served as my surrogate parents for all of my teenage years. Trying to grieve both of their deaths and the gaping hole they left in our family overwhelmed me to the point that avoidance of my emotions felt like a better route, certainly a safer one.

Although many of my family members thought I would be the natural person to fill Lillian's shoes, I just couldn't face the idea of raising the children alone. I might have been the closest person in their young lives, but I didn't have the strength to do the job well. Thankfully, a couple from the church, Bob and Phyllis Carpus, offered to take in all six of Mark and Lillian's children.

THIRTY-ONE

ONCE I RETURNED TO SCHOOL, though, I came unglued.

I thought that returning to my normal schedule might help assuage the pain of losing my second mom. I was wrong. Instead, I fell into a deep depression. Though I slept most of the time I wasn't in class, I never felt like I could get enough rest. Whereas I had once been a conscientious and attentive student, now I nodded off in my classes when the teacher was up front lecturing, which meant most of the time. At certain periods during the day our dorms were off limits, but I would sneak back in to take a nap.

Mrs. Hester, our dorm mother, caught me several times. On the fourth or fifth incident, she cornered me. "I know you must be grief stricken over your sister's death, but sneaking around won't help. I want you to go see Mrs. Johnson."

I just stared blankly and nodded.

While I was waiting to see Mrs. Johnson, the dean of women, I dozed off in the reception area. Her assistant gently shook me. "Keturah, Mrs. Johnson is ready to see you now."

I grabbed my book bag and purse and went into her office. She greeted me at the door with a side hug. "I'm glad you came to see me, Keturah. Have a seat."

I sat across from her, a number of folders neatly stacked on her desk between us.

"I can't even begin to imagine what you're going through. The death of a loved one is always difficult, but a suicide . . . well, that takes grief to a whole different level."

I nodded, willing myself not to cry.

"Mrs. Hester told me you've been sneaking into the dorm during the day to sleep. Your teachers said you can't keep your eyes open during their lectures. Listen, I don't want to pry. I simply want to help. Will you please let me?"

I uttered a barely audible, "Yes."

Mrs. Johnson recommended herbal remedies to help me sleep and give me more energy. I tried them, but they had little effect. Bob and Phyllis Carpus were concerned about my well-being and got involved too. Together, the three of them decided I would get more rest if I lived off campus for a while and arranged for me to live with a family nearby named the Meltons. Though I slept much better at night in my new living situation, I still fell asleep during class. The problem wasn't that I wasn't getting enough rest. The problem was depression, not easily solved and certainly not by attacking only one component. Yes, I was always tired, but I was also numb.

The Carpuses and Mrs. Johnson suggested plan B—counseling sessions with Pastor Burnside, the pastor of the church I attended at the time in Denton, Texas. The Burnside family invited me to stay with them for a week while I underwent intensive therapy. They reasoned that I could rest as much as I needed in between counseling sessions. During this time, I slept as much as eighteen to twenty hours a day, waking up only for therapy sessions and sporadic meals.

During one session, Pastor Burnside placed an empty chair in front of me and asked me to imagine Lillian sitting in the chair and talk to her. Even though the exercise felt pointless, I did as he asked. I have no idea what I said to the chair. The pastor prayed at the beginning of each session. I don't remember praying; I just remember going through the motions and trying to say the right things so that everyone would just leave me alone.

At their wits' end as to how to help me, they asked my former youth pastor, the man who had led me to Christ, to intervene. He had moved to the Dallas area years before, and when he showed up at the house for a "surprise" visit, I managed to make us both a sandwich. We talked about our mutual friends and "the good old days" of the youth group. As soon as he left, I realized that Bob and Phyllis had asked him to stop by and see me. I knew everyone was worried about me coming out of my depressed state. I wondered if I ever would. It seemed like it could go on forever.

One afternoon, I woke from a marathon nap, my head groggy, stuck halfway between sleep and being awake. Somewhere deep inside me, a thought formed: *You will never feel happiness again.* I never questioned the idea, which I would normally do. Instead, in a matter of seconds, I accepted it completely as fact. In the same moment, I accepted that fate. Somehow it didn't bother me to know I would live "lifeless" for the rest of my days. I acknowledged that I would never again feel joy or happiness coursing through my body. Such light, airy feelings didn't seem possible, given the tragedies that had occurred in my life.

The deadness within me permeated every aspect of my being— mind, body, and spirit—to the point that I had no desire for anyone or anything. I couldn't care less about what happened around me or to me. I only went through the motions of life because others required that of me. Otherwise, I slept. Weeks passed, and yet the loss of anything resembling a life didn't bother me in the least. I didn't want to go anywhere, do anything, see or talk to anyone.

Things I had once enjoyed doing with friends held no appeal. Instead, a deep heaviness hung over my every step, which made simple tasks—such as getting out of bed to go to the bathroom—seem daunting. I wore no makeup when I went out and barely bothered to comb my hair. I did the bare minimum to get by. This went on for months.

x x x x x

Spring arrived, but I hardly noticed, since I rarely went outside other than to class when I was able to. One day in class, a teacher announced a group field trip. The school had purchased tickets for every student to attend a Sandi Patty concert at Reunion Arena in Dallas. Even though Sandi Patty was one of my favorite artists at the time (second only to Amy Grant), even though I knew every one of her songs by heart, I didn't feel like going.

I had attended a Sandi Patty concert just the year before, after begging Lillian to purchase the concert tickets for me and my friends on her credit card, and then quickly collecting money from them to pay Lillian back. I had no interest in going this year. I told the organizers of the field trip that I wouldn't be attending.

The day of the concert, I returned to the Meltons' house after class and immediately got in bed. The clock beside the bed read 5:15 p.m. Ten minutes later, I heard someone knocking on the front door. I ignored it, hoping whoever it was would go away.

The knocking continued, and I continued to ignore it.

Finally, the knocking became so frequent and persistent that I knew I wouldn't be able to sleep until whoever was doing it went away. I opened the front door to see my friend Kelli Green standing there.

"Hey, aren't you coming to the Sandi Patty concert with us?" Kelli gestured over her shoulder to the car parked on the street.

"No, I already said I didn't want to go. I asked them to give my ticket to someone else."

"But you love Sandi Patty! Why aren't you going?"

"Because I don't feel like it. I'm tired, and I want to sleep." To emphasize my point, I closed my eyes and leaned against the doorjamb.

"You've been sleeping an awful lot lately. It will do you good to get out and do something fun for a change."

"I really don't feel like it. You guys go on ahead. I don't want to go."

"Well, you've been cooped up in this house for months, just sleeping. It's time you got out and had some fun." Her eyes pleaded as much as her words.

"Don't you get it? I want to stay here and sleep."

"Well, you really need to get out and do something. I'll wait while you get ready."

I stared at my friend. I was sure she meant well, but she was starting to tick me off. "Look, *I don't want to go! I don't feel like doing anything!* I'm not fun to be around, and I don't want to bring everyone else down by showing up. Thanks for what you're trying to do, but I'm going back to bed." I turned to go back inside.

Kelli grabbed my arm and pulled me back to face her. "No. You aren't going back to bed, Keturah. You're coming with us."

I yanked my arm free. "No. I'm not!"

"Go get dressed." Kelli extended her entire arm and pointed into the house.

"I'm not going. I'm in my pajamas, and I'm staying here. See you later." I started to shut the door.

"*Keturah.*" Kelli said my name in an authoritative tone I'd never heard her use before—ever. "You are coming with us. Go get dressed, or I'm dragging you to the concert in your pajamas. You don't have a choice here. Go. Get. Dressed. *Now.* I'm not leaving without you, you can be sure of that. Now *go.*"

My entire body sagged in defeat. "Fine. I'll go get dressed. But you're going to regret this. I'm not a lot of fun to be around these days."

Undeterred, Kelli offered a parting shot as I went back inside. "And pack a pair of jeans. We have off-campus passes for tonight, and a bunch of us are going to West End and Reunion Tower after the concert." Jeans were forbidden at our conservative Christian college, and so were the post-concert activities they had planned for us.

I hardly remember the concert itself, but afterward my friends insisted on moving forward with their plans as Kelli, our friends Debbie and Becky, and I entered the parking garage. "Girls, we're going to change into our jeans in the backseat of the car. We can take turns watching out for other people."

Modest me was grateful for the cover of darkness the garage provided, but the possibility of getting caught invigorated me, the first time I'd felt like that in months. Anna, the rule follower, chose to break all the rules that night, and the accompanying adrenaline rush let me know I was still alive. I hadn't died along with Lillian back in January.

In the same way I'd accepted that I would never feel happy again, I realized that any feeling whatsoever—even happiness—was possible. That rush of adrenaline broke through the deadness I'd been experiencing for so long. I felt as though a doctor had yelled, "Clear!" and used shock paddles to jump-start my heart. I felt alive again. That night showed me I had the potential for happiness and joy on the horizon and that I would go on to live a full life.

I woke the next morning still feeling the rush of the night before. Breaking the rules had brought me back to life. It dawned on me that my Savior had done the same thing. When Jesus walked the earth, He broke the rules that the Jewish leaders had established for God's people, and they hated Him for it.

I remembered the Bible story of Jesus healing a paralyzed man after the man's friends lowered him through the roof into the crowded room where Jesus was teaching. I viewed my rescue in much the same way. My friend Kelli's persistence and rule-breaking initiated the healing process in my life. Jesus didn't follow the status quo, and He paid the ultimate price for it when He was crucified. Many times, my friends and I paid the price for breaking the rules at the Institute, getting "campused" for our infractions. We regularly got into trouble for not adhering to the rules and restrictions the administration imposed on us—rules that we had agreed to follow when we'd enrolled. But rules and regulations, laws and teachings, didn't save my life that day; breaking the rules set me free from the bondage of depression. Sometimes breaking the rules is necessary.

THIRTY-TWO

Bob and Phyllis Carpus had just become empty nesters when they became the legal guardians of Mark and Lillian's six children. In January of 1990, the family moved from Houston to Lewisville, Texas. In an act of selflessness, the Carpuses sold or gave away most of their home's furnishings and packed up Mark and Lillian's furniture and décor items for the new address. They wanted their house to feel as much like home to the children as possible. I was touched by their thoughtfulness.

Once the family was settled, I moved in with them as well, to be a source of stability and comfort to the children. Still, the grieving, which was raw and real for all of us, continued.

I was thankful for my boyfriend back in Houston, David, who regularly wrote to me. His words made me feel accepted and worthy. But our relationship had been a roller-coaster ride since high school. David and I developed an unhealthy pattern of "going together" and breaking up. We would spat over various things—sometimes silly or inconsequential, but more than a few times over more serious matters. Several adults warned me not to consider marriage yet, saying I was too young and inexperienced with male-female relationships to make such a commitment. And others pointed out that the off-again times in my relationship with David were warning signs. "You need more emotional healing from all of the trauma in your life first" was their advice. To be perfectly honest, neither of us was ready to get married.

But I was so in love. When David and I were together, I couldn't see past my feelings for him. And yet when we were apart, I wrestled with doubt and insecurity. Would marrying him be a mistake? Would anyone ever love me as much as David said he did?

David's presence in my life had become familiar and comfortable. I fantasized again about the kind of life we could have together. As proof that I'd broken free from my childhood chains of polygamy, I would be David's one and only wife. I wouldn't have to share him with anyone. And we would have lots of kids.

David decided to join the Marine Corps. Right before he left for thirteen weeks of basic training, he visited me for a weekend. Being with him again, in person, felt so right. He had always been a gentleman, and I appreciated that about him. We had committed to remaining pure while we dated, and we kept that commitment to one another. I felt like that promise alone spoke volumes about how he would treat me after we were married. I knew he would love and respect me. And I believed David would help me unravel my tangled emotions following Lillian's death.

I was thrilled to go to the Marine Corps recruit depot in San Diego for David's graduation, appropriately fancy in my new outfit and three-inch heels. The next day, we flew back to Houston, where the celebration continued.

David's mom, Sandy, had prepared his favorite meal of chili beans and Mexican-style cornbread, with Mrs. Smith's Deep Dish Apple Pie and Blue Bell Homemade Vanilla ice cream for dessert. We both enjoyed being with his family, including his younger brother and sister, Ben and Emily. I slept at Celia's apartment, but I spent every waking hour with David.

One night after dinner, we were alone at his mom's apartment, relaxing on the couch together. Suddenly, David pulled out a little black box, opened it, and held it in his hand in front of me. I gaped at the diamond ring inside.

"Anna, will you marry me?"

My heart missed a beat at the question. I couldn't wait to begin our happily-ever-after life together.

"Yes, of course I'll marry you!" I couldn't wait to tell Celia and begin planning my wedding! I thought, *I wish I could let you know, too, Mom. If only I knew how to reach you.*

After David returned to San Diego to complete the rest of his training, I began to plan our wedding. Every time we talked on the phone, I asked his opinion about wedding details—the colors I was choosing, flowers, music—and he assured me that whatever I decided was fine with him.

"All I really care about is seeing you coming down that aisle toward me. I can't wait for us to walk out of that church as husband and wife."

Thankfully, I had Celia, as well as lots of friends and stand-in "family" like Bob and Phyllis, who were willing to help with the wedding plans. Neither David's parents nor my mom could help us with the expenses, so the words *shoestring budget* became a reality we worked around.

Celia, my maid of honor, already had her dress—a sky-blue Cinderella-style ball gown I had made for her when I was a senior in high school. The dress took first prize in the state ACE international student competition and a fifth-place ribbon nationally. But having Celia wear it on this day was the most meaningful to me.

To honor Lillian and Mark, I asked their youngest daughter,

Hannah, to be my flower girl. She had just turned seven years old. I couldn't afford a fancy dress for her, either. A friend from work, Nancy McGee, offered to make a simple, elastic-waistband skirt. I didn't hold much hope of finding the same color as Celia's dress, but I thought the same taffeta fabric in a complementary color would work well.

One night after work, Nancy and I went to Cloth World to pick out the fabric. As soon as we walked into the store, I began scanning the bolts of fabric, looking for a pale shade of pink. One of the employees had a shopping cart full of rolled-up fabric remnants. As she picked up a bundle of remnants, I couldn't believe my eyes. In her hand was a small roll of the exact fabric and color I had used for Celia's dress—just enough fabric to make a fancy skirt for a little girl. Nancy took the fabric home and brought the finished skirt to my house the following day.

More than anything, I wanted to find a beautiful wedding dress. I went to several bridal shops and tried on gorgeous gowns, but the price tag on every one far exceeded my budget. I had no idea how I would pay for such an extravagant purchase on my meager earnings working for ACE. I lamented my situation to Celia during one of our many long-distance phone calls. "Even though I love this one particular dress, I can't justify spending that much money. No, that's not true. I don't have the money to spend."

Celia offered a suggestion. "Why don't you rent a gown for the day? That way you'd get something beautiful, and it wouldn't break the bank." That was an idea I hadn't even considered.

I heard another voice on the phone in the background.

"Hold on," Celia said.

"Well, if my wedding gown fits her, she can have it!" said the other voice.

Celia came back on the line. "Anna, my boyfriend's sister just came by the office, and she heard me talking to you about a wedding dress. She said you're welcome to wear hers." Later, Celia elaborated, saying that the young woman's wedding day wasn't a good memory for her, and she was delighted that her dress might make someone else happy.

Celia confirmed the size, and that sealed the deal. Celia sent me the dress by FedEx just days before the wedding. I still had a rental gown in reserve, but I was hoping I could cancel the rental with minimal fees if this dress worked out.

When the package arrived, I held my breath as I pulled it out of the box and slowly unzipped the protective bag it was in. I stepped into the dress with Emily's help. As I stood in front of the mirror, I couldn't believe my reflection.

Not only did it fit perfectly, but it had the same type of sleeves that were on the dress I had picked out to rent, and a bodice and high neckline made of beautiful lace. Nancy loaned me her wedding veil. I look back now and marvel at the miracle dress—perfectly styled, formed, and fitted just for me. I knew that my heavenly Father had provided this gift to make my wedding day special.

Another friend from work made us a wonderful three-tiered cake and created all the silk flower arrangements for the wedding party. Immediately after the ceremony, she would repurpose my bouquet as a decoration for the bridal table at the reception. I valued her frugality and understanding.

David finished his training and flew to Dallas the night before our wedding. On December 16, 1989, Bob Carpus walked me down the aisle. I carefully measured my steps, looking around at all the family and friends that showed up for us that day. I was sad that Mom couldn't be there, but I was grateful for everyone else who came. It was a day of celebrating young love, and everyone was happy for us.

A family friend paid for my honeymoon attire, and my college friends, led by Madlin, pooled their funds for David and me to stay at a nearby hotel on our wedding night. As we began our life together, I reveled in the joy of the moment.

We spent the last part of our honeymoon celebrating Christmas with David's grandparents, retreating to "the honeymoon suite"— the guest bedroom in their home—at night. Grampa Roger and Grammy Nancy's generosity made our shoestring-budget honeymoon everything we could have hoped for and more. As we got ready to leave, Grammy packed up our car with brand-new bedding, household items, and yummy treats for the road. There was barely room for us!

Soon David shipped out to Okinawa, Japan, to begin active duty, and I was left in Lewisville trying to figure out how to obtain a US passport and a visa so I could join him overseas. I only had a Mexican birth certificate from Chihuahua, Mexico. I went to Congressman Dick Armey's office in Denton, Texas, to ask for his help. I sat down with one of his assistants to recount an abbreviated version of my life story.

When I was done, the assistant asked, "Can you get in touch with your mother?"

"I don't have any idea where she is," I said.

"Okay, we'll get this done another way." We based my citizenship off of my mother, since that would be proof enough, and less complicated than my father. I spent the next few months sending off for my mom's high school and college transcripts and the birth certificates of her first five children, all born in the United States. After two trips to the passport office in Houston, I was finally issued a passport.

"This is your only proof of citizenship," the kind lady at the agency told me. "Be sure never to let your passport expire." My passport is still my only proof that I am a citizen of the United States.

Finally, in April 1990, I bought a one-way ticket to Okinawa, Japan. I believed all my dreams were coming true.

x x x x x

We started our family in Japan with the birth of our son, David Joziah. After experiencing pregnancy-induced high blood pressure, among other scary symptoms, and then thirty-six hours of labor, I finally gave birth to him by C-section. Even after tending to all of those babies as a young girl, when the nurse came to discharge us from the hospital, I thought with a touch of alarm, *What do I do if he cries?* Not having family around to help left me feeling a bit vulnerable, especially in a foreign country.

I felt a strange dichotomy in Japan. Being away from Mark and Lillian's children had its benefits, namely that I wasn't reminded of their parents' tragic deaths on a daily basis. But I missed being connected with my large family and knowing everything that went on in the lives of my siblings, nieces, and nephews. Though David and I enjoyed living abroad, as months passed, cracks in our marriage began to surface, much like cracks in the walls of a house when the foundation starts becoming compromised. I chose to ignore these marital cracks, thinking things would get better in time. I couldn't wait to return to the United States, which we did in January 1992.

That same year, our son Caleb was welcomed into the world by Amy Grant's new song, "Breath of Heaven," which I had on repeat mode on my CD player. We brought him home from the hospital on Christmas Eve, the words of the song echoing in my heart forevermore.

Be forever near me, Breath of heaven.

Celia surprised me by buying my mom a plane ticket to come help me after Caleb was born. Celia joined us for part of the visit as well. Any bitterness I might have felt toward Mom began to lessen once I saw her interacting so tenderly with my children and caring for me. I was tandem-nursing the two boys, and my mom's concern that Caleb wouldn't get enough breast milk was so endearing to me. She had tried to breast-feed her children, but would "dry up after a few weeks," she told me. The tension in our relationship eased a bit.

When my son Jacob was born in 1994, within months we realized he needed surgery on his skull because his soft spot had closed up too quickly. I asked Mom to come help me again. She told me she would pray about it. I fumed at the notion that she would have to pray before deciding whether to come help one of her children. My own mothering instincts couldn't fathom such a response. She did end up coming after all, and I was thankful she was there.

In 1995, I headed for Dallas with my three sons to attend the wedding of Mark and Lillian's oldest daughter, Emily. Suddenly the drought ended, and family surrounded me—Celia, Rena, and several of my brother Heber's children I'd never met before. We greeted each other warmly, made introductions, and snapped pictures at a frenetic rate.

But the joyous event was a stark reminder of the losses we had endured. As Emily walked down the aisle with a surrogate for Mark, my efforts to choke back tears proved futile. Celia and I both cried through the entire wedding as we faced afresh the pain of losing Mark and Lillian. A photo of them on their wedding day positioned in a place of honor magnified their absence.

My decision to attend Emily's wedding wasn't motivated by obligation—I wanted to be there. In some respects, I felt as though my presence somehow represented Mark and Lillian and kept their spirits alive. For years I carried within me the self-imposed weight of being their representative at these milestone events. Nothing would have kept me away from the children during that time period. Embracing them and watching them grow brought me great joy. But sorrow always accompanied the joy, inseparable twins at every event. Tears of joy and sorrow welled up and spilled over because I had never properly grieved Mark's and Lillian's deaths. Back then, I didn't know how. I only knew how to compartmentalize the ache in my heart as I numbed the pain of my grief.

With a husband and three little boys to care for, life never slowed down. Consequently, I allowed busyness to push aside my grief. But Emily's wedding, and every other happy event that followed, like summer visits from the children and all of their graduations from high school and college, reopened my wounds, ushering in the worst heartache I'd ever known.

When we returned home from the wedding, I was exhausted. That night, I had a dream that I was standing at the sink washing dishes, watching birds through the window dodge and weave in an airborne game of tag. Suddenly, a brown van screeched to a halt in the driveway in front of the house. Out jumped members of the "bad side" of my family, including my brother Heber. Each of them carried guns and assault rifles. They stormed into our house before I could run to lock the front door.

Just as I entered the living room, they sprayed the entire area with bullets. Shot in the stomach, I fell to the floor, face first. The shots hadn't killed me, and I felt thankful to be alive. Still, I knew that if I got up, they would simply shoot me again. But if

I pretended I was dead, maybe they would leave me alone and I could go find my children and protect them from this evil.

I have to get to my boys. But if I move, it's all over. I felt powerless to help my own children. Heber and my other family members could have already found my sons asleep in their rooms and killed them all.

Just as I started to push myself up off the floor, I woke up from the nightmare, drenched in sweat, my heart racing. I lay awake the rest of the night, covers tucked up to my chin, the horrible scenarios playing out in my mind.

THIRTY-THREE

A FEW DAYS LATER, I was with my friend Diana at the park. She had three young boys, too, and when we could, we arranged play-dates with each other for our kids. As the boys played, we sat on a bench and I told her about the nightmare. She listened intently, her face registering an array of emotions. I valued her empathy and thanked God that she was kind enough to listen.

As soon as I reached the end of the narrative, Diana reached out and placed her hand on my knee. "Do you have someone at your church you can talk to? Like a women's ministry director?"

"No," I responded. "I don't think so."

"A woman at our church does lay ministry counseling. If I make an appointment for you, would you go?"

I stared at her, shocked yet hopeful at her offer. It had not occurred to me that I might need a counselor, and I wouldn't have known where to begin looking for one. Diana understood that I wasn't even capable of following through on contacting this woman and scheduling a time to meet. I whispered, "Yes."

"Would you like me to pick you up and take you? Or could I babysit the boys while you go?"

I glanced over to the swings, where our sons squealed with

excitement the higher they went. *Diana isn't simply suggesting I get counseling. She wants to facilitate the process.* I was touched by this caring friend. "If you can babysit the boys, I'd be so grateful."

Two days later, Diana watched my boys while I went to the morning appointment she had scheduled for me while David was at work. He was glad that I was going to talk to someone. As I drove to the church, I wondered what I would say. To this day I can't remember the name of the lay counselor, or the name of the church for that matter, but I poured out my heart for a solid hour. I told her about my unbelievable family of origin and the vivid nightmare I had just experienced days before.

The woman wisely told me, "Anna, you need more help than what I can offer here." She handed me the business card of a licensed therapist. "Joy, with Samaritan Pastoral Counseling Ministry, did her doctoral thesis on cults. She will not only understand what you need in order to heal, but she'll also understand and empathize with where you've been."

The counselor offered her services on a sliding scale, making them affordable, and I started meeting with her every week.

At our first appointment, she wasted no time getting to the root of the issue. "Tell me about your relationship with your dad."

"He was never around, and we dealt with it." Stoic Anna took over, my last-ditch effort to protect myself from baring my soul and facing my tragic past.

"Tell me more about that. What do you mean when you say, 'we dealt with it'?"

I literally felt my defenses wavering, the walls I'd built up and hidden behind for two decades crumbling before me. I told her about being abandoned in Mexico by my mom, about Rafael's advances and Antonia's humiliation of us children, about working like a slave for Dan Jordan, and about not having anyone around to protect me.

Joy listened. She nodded at appropriate times. She asked probing questions to lead me further and further along the path of self-examination. I wasn't exactly a willing participant, but I felt I didn't have any other choice. Though I found it difficult to open up my heart about the experiences I had endured, little by little I cracked open the spaces that had been locked down tightly for decades. I felt exposed and unprotected as I allowed the emotions to surface. Oftentimes I felt like I was drowning and couldn't breathe as I became overwhelmed by the experience of actually speaking aloud the atrocities we had endured as children.

One afternoon early in the process, Joy explained in her soft voice, "I call it peeling back the layers of an onion." Each time we met, I progressed a little bit more. I came to understand that it wasn't just about growing up without a dad. Yes, that was part of it. But my experiences went far beyond that. Obviously, my dad didn't protect me. But even more than that, he didn't care about *any* of his children or our well-being. He actually *put* us in harm's way. He allowed others to demean and abuse me and to treat me like a slave. He gave orders to have us sent to Mexico and allowed me to be groomed for sexual abuse and for an eventual marriage. Joy helped me explore how that abandonment and lack of fatherly provision and protection still affected me.

I slowly and painfully morphed from the unemotional person I'd been trained to be my entire life into someone who knew how to shed appropriate tears about the incredible losses I had endured. Women who live in a polygamist culture can't possibly bear up under most of what they have to endure without shutting down emotionally. What woman of sound mind can wholeheartedly deal with her husband having sex with other women on a regular basis?

When a powerful, narcissistic man manipulates multiple women into marrying him and sharing him with their "sister-wives," they learn to cope with the sheer lunacy of it by compartmentalizing their emotions. Suddenly so many aspects of my life crystallized— why my mom never cried, why she always defended my father, why she obeyed him without question. I'd been raised to act the same way.

In the beginning, I never cried during counseling. Like any good cult follower, I had learned to keep my emotions in check. I think the feelings side of me had been suppressed for so long that I didn't know how to express emotions, especially sadness and grief. I sat in Joy's office for months sharing only surface events and feelings. As she gently probed and chipped away at the walls I'd erected, I occasionally shed a tear or two, but that was it. As soon as a tear fell, fear or instinct kicked in. I would quickly change the subject to avoid going deeper and confronting the core issues and emotions. Bottom line: I didn't want to go there because I feared it would be like a breaking dam—uncontrollable once the water broke through.

Over time, my defenses wore down. Joy's insightful questions and empathetic responses helped me learn to trust her. With that trust came authenticity. I began to share more intimate parts of my journey. And with that sharing came the tears. So many tears. Once I opened those floodgates, my worst fears came true and I felt like I'd never be able to shut the gates again.

Joy and I met together for almost five years before I reached the point where I could sit in her office and grieve, freely letting the tears flow. Not the pretty, photogenic tears that a leading lady sheds when her boyfriend goes off to war, but gut-wrenching, heaving sobs that smeared my makeup and left my stomach muscles sore. David supported my efforts to deal with my past, though he couldn't understand the depth of the anguish I faced confronting such emotional experiences.

And so we went on. Joy helped me peel off the layers. I shared intimate aspects of myself—deeply rooted fears and insecurities. I cried. Occasionally, I cancelled appointments in a futile effort to avoid the pain of another layer being exposed. During that time, the cracks in my marriage reappeared, and again I plastered and painted over them, ignoring the signs that the foundation needed repair. Neither of us knew how to face the issues head on.

Two other great blessings came into our lives during this time. I gave birth to our two precious daughters, Kristina in 1996 and Hannah in 1998. I loved my boys, but having daughters seemed to complete me as a woman. I would joke and say, "We have a 'full house'; three of one kind and two of another." I was mostly a stay-at-home mom during those years, though I took odd jobs at times to help make ends meet. I was a good seamstress and took in sewing work often. Once I used leftover fabric to make matching dresses for me and the girls for Easter. David's salary as a sergeant in the Marine Corps barely kept our meager bills paid. I gladly gave up small luxury items to be able to stay home and raise my children. During that time, I taught the boys to read as they became old enough, and I loved homeschooling them.

I continued meeting with Joy and pursued my wholeness and healing. At the same time, the foundation of my marriage was shaken to the core, and in the spring of 1999 David and I separated and eventually divorced.

It was at that point in my counseling that Joy urged me to lighten my load so I could concentrate my efforts on my grief journey. "I encourage you to take everything off yourself. Think about it. Grief requires a lot of energy. So give yourself permission to not take on anything new. Instead, learn how to say no.

Minimize and simplify. Allow yourself time and space to take care of Anna and your kids."

I did as she suggested. I stopped volunteering at church on Sunday morning and Wednesday night and let go of outside commitments one by one, until I was left with no place to hide.

Finally, as a divorced, single mother of five young children, I arrived at a point where my defenses were completely removed and I was left utterly exposed. I reached a place where I could grieve my fatherlessness. Though I'd always known I never had a father who told me I was beautiful or called me his princess, or placed my feet on his to dance around the living room, or cross-examined a boy who came to pick me up for a date, I finally understood how that extreme lack affected me as a grown woman—how it impacted every aspect of my marriage and parenting.

When I finally allowed myself to acknowledge what I'd missed out on, it took several more months to fully grieve the process and heal. Those aching, turn-myself-inside-out months hurt as much physically as they did emotionally. I cried so violently during appointments that my abdominal muscles hurt for days after. I would compose myself before leaving Joy's office, but regularly found myself crying again. Sometimes I cried so hard I couldn't see straight to drive. I remember pulling over and sitting in my car sobbing, and then willing myself to regulate my breathing and stop the tears so I could finish my drive back home.

Once home, I would do my best to pull it together. But the emotional toll that my counseling took on me left me tired and needing rest for days following each appointment. Then, as I slowly recovered, my energy levels would rise, and I'd begin to dread my next appointment.

Eventually I came to realize how necessary the grieving, the pain, the introspection were to my healing. Instead of stiff-arming it like I had for so long, I finally began to embrace it, to throw myself fully into examining both my past and my present to help myself get better.

x x x x x

A few months later, I smiled as I drove into the parking lot of Samaritan Counseling. Walking into Joy's office, I felt physically light, cleansed, liberated. I greeted Joy as she led me into her office. "Good morning!"

"Someone's in a good mood." Joy returned the smile. "Want to share?"

"Actually, I do." I paused and looked out the window. The sun shone bright on that hot Texas afternoon. "I am finally beginning to understand what it means to have a relationship with my Father."

Joy looked at me quizzically.

"My dad did horrible things to me. He abandoned me. He never once protected me. He couldn't have cared less about me. He actually ordered the deaths of people I loved. Ervil LeBaron was a truly despicable person. But my dad is not my father."

My voice quavered, and I choked back tears before I continued. "God is my Father. Even before I knew Him, He called my name, He cared about me, and He protected me. God has never required anything from me. I don't have to try to be good enough for Him. He loves me anyway. He loves me no matter what. That's what unconditional love is. I've come to the realization that I'm not fatherless. I never was."

I closed my eyes and heaved a deep sigh. "I finally feel like I'm finished crying about this."

When I opened them, Joy leaned toward me, both elbows on her knees. "You did it, Anna."

I grabbed a tissue from the box on the coffee table in front of me. "Did what?"

"You finally got to the core. You peeled back all of the layers." I sensed her joy and pleasure at having helped me walk to the end of this part of my very difficult journey. I could see in her eyes how proud she was of me for having done the hard work. This evoked a few more tears—not tears of sadness but of joy at having reached the end of a long journey. The last words I remember her saying to me were, "Now go live in your skin."

Months passed, and I watched as David began intensive personal counseling, leading eventually to our decision to remarry, only this time with the help of a marriage counselor.

About this same time, my friend Yoby loaned me Dallas Willard's book *The Divine Conspiracy: Rediscovering Our Hidden Life in God.* I was especially challenged by these words:

I occupy my body and its proximate space, but I am not localizable in it or around it. You cannot find me or any of my thoughts, feelings, or character traits in any part of my body. Even I cannot. If you wish to find me, the last thing you should do is open my body to take a look.*

People are spiritual beings inhabiting physical human bodies. It dawned on me that it is the breath of God that really makes us come alive. Our spirit gives us life, so when the spirit leaves the body, our body is no longer alive. Embracing this gave me hope for life, a hope that's available to everyone. Your spirit is that part of you that dreams and hopes and has aspirations. No doctor performs open-heart surgery and finds your dreams and longings inside you.

---

*Dallas Willard, *The Divine Conspiracy* (New York: HarperCollins, 1998), 75.

Nothing like that can be found in your physical being. In much the same way, a brain surgeon doesn't open your brain and find your intelligence. The doctor wouldn't see 2 + 2 = 4 inscribed on the gray matter.

I couldn't stop thinking about what I read, and I awoke with a jolt at four o'clock the next morning. Though I wasn't familiar with the practice of meditating, that's what I was doing as I sat there contemplating these new ideas. We are spiritual beings, and we have spiritual power. By 6:30, I found myself on my knees on the floor, facedown on the carpet with my hands covering my face, not quite sure how I had ended up there. I firmly resolved as I prayed, "God, my earthly father used his spiritual power for evil. But from this day forward, my spiritual power will be used only for good—and for You."

Even though I didn't have a spiritual "grid" or reference point for what happened that morning, I knew something important and impactful had taken place. The spiritual trajectory of my life had changed forever. I didn't know how to formulate the words to describe to anyone what had taken place that day, but what happened was real and deeply personal. It was transformational. I couldn't have explained to another human being what had occurred, and I didn't for a long time. I believe that was the day that I cut ties with the influence of my father. All spiritual ties. All spiritual influence. God's power began to influence me in new and powerful ways, and my life hasn't been the same since.

I've heard people refer to such bondage as generational sin or as a generational curse. That morning, God not only broke my ties with the horrific generational sins and far-reaching impact of Ervil LeBaron, He also began teaching me how to move forward on the path He had for my life through dependence on the Holy Spirit. As I yielded to Him, I became more and more able to trust God and His Fatherly care for me. Deep in my soul, I felt a sense of contentment with the spiritual commitment I had made. For the first time in a long time, I felt like my feet were on solid ground, and I had hope for my future.

THIRTY-FOUR

IN 2000, I ACCEPTED AN OFFER to work full time as an executive assistant for my best friend, Madlin, in Austin, Texas. David had begun selling insurance, which he could do from anywhere in the state of Texas. Unlike the frantic midnight getaways I'd known as a child, our family carefully packed our belongings and stopped as needed on the long drive. Once we arrived, I worked hard to create a homey atmosphere in our rented house.

Not long after we got settled in, I went to the local H-E-B store to pick up some groceries. At the meat department, I pointed out a great cut of beef and asked the man behind the counter to slice it for me while I went to pick up milk and eggs. When I got back, he handed me the wrapped bundle, which I realized had not been sliced. I placed the meat back on the counter. "Excuse me. Remember, I asked you to slice it?"

"My apologies." He picked up the package and grinned at me.

The moment he smiled, I knew. Strangely enough, I recognized his teeth. *His family had married into our family.* I couldn't see his name tag tucked inside his butcher's apron, but I took a chance. "Your name is Harvey, isn't it?"

The man's eyes bugged out at hearing the name Harvey, and

his smile disappeared. He stared at me intently, and I watched as a flicker of recognition grew. "You're—um, aren't you . . ."

I patted my chest. "I'm Anna."

We just stood and stared at one another. Neither of us knew what to do. I felt fear prickling up the back of my neck as I imagined the connections he might still have with our family members who may have committed murder. He pulled his name badge out from inside of his butcher's apron. The badge read: STEVE.

He finally cleared his throat. "I changed my name many years ago. I haven't heard the name Harvey in a long time. I didn't know you lived in Austin."

"My family just moved here from Amarillo. I didn't know you lived here, either. Or that you had changed your name," I said, laughing nervously.

"Have you talked to Rena since you got here?"

Rena. My fear left as quickly as it had come. I suddenly felt safe because she had always been someone I could trust. I'd heard that years earlier Rena, the sister-wife who had sung Celia and me to sleep in Mexico, had moved to central Texas. After Rena left my father, she married her current husband, John. In addition to her own family members, she felt a burden to take in the children of those left fatherless and motherless, either because their parents had been victims of the crimes and were dead, or because their parents were perpetrators of the crimes and were now serving prison sentences. My closer siblings and I had always referred to this group of LeBarons, excluding Rena, as the "bad" side of the family.

"Here, let me give you her phone number. I know she'd love to hear from you." He grabbed a pad of paper, scribbled down the number, and slid the paper across the counter to me.

After he sliced the meat, I thanked him and quickly left.

I called Rena as soon as I got back home. We talked for almost an hour, catching up on each other's lives. I was shocked to find out that so many of my siblings and their children lived nearby.

At the close of our conversation, Rena said, "I hope you'll consider joining us for our annual Christmas get-together."

"I would love to come, but it's our busy season at work, so I'm not sure I'll be able to make it." Though I heard only sincerity and love in Rena's request, I still had a nagging residual fear of this part of my family.

"I understand. We'll get together another time. In the meantime, let's keep in touch."

Although I wasn't ready to see her in person, Rena and I talked numerous times over the next several months. With each conversation, my fears began to dissipate. So when Rena invited me to join the family for a Fourth of July celebration, I said yes. *What will it be like to see my half-siblings?* The last time we'd been together had been decades ago, when we were kids relying on the sister-wives to teach us, feed and clothe us, and protect us.

When I asked David to come with me, he hesitated at first, but then agreed to go. As we pulled up in front of Rena's little house, I thought, *My husband is a Marine. If there's any trouble, he can handle it.* But at the same time, I convinced myself the get-together would be safe. After all, if anyone in that group had wanted me dead, they could have accomplished that a long time ago.

I tilted down the visor in the car and reapplied my lipstick. As I got out of the minivan and stepped out onto the dry grass, I smoothed out the wrinkles in my shorts and straightened a few things on my children's clothes and hair. Before we got to the front door, it swung open and Rena ran out. "Anna! I'm so glad to see you!"

She had a few more wrinkles on her face and shorter hair than I remembered, but I would have recognized Rena anywhere. She wore jeans and a classic polo shirt. My mind flashed to happy times with her in Mexico, learning to cook beans and caring for her children while she made proselytizing trips with my father. My fondness for Rena was the only thing that could make such a reunion possible. Seeing her for the first time in a long time brought a flood of emotion, which I kept in check, as usual. I kept reassuring myself that Rena was safe, even though doubts plagued my mind.

We hugged for a long time, so tightly I didn't want to let go.

Rena finally pulled away. "And here are your beautiful children."

I introduced her to David and each of the kids, whom she fussed over equally. "Come on in! There are a lot of people very excited to see you." As she went around the room pointing out relatives and saying their names, I couldn't keep from smiling. I didn't need her to tell me their names, because I recognized each person in the room. One by one, they came forward to hug me. I remember that moment as such a precious time—tears, hugs, and more introductions. Through that initial time together, I was able to reestablish contact with many family members.

At Christmastime, my half-brother Robert, one sibling who had been estranged from me for decades, came to the annual family gathering. We hadn't seen each other since we were kids, and far too much had happened in the years since. Robert paid a high price for his part in our family history. Seeing him brought back all the devastation I had experienced years earlier. As I embraced my long-lost brother, the emotion I had held inside for years came out in a torrent of tears. He held me in his arms in a giant bear hug as my grief threatened to overwhelm me. Like many others affected by those who had done my father's bidding, I had come to understand that on their own, these people would have made very different choices. I also knew I finally had nothing more to fear.

On Christmas night, I took a short walk by myself. As I stared at God's handiwork in the stars, I thought about all He had accomplished in my healing journey. His timing was perfect. I'd finished my therapy with Joy and had moved to Austin because He knew I was ready to begin reestablishing ties with my estranged family.

x x x x x

We spent several years reconnecting, and God used me as a bridge for other family members who initially wanted nothing to do with certain relatives I had reunited with. The holdouts expressed curiosity, but they didn't want to forge a connection. Not yet, anyway. All that would take time, but it turned out to be another big piece of the healing journey.

In October 2002, my brother Hyrum's wife gave birth to twin preemies who tragically passed away soon after they were born. While I was making arrangements to attend the funeral, I called Mom to coordinate my trip with hers. "When do you plan to be there for the funeral?" I asked.

"I'm praying about it."

Those words triggered something deep inside me from my counseling days with Joy. I let Mom have the full force of my pent-up fury for all the times she hadn't been there for me and for my many siblings. I leveled all my palpable tension at her. "Mom, what kind of religion makes you question whether you should show up during the darkest hours of your children's lives?"

Knowing she had no defense, Mom eventually relented and allowed us to buy her a plane ticket to attend the funeral. I found myself revisiting this moment again and again in my mind. That conversation served as a pivotal moment for me—one in which I stopped being afraid of my mother and began to speak truth, to say to her what needed to be said.

x x x x x

On December 31, 2004, David and I moved to Dallas for my job. We started attending Gateway Church in January, and I read about a program called Freedom Ministry that was offered at the church and taught by Bob Hamp. Nervous but excited, I showed up for the introductory session titled "Levels of Change," which asserted that in order to be set free, believers must understand their identity in Christ. *If I want change to happen, I need to be secure in Christ.*

I left class with a bookmark that read: *I am accepted. I am secure. I am significant in His Kingdom.* I repeated this mantra to myself several times every day, allowing its message to burrow deep into my heart until I came to accept its truth. The Freedom Ministry class impacted me so deeply that I dived in and absorbed it as if it were my job. I eagerly pressed in to God and grabbed hold of every ounce of freedom in Christ.

Over the following weeks and months, the idea that I was accepted, secure, and significant in His Kingdom slowly moved from head knowledge to heart belief. *Nothing can ever separate me from the love of Christ.* During that period of time, I really came to believe—and not just repeat something because it was the right thing—that I was secure in His grasp. *Nothing can ever separate me from Him! I belong to Him! I am His daughter.*

That message became palpably real one day. I was having a tough time, overwhelmed by work and mothering five children. I knew all the plates I had in the air weren't spinning correctly— some were more wobbly than others and a few had already crashed to the ground. I was in a hard place emotionally and felt like I couldn't keep it all together much longer. I condemned myself for being inadequate and unable to measure up to my own standards.

Immediately God spoke to my heart. "Anna, if you keeled over dead right now—smack-dab in the middle of the mess of your thoughts and emotions—I would say to you, 'You are my beloved daughter, and I am well pleased with you. Well done, my good and faithful servant.'"

In the span of a few seconds, I understood completely, for the first time since I'd invited Jesus into my life at youth camp all those years before, that my relationship with God had nothing to do with my performance or with my being able to handle all of my obligations. Instead, it was about knowing Him and being loved by Him. I also understood that God knew He could finally say these wonderful things to me because, at last, I was able to receive them, know them, and believe them. That's when the transformation began. For the first time, I realized I didn't have to do anything to make my heavenly Father love me. He loved me and accepted me just as I was.

I sank to the couch, burying my face in my hands and letting healing tears flow down my cheeks. I could almost feel the arms of God embrace me as I sobbed deeply, recognizing what He had always seen—my righteousness in Christ. Finally, I accepted that the Cross of Christ was enough. I didn't have to work to be good enough; I didn't have to perform to an impossible standard. He accepted me because of what Jesus had done for me. I sat there, overcome by His deep love for me, possibly for the first time ever.

God had finally completed the work He had begun in me decades before at J Bar J Ranch.

THIRTY-FIVE

"ANNA? Anna!" Madlin's mother, Estella, abruptly interrupted my thoughts as she turned sideways in the passenger seat and patted my arm. I had been in Houston on business, and Madlin had asked if I could give Estella a ride back to Dallas.

I tapped on the brakes to slow the car.

"What is it?" She stared at me, her eyes quizzical.

"It's—well, um, I recognize this cemetery."

"You do? Has Madlin brought you to Alex's grave before?" Estella's face pinched slightly when she mentioned her son's name. Alex, who had died in a car accident at twenty-five, was her oldest son. I had many fond memories of Alex from our days at Spring Branch Academy, where I had met Madlin, my best friend for more than thirty years now. The smallness of the school meant our relationships with each other were close and our lives were intertwined. Understandably, Alex's untimely death devastated his entire family. Alex had been my friend, too, and I had not been able to attend his funeral. This was my opportunity to pay my respects.

I could sense my emotions building quickly. *Alex isn't the only person I know who is buried here.* My mind was flooded with snapshot memories of a notorious funeral in 1981—my father's.

My thoughts became jumbled, but I didn't feel like sharing them with Estella. At the same time, I knew her tenacity. She wouldn't let it go until I told her what was making me zone out.

I pulled inside the large iron gates at the cemetery's entrance, stopped, and slipped the car into park. "This is the same place my dad is buried."

I had been to my father's gravesite exactly three times—in 1981 for his funeral, in 2001 during my self-titled "journey of remembrance" after reading the book *The Sacred Romance*, and now today. Three times I had been here, the same number of times I recall seeing my father when he was alive.

"Ervil LeBaron is buried here?" She practically spat when she spoke his name aloud.

Tingles ran up and down my spine at his name, and I saw goose bumps on my arm. I felt as if I'd swallowed a rock and it was sitting in my stomach.

"Listen, I'm sorry I said anything. Let's just find Alex. I mean, let's find his grave marker." My voice sounded uncharacteristically high.

Estella looked away for a long moment before squinting at one of the little metal signs where two lanes intersected. "Take a right here. And then another right."

We drove ahead in silence, each of us deep in thought for very different reasons.

Estella reached for her car door even before she spoke. "Stop. This is it." She pointed in the direction where we would find a small headstone with Alex's name on it.

I jammed on the brakes, and she stepped out of the car. *I'll give her a few moments alone before I join her.* I turned the rearview mirror to steal a glance at myself. Tired eyes and a furrowed brow greeted me. That's how thinking about my dad always affected me. I quickly readjusted the mirror.

The cemetery was deserted except for us. When I glanced at Estella, I saw her body language had changed. I got out of the car and hurried to her, reaching her side just as she began to sag to her knees.

Estella wept quietly, not wanting to draw attention to the grief that consumed her. We both knelt on the grass, and I wrapped my arms tightly around her. Her breaths became ragged as she sobbed, lamenting in Spanish—"Alex!" and "Why, God?" I don't know how long we were in that position. I could feel my knees going numb, but I wasn't about to move. I spoke in soothing tones and reassured her that it was okay to cry, to let it all out.

Finally, she sat up straight and retrieved a handkerchief from her small purse. She blew her nose, then breathed in and out slowly and deliberately. "I'm okay now, really. Thank you, Anna."

As I helped her to her feet, she touched Alex's headstone one last time and walked back toward my car. I followed in silence. We had no sooner gotten inside when she said, "Why don't we see if we can find your father's grave?"

Now it was my turn for my breath to get caught in my throat and my pulse to quicken. *I don't want to visit my father's gravesite, even though Estella wants to bear my grief with me, as I have just done with her.* I willed myself to become calm before I answered. I couldn't find the words to explain my hesitation, so I simply responded, "I don't think that's a good idea."

"It might be good for you." She stared at me as though she could see right into my heart.

"I disagree. When I think about him, I don't feel much of anything. I've been to his gravesite before, and it didn't do anything for me. There's no reason for me to go there again, you know?"

"I understand. I really do. But sometimes people find great comfort by confronting their fears."

I laughed awkwardly. "I don't *want* that kind of comfort."

"Then would you do it for me? Please?"

Why did she have to say that? As much as I wanted to start the car and get out of the cemetery at that moment, I couldn't disrespect her by dismissing her suggestion. I smiled at her. "How can I refuse? Besides, I don't need you tattling on me to Madlin."

I looked left, right, and then behind me to get my bearings. "I know he's buried in section 13."

"Let's go find it."

Easier said than done. The setting sun made it difficult to see any section markers, and the shade from the trees scattered throughout the cemetery added to the darkness. We finally found section 13.

I stopped the car, and we both got out, met by the sweet smell of honeysuckle wafting in the warm Texas breeze.

I knew my father's grave was located somewhere near a towering pine tree, but there were so many of them. We walked up and down rows and rows, and then spotted it at the same time.

Estella pointed and exclaimed, "Here it is!" My throat constricted. I had never experienced any emotions here before and was confused about what was happening now. *It has to be because I was just grieving for Alex.*

Estella came alongside me, clutched my right hand, and pulled it to her chest. We silently read the words etched into the stone.

Beloved Father

Ervil M. LeBaron

Feb. 22, 1925

Aug. 15, 1981

I nearly laughed out loud. Beloved father? Beloved by whom? I gently pulled my hand free from Estella's and crossed my arms on my chest, as if defending myself against the situation. *I don't want to be here. I don't know what to say.*

I certainly didn't mourn my father. Not since I'd learned about the kind of man he was. Not since family members had told me how he had manipulated others for his own agenda. Not since I understood that he'd ordered numerous deaths of people I loved and cared about, only because they tried to get away from him and his cult. I wished I had a way to obliterate the word *Beloved* from the marker. I ached inside to feel something—anything—about my dead father, other than the deep-seated anger that surfaced on occasion.

Empty. That's how I feel. I didn't say the words that screamed in my mind. *You were never there for me. I was raised fatherless. How dare you put all of us in danger!* I willed my accusations to reach his ears beyond the grave.

I closed my eyes and prayed silently, begging God for strength and for a forgiving heart. I asked Him to help me be a better parent to my children than my dad had been to me. I vowed once more to love them well and protect them with everything inside of me. When I opened my eyes, I saw Estella had moved two steps closer to the grave.

She held one hand over her heart, breathed in deeply, then started mumbling in Spanish.

I caught a word or two, but most of it was unintelligible. I watched, transfixed, as she seemed to rally all her strength—for what, I didn't know.

Finally she spoke clearly, still in her native Spanish, her voice growing louder as though she gained power from quiet places inside herself. "Mr. LeBaron, here is your daughter. What do you have to say for yourself?"

I gasped as I watched her stand up to my father. She pointed an accusing finger at the gravestone, gesturing in a staccato motion, as though she were poking him in the chest.

"You're lying there—dead for many years." Then she turned and motioned toward me in a sweeping gesture. "But here stands your daughter! She has overcome."

I had no idea I was crying until I tasted the salt of my tears. I watched in awe as this tiny Guatemalan woman set aside her own grief for her son to be my advocate. Her words touched ravaged places in my heart I didn't even know existed. Her strong words spoke to *me* more than they did to my dead father. It was as if we were in a courtroom and my father was on the stand. I couldn't believe it. Someone had stood up to him.

Finally.

Someone called him to account for the pain of my childhood and the anxiety that had consumed my life and still threatened my ongoing happiness. Someone understood how he had devastated our lives by his calculated choices. Someone understood and spoke out about what he had done. Estella's words flooded my head, my heart, and my soul, washing away my fear and ushering in a strength I'd not known before. She pronounced my father guilty of his offenses against me and my family.

I knew Estella's words came from a place deep inside. Since I was Madlin's best friend, Estella treated me as one of her own daughters. This woman, small in stature, loomed large before me that day.

When she spoke those words, overcoming her own reluctance to challenge my dead father, I felt release from his bondage. *Finally someone has spoken the truth to him and said what needed to be said.* This woman had an economy of words, but every word had power.

Estella's undeniable challenge fueled a growing fire within me that spread throughout my body. I had lived long enough with myriad uncertainties swirling around my life, questions that kept me from embracing the present, fears that held me back emotionally. I had longed for answers. For closure. For peace. God had used Estella as the catalyst for all these things and more.

I breathed in until I thought my lungs would burst and held it while I spoke a prayer inside myself.

God, thank You. You knew I didn't want to come here, but You knew who needed to be at my side, and then You gave her just the right words to speak on my behalf. Thank You for redeeming my childhood and my story as only You could. I am Your daughter forever.

I let out my breath slowly, eyes still closed. I could feel strength and resolve pulsing through me. I hugged Estella tightly before we headed back to the car.

A weight had been lifted off my shoulders, and I felt like a different person. Because of God's power that had been at work in my life long before I knew Him, and through His unconditional love, I was who He created me to be.

EPILOGUE

THE SMALL WHITE HOUSE came into view as I rounded the corner. I pulled into the driveway and heard the sound of gravel beneath the tires of the rental car. My eyes were drawn to the apricot tree in the front yard as the memory of my mom singing to me flooded my mind: "I looked out the window and what did I see? Popcorn popping on the apricot tree . . ."

This trip had been a distant milestone on my journey of writing my story, so knowing that it had finally arrived was a bit daunting. My mom and I had been discussing this trip since I'd begun writing the first draft of this book in January of 2014. *What will she think about what I've written, since she still believes in polygamy? Will she understand why I had to tell my story? How will she react to reading about the things she did not know had happened?* So many questions ran through my mind as I approached her home, steps closer to our highly anticipated visit. I had struggled over the years with wanting to lash out at her in anger while at the same time wanting to protect her.

It's a dichotomy I still struggle with. I hid my suffering from her for the same reason others who have experienced hardships do: We don't want to cause more pain. I had reconnected with my mom as an adult with the realistic understanding that a sense of disappointment would be inseparable from the love I have for her. She simply could not be the mother that I need her to be while still maintaining her beliefs in the religious system that has caused such devastation to so many. Her duty and loyalty to her religion had already been firmly established. That is evidenced by her inability to refrain from talking about her beliefs to her grown children even though it causes us pain to hear her go on. In spite of all this, she and I have cobbled together the best relationship possible under the circumstances.

As much as the prospects of this visit filled me with trepidation, I was determined that my eighty-five-year-old mother would not read my story alone. Some of the events I'd written about would prove painful for her to read, and I wanted to be physically present so we could talk about those hard things together. My intention all along was to be the hands and feet of Jesus to her, to comfort her heart with my very presence. I wanted her to see me, alive and well, with her own two eyes. I wanted her to know that I had matured—both physically and spiritually—and would not allow the pain of having grown up as the polygamist's daughter to determine the outcome of my life.

I rolled to a stop in front of the house, shifted the car into park, and opened the door. I took a deep breath, reached into my bag, and pulled out the manuscript I'd had bound, complete with a color photo of the book cover on top. I wanted to show it to Mom immediately. I walked over to the apricot tree and plucked a ripe, juicy fruit, warm from the sun, from its bountiful limbs. Just holding it in my hand was comforting. Then I walked up the steps to her front door.

Mom's sister-wife Elaine answered my knock with a chuckle and playful reprimand. "You're late! Your mom has been waiting for you!"

"The drive from Salt Lake City took me twenty minutes longer than I anticipated," I explained.

I made my way through the home shared by three of my mom's twenty-one sister-wives. I found Mom sitting in her recliner in the back bedroom. She greeted me with a smile and a little bit of nervous laughter as she anxiously anticipated the task before us. She could imagine the challenges ahead of us, based on the few sample chapters I'd read to her during my visit the previous year.

I handed her the completed manuscript, and she began leafing through the pages. Then she looked at me and said, "You did it, Anna. You said you would come see me when you were finished, and here you are."

We wasted no time in getting me settled in so we could begin. Over the next few days, we spent hours sitting together while I read the manuscript aloud to her. Sometimes Elaine sat in on the readings. Even though she got tired, Mom didn't want me to stop. She and I both shed many tears as I read.

At times, it was uncomfortable for me to read things I had revealed about our family and about my own life—things that she had never known about until that moment. It was excruciating for us both to relive the day I ran away from home. We paused frequently, as she was often surprised by parts of my story. "Anna Keturah, did that really happen to you?" she asked.

"Yes," I had to answer every time.

x x x x x

I turned the last page of the story and closed the manuscript. Mom took it from me and sat with it in her lap, silently caressing the picture of a younger me on the cover. I watched her hands repeatedly brush back and forth as tears fell from her eyes and she wept quietly. Ten minutes passed before she was able to speak.

"What was it like for you hearing the things that happened to me?" I asked carefully.

"It's awful. I didn't know . . . I don't even know how you still love me," she replied.

"Mama . . ." I began.

"I'm glad you do," she continued. "And I'm so glad you're here."

She lowered her eyes before wiping away more tears with the back of her age-spotted hand.

"I just don't like your eyes covered up, or your mouth. I still think the publisher ruined a perfectly good picture of you!"

She was alluding to a conversation we had had months before this visit, when the design for the book cover had just been finalized. I had sent a photo of it to her. She didn't understand it, so I explained by phone, "Those are censor bars."

"Why would they do that?" she asked indignantly.

"Because I was censored, Mom," I stated matter-of-factly.

"You were not censored!" she argued in her high-pitched tone I was so familiar with.

"I think you are remembering a different life than the one I lived," I said as gently as possible.

Now that she had read the entire manuscript, she said she understood the cover.

"Well, I'm glad for you because it heals your heart. But reading all this hurts me." She gestured toward her heart. "I'm not going to lie about that." I'm not sure my mom had ever been forced to face the pain that her choices had caused her children. She voiced regret about following Ervil and went so far as to condemn him as a false prophet.

When she immediately followed that declaration with her strongly held belief in her most recent late husband as the true prophet, I drew in a deep breath. Deep breathing was one of the many tools I had learned in counseling to manage the anxiety and the triggers I experienced. I did not have any expectation that her beliefs had changed. But I needed her to hear my story and to know that in spite of everything, my heart was still tender toward her.

Mom read the manuscript twice more on her own while I was in town that week. We discussed at length events she had not known about, both of us acknowledging that there were aspects of our respective beliefs that we disagreed upon—namely tenets of polygamy that were important to her and caused me to question how she could still believe in them. We had agreed to disagree years before. Her beliefs about who Jesus is and who I have come to understand Him to be are miles apart, stretched to a thinness I did not know was possible. The connection between the two is in name only.

On Friday, as I prepared to depart for the airport, I walked across the front yard to the apricot tree. I picked several pieces of fruit from the tree to take with me, humming softly to myself. "I could take an armful and make a treat, a popcorn ball that would smell so sweet."

x x x x x

After arriving home, I stood at my dining room window and gazed at my backyard, recalling my visit with my mom. This house is the one I've lived in the longest of my entire life. It is the house I've made into a home for my five children. I've put down roots here, both literally and figuratively. When we moved in ten years ago, we planted a tree in the backyard—one that I hoped my future grandkids would climb one day. A few years later, I planted an apricot tree to remind me of my younger years with my mom. The leaves on the apricot tree danced in the summer wind as I peered at it through the window. "It wasn't really so, but it seemed to be, popcorn popping on the apricot tree."

The weight of all the questions I'd held in anticipation of sharing the words I'd written with my mother had lifted. Relief that the task was done washed over me. Our phone calls and infrequent visits will continue as long as she remains with us. She doesn't understand the conflicting feelings her children carry within themselves toward her, and we cannot fathom how she can continue holding on to her revised and updated fundamentalist Mormon beliefs. I listen to her say things she feels compelled to say, not shutting her down or shutting her out completely, as others of my siblings have chosen to do for their own well-being.

With this visit and its painful revelations, my mom and I had reached the beginning of the end of my healing journey. I said the things that needed to be said—even though it hurt her to hear me say them—and found steady ground for us to walk on. I know that because of both my father *and* my mother, I was born the polygamists' daughter.

But that truth has been redeemed by a bigger Truth. I am a child of a God who loves me unconditionally. He knows my name. He knows my story.

And He has set me free.

SNAPSHOTS OF MY STORY

DESPITE THE FACT THAT I rarely had money, at the age of ten I saved up enough to buy my own camera. I gladly passed up purchasing other treats so I could pay for film and developing. Every image I captured was so costly that I couldn't throw out a single photo, not even the blurry ones.

These images offer a peek at my lifetime of memories. I hope you enjoy these glimpses of my story from behind the lens.

My mother and me. When this was taken, I was the youngest in my family and the only one of my siblings to have a professional photo with just my mother—I treasure it greatly. ▼

▲ My father had an undeniable presence wherever he went.

This is the home where I was born in Chihuahua, Mexico. It was originally built out of stones, so we called it "the rock house." But later someone finished the outside to make it look more "normal" and painted it bright blue. If only walls could talk . . .

My sister Celia (on the right) and me in front of our home. ▼

▲ Whenever my mother was with us, she always made sure a photo was taken of her children. I love this one from 1972 because of our smiles . . . and because of the cloth diapers filling the clothesline. Left to right: Mom (holding Hyrum on her hip), Heber, me hidden in the shadow next to Kathleen, Marilyn, Celia.

▲ Family photo taken in Houston in 1981 right before my father died in prison, leaving my mom to care for many of his fatherless and motherless children. Back: Virginia, Manuel, Celia, me, Mom, Megan, June, Amy, Sean. Front: Hyrum, Eric, Adine, Tiffany.

Ramona and Faye, full sisters, both married to Dan Jordan as teenagers, making them sister-wives as well. ▼

▲ My mother and Rosemary, sister-wives of Ervil. They were both redheads and had their differences, but they did their best to get along. Taken in Houston, 1982.

A rare photo of my mother and father together. Chihuahua, Mexico, mid-1960s. ▼

▲ Rena and Lillian on Rena's wedding day in Houston, 1981. Rena was originally married to my father—and she even killed for him—but later "divorced" him so she could marry her current husband, John.

My half-brother Ed and me, all dressed up for church, which was held in Mark and Lillian's finished-out garage. ▶

◀ Lillian in 1982, shortly after I ran away from home to live with her. Houston, the Campbell Road house.

My half-brother Ed with his favorite truck outside Reliance Appliance, where we all worked. Ed was killed during "The Four O'Clock Murders" in June 1988, along with Mark Chynoweth, Duane Chynoweth, and Duane's daughter Jenny. Houston, early 1980s. ▶

My father's mugshot from 1979, when the Mexican authorities turned him over to the FBI on murder and conspiracy charges. ▼

▲ Various children and grandchildren of Ervil LeBaron at his gravesite. It was a complicated grieving process for us all, as we lost a father we'd never really had in the first place. ▼

Shortly after the funeral, a gravestone was laid. As an adult, seeing the words "Beloved Father" makes my heart ache because the description isn't true. For me, it is a stark reminder that I grew up fatherless. ▼

▲ One of the last photos of my mother and me before I ran away in 1982. My shirt reads "Daddy's Girl," revealing my heart's true desire.

After I ran away to join them, Mark and Lillian enrolled me in a Christian school in Houston. At only thirteen, this decision would change the trajectory of my entire life. ▼

Even after I escaped the cult, its shadows still haunted me. Here, celebrating my half-brother Tony's wedding and dressed to the nines, I couldn't hide the tumult going on inside my heart. ▶

◀ Me at the Campbell Road house, where Reliance Appliance was located at the time. I worked every day after school and all day Saturday the entire time I lived with Mark and Lillian. Whenever they went on vacation, I felt a sense of freedom: Though I had to manage the store, I could also call my boyfriend, David, a strictly prohibited activity.

Following Lillian's death in 1989, I became severely depressed. My former youth pastor came to visit and encourage me. I will always be grateful to him for leading me to the one true Christ. ▶

An aerial photo of Reliance Appliance, the place where Mark was gunned down in his office by cult members. If you look carefully, you can see the ramp we used to bring appliances into and out of the showroom—and later where the coroners would wheel Mark's body down on a gurney. This image, spread all over the news, haunts me still. ▶

◀ A candid photo on the day of the combined funeral for Mark, Ed, Duane, and Jenny. It was a dark, dark time of grieving for all of us.

One of the last family photos of Mark and Lillian with all six of their children. After Mark's murder and later, Lillian's suicide, their children struggled to piece their lives back together. ▶

My children loved playing with my sister Celia's children. Watching them grow up together brings beautiful restoration from our own fractured childhood. ▼

▲ Having children of my own was powerfully redemptive, in light of my upbringing. After having three boys in a row, I was delighted to have my own daughter—I often dressed Kristina in outfits to match mine!

▲ My family in 1998, soon after my last child, Hannah (in Granny's arms) was born. My mother-in-love, Sandra, lived with us for seven years. We get along well to this day, and she was a great help to me as I was raising my children.

Today my children, surrounding me here, are all grown. To see them succeed and mature is one of my biggest and most treasured accomplishments. It hasn't always been easy, but it has always been worth it. They have my heart forever. ▶

◀ Recently, Wendy Walters invited me to share my story at the Release the Writer conference as an alumnus. I love being able to use my experiences to help others.

In July 2016, I went to visit my mother, who still believes in polygamy and lives with two of her sister-wives. Reading my manuscript to her was difficult for both of us, but for me, it was the culmination of a long journey to freedom and healing. ▶

Q&A WITH ANNA LeBARON

Q: *Looking back, what was your scariest moment of living in a polygamist cult?*
A: You want me to pick just one? All of them combined is the reason I don't watch movies that fall into the horror, thriller, or suspense categories—I lived that! Narrowing it down, one of the scariest moments was being forced to go door to door in Mexico selling slices of cake. I was well aware that American children were being kidnapped. Every time I ventured out onto the streets, I knew I was vulnerable. I felt the anxiety in the pit of my stomach.

Q: *Was there a specific moment when you began to have a personal relationship with God? How did you separate the true God from the one you had been raised to worship?*
A: I became aware of God and Jesus the few times I attended Sunday school at a local Christian church. Later, when I was thirteen and enrolled in a Christian school, I became aware of others who had a personal relationship with God. When one of my classmates, Marsha Mosher, prayed out loud and began with the word "Father," I recognized the difference instantly. She *knew* God intimately. I longed for that kind of loving expression to be authentic and real within my life.

I had been raised to revere Joseph Smith and worship my dad, Ervil

LeBaron, as the "one mighty and strong," the one on earth designated to speak for God. When I understood how I had been misled, I began questioning myself. *Is God's love really genuine and available to me? Can I really be a part of His family?* Answering those questions are what helped me know God, the Father, in an authentic way and gave my spiritual expression a genuineness I hadn't experienced before.

Q: *When you first ran away from the cult, you mention the safety you felt at Mark and Lillian's house. How did you begin to process your experience? What was your first step toward healing?*
A: I did my best to fit in, and much of that was done by putting on a happy face, even when that didn't reflect what was happening on the inside. Although I appreciated the chance to live at Mark and Lillian's house, I don't think I began truly healing until 1995, when I started seeing a professional counselor. The healing process has been a long journey and has taken decades. I am still on that journey and continue taking steps in the right direction.

Q: *If your dad were alive today, what would you say to him?*
A: I'm not going to lie—this is a hard question. I don't believe that my dad was in his right mind for most of his adult life. Mental illness runs in our family. I believe things could have been different had he received the care he needed. As it stands now, I'm like every other person who longs for the approval and blessing of his or her father. I'd want that from my father, if he were capable of giving that to me. I would want him to say he is proud of me.

Q: *Do you think of the children of Ervil and his other wives as your family, even today? Do you keep in touch at all?*
A: Yes, I consider my fifty-plus siblings and their mothers my family. Naturally, I feel closest to my six full siblings and my mother's older children from her previous husbands. That said, I have siblings from my mother's sister-wives that I'm very close to, and I would do anything for them. I also have several siblings where the relationship is strained, and we aren't in close contact. Our family has been through such trauma that having close relationships with everyone is all but

impossible. I navigate those relationships with trepidation and continue hoping for healing and reconciliation for all of us.

I am in touch with all the family members and siblings who want to be in touch with me. However, some choose to keep their distance for a variety of reasons, and I respect their decisions. I maintain some measurable distance from a few family members, while I continue to pursue my own healing. My relationship with one of my brothers is a good example of this. He is in prison for the misguided "blood atonement" killing of my brother-in-law Mark. Even though this brother accepted Jesus Christ as his Savior in prison, I have put a healthy boundary around my heart regarding our relationship. We talk on the phone occasionally, but that is as much as I can do right now. I don't think he knows the full measure of how his actions affected my life. I hope that after he reads this book, we may be able to cobble together a closer tie.

I know there are people in my family who will not be happy that I have written this book. Some may have a different perspective on or recollection of the events that I describe. Being a peacemaker at heart, it took me a while to gather the courage to tell my story, knowing that others would question me—and my motives—for writing. I hope they will tell their stories one day as well.

Q: *How prepared did you feel going into marriage and motherhood? What aspects of each do you think you have done well? What aspects of each needed work? How do you think your upbringing affected these roles and relationships?*

A: My upbringing definitely affected my role as a wife and mother, both positively and negatively. I really thought "love conquers all" going into my first marriage and later into my second marriage. I was wrong, and it broke my heart both times. I believe that my children's father and I were both ill-equipped to enter our marriage. Neither of us knew how to create a safe space for our love to grow and develop. By the time we looked outside of our relationship for help, there was too much damage already done to save the marriage. We divorced after almost ten years and having five children together. We sought individual counseling and then later we got marriage counseling and remarried. That relationship ended after another seven years of working hard to figure it out. I'm glad for my children's sake that we remarried, since they got to have their father present in their lives for those additional seven years. David passed away in 2016 after a short battle with cancer. He and I were able to share a few moments in the hospital right before he passed, and he asked me to forgive him "for everything." I was able to honestly tell him that I did.

As for my role as a mother, nothing has brought me more joy or more pain. The joys come from having raised my five children and watching them now, all grown up. The pain comes from all the ways in which I know I messed up. It's glaringly obvious to me where things went sideways in my parenting. I own up to the ways in which I have caused them harm, even with my best intentions to mother them well.

I dreamed of being the quintessential stay-at-home, attachment-style-parenting-with-a-side-of-James-Dobson mom. I did my best, until I couldn't anymore. When my kids' dad quit his job, I became a working mom and, of necessity, I became the provider for our family. Later I became a single mother of five children and worked outside the home full time. Those difficult years brought stress on us all. The loss of my dream of being a stay-at-home mom left me grieving for years. I lost a lot of time in the denial and depression stages of the grief process. I became detached emotionally as a coping mechanism and have plenty of regret about that.

Q: *You now have a beautiful family. What do your children know about your childhood?*

A: I love my children! When they were little, I wanted to protect their young minds from having to carry the weight of knowing about my family of origin. They grew up not knowing anything about my father, except what they may have overheard in bits and pieces. It wasn't until my oldest was a teenager that I began to openly discuss the events of my childhood, leaving out many details. Most of what I tell in the book will be a surprise to even those family and friends I

ANNA LeBARON || 301

feel closest to. I'm hoping that my children will understand me better when they decide to read this book.

Q: *Do you have family/friends who are still practicing a polygamist lifestyle (besides your mother)? How do you reconcile that and still have a loving relationship with them?*
A: Yes. Several close and extended family members still practice; others still believe in but don't currently practice polygamy as an expression of their faith. We have all pretty much agreed to disagree. I also have close and extended family who are modern-day LDS Mormons, as well as some who are atheists, agnostics, new agers, Buddhists, and several different denominations of Christianity. Some describe themselves as spiritual but not religious. My family has navigated the choppy waters of our spiritual expressions within the context of our relationships with one another. Lots of love and grace have been extended and received.

Q: *What was the book-writing experience like? I can't imagine the courage and vulnerability it must have taken.*
A: I have known for decades that I wanted to write a book and tell my story. The book-writing experience was more difficult than I ever expected. The amount of detail, storytelling, and editing needed was more than I had bargained for.

Writing a book is in so many ways like having a baby. I'm convinced that no one is ever "prepared" to have a baby, no matter how well-read or experienced you are with other people's babies. I'm eager to "deliver" this book-baby to the world and am hoping for the best possible outcome and reception.

Q: *Can you see ways that God has used the bad things in your upbringing for good today?*
A: Definitely. First, I speak Spanish fluently, which has been invaluable in my business and professional life. It also comes in handy when I need to talk to my siblings and don't want my kids to understand what I'm saying. I have learned to be a peacemaker because I can see two sides of a situation clearly. My experiences have made me

relatable, empathetic, and compassionate toward others. My upbringing gives me credibility when speaking to others, and I feel very comfortable in front of a crowd. I'm told that I inherited my father's intelligence and charisma.

Q: *Over the past few years, there have been television reality shows featuring polygamous families, such as Sister Wives and now My Five Wives. Also, Escaping Polygamy features the efforts of three sisters who escaped from their cult and are helping others to do the same. What do you think about these shows? How do they differ from your experience?*

A: My experiences were very different than what is currently portrayed on television. My life was closer to the fictitious drama *Big Love* that ran from 2006 to 2011. I could only watch a few episodes because of the strong reactions it triggered within me. The series portrayed life with a more violent, fundamentalist cult-like atmosphere.

When I've watched *Escaping Polygamy,* I am reminded of my own escape from the cult. The heart-pounding, sweaty-palm feelings come right back to me as if it were yesterday

As for the show *Sister Wives,* Christine Brown is my cousin. Her grandfather and my father are brothers. She doesn't know me—yet. I follow her on Twitter, but that's the extent of my connection with her as of this writing. I'd love to meet her, of course! I do wonder about her early years, where she grew up, and if she knew about my dad or had any experiences with him.

It seems to me like the show wants to portray the polygamist lifestyle as normal. My experience was that this kind of life is anything *but* normal, especially for the kids. However, I escaped prior to becoming a child-bride or being married off to a man with multiple wives. I'm grateful that I was never a sister-wife and that I won't have those experiences to compare notes with Christine about.

Q: *What is one thing you hope your readers take from your story?*
A: Hope and courage. I especially desire this for them if they have experienced trauma or abuse of any kind in their life. There is a lot of living left for all of us to do. Pursuing true freedom and healing in a holistic way that involved my body, soul, and spirit was what worked for me.

ACKNOWLEDGMENTS

To MY CHILDREN. Words are not enough. From the beginning, you have supported me and cheered me on throughout the writing of this book, each in your own way. You have risen so far above what I could ever have dreamed, considering my upbringing and all the ways I could have done better by you. That you don't hold those things to my account is the greatest gift I will ever receive. David, Caleb, Jacob, Kristina, and Hannah, you are my most precious treasure and purest joy. You have my whole heart forever.

To my family—every one of you. We've suffered and lost way too much. The losses were unbearable for some, and we lost them, too. The weight of it all hangs too heavily on others. I am fully aware that many of you experienced unimaginably worse than anything you will read here.

Ramona, Faye, Kathleen, Celia, Hyrum, and Adine, I couldn't have done this without you, nor would I have wanted to.

Celia, you taught me to love reading and learning before I started kindergarten, which helped me become who I am today. You've continued teaching me throughout the years. We've spent countless hours talking, in person and by phone, and it won't ever be enough. I can't imagine living life without you. I love it that we grew up together. I love it more that we made sure our children did too.

Madlin, you've been my best friend and the sister my heart chose for what feels like forever. We've been through it all in the three-plus decades we've shared. You and your family are precious to me. Praying with you and Mark until Joshua was born and then fasting from *dessert* all those months until Alexandra joined your family are my two favorite stories about us. I also love the legendary 9-1-1 stories, and we have a slew of them. The best is always yet to come.

Kelli, you were the wind beneath my wings even before chapter 31 had been written in this book. Yes, we were breaking the rules when we went to the movie theater to see *Beaches*. Your irrepressible and resilient spirit is what I love most about you.

To my high school (SBCGA) and "college" (I.I.) friends. You embraced the new girl and included me in all the shenanigans, which only got better as time went on. Your friendship changed my life forever.

Jessica Kirkland, you believed in my story from the first time we talked. You demonstrated that when, for our next call, you blocked off your entire morning so you could listen to me unravel the tangled tale front to back. I'm forever grateful.

Leslie Wilson, you took my first draft—the "dry bones" of my story—and breathed life into them. This was truly a collaborative effort. By the time we were finished, I felt like you knew and loved me and my family, just as if you had been born into it yourself, though I'm sure you are glad you weren't. The tender way you shepherded me and held every story I told as sacred and worthy of being heard was mothering to my heart.

The Tyndale Momentum team. Sarah Atkinson, thank you for hearing my heart and allowing me to tell my story. Bonne Steffen, your guidance through the endless rounds of edits was steady and sure. Nicole Grimes, you nailed the cover. Sharon Leavitt, you made me feel like part of the Tyndale House family. Jillian Schlossberg, Katie Dodillet, Cassidy Gage, and Nancy Clausen, thank you for your enthusiastic partnership. Jan Long Harris, I have more books inside me. Here's to more yeses.

Bob Hamp, your pastoral influence set me free to become the

person I was created and redeemed to be. I think, live, lead, and learn differently because of you. You taught me how to hear God speak and then how to receive, internalize, and broadcast what He speaks to me. This book is my favorite broadcast so far. Knowing you're proud of me is fathering to my heart.

Joy, my first counselor. I'm learning to "live in my skin" and can say it's quite nice.

Tiffany, my current counselor. You had your work cut out for you the day I inadvertently ended up in your office. You walked some pretty rough terrain with me as I blazed new trails for my life.

The Dirty Dozen (My Covering). I was knee-deep in the soil of my heart in counseling when I pulled you all together and asked you to pray. I knew Tiffany meant business, and so did I—and things got messy fast. So much was being uprooted to make room for the beautiful and nourishing seeds that God wanted to plant. Then I started writing this book, and you have kept right on praying to this day.

Wendy Walters, this book-baby was growing inside me for decades when Release the Writer came along. Now look what you've unleashed! Some debts of the heart can never be repaid. This is one of them.

Mary DeMuth, I've read so many memoirs. Then I read *Thin Places*, and my heart healed in ways I didn't expect. I knew that if I ever wrote my story, I'd want to have the same impact on my readers that you had on me. Your early input on the manuscript and (later) your endorsement mean the world to me. The little girl inside of me sees and acknowledges the little girl inside of you. A well-Fathered heart is my best prayer for you and for all those touched by our stories.

Ticcoa Leister, you came along at just the right time and extroverted your heart out. Thank you for helping me edit when I was Done with a capital D. About the epilogue, you heard my heart and then put words on paper that my heart had not yet spoken. I hope Sunshine and Jess forgive me for your newfound love of Texas.

#the4500, *I can't even.* Can you believe all that's happened since we met online in March 2015? I love you all more than the telling of it. I hope to meet every single one of you #IRL one day. So many women, from every walk of life, and every brand and flavor of crazy people who dared to believe that Jesus was who He said He was and decided to follow Him so they could become more like Him. You, heart friends, are a modern day Jesus-turning-water-into-wine miracle when the best wine was saved for last. I'd like to propose a toast: #the4500forLYFE.

Tracy Lynn Page, your hashtag-thieving ways began a new chapter in my life. I will never get tired of telling our epic story. I wrote that sentence sitting in your living room with you and Dobie.

My Launch Team—#the4500launches—where to start? You matched my boundless enthusiasm for book launching and cranked it up a few notches. I'm over the moon that you came alongside me. You embodied my favorite Jessie Kirkland quote: "Behold, the power of social media!"

The Olivia Newton-John album cover sleuths, those sentences survived the final edits! That was the most crowd-sourcing fun I've had on the Internet.

My very early readers: Celia Manila, Mary DeMuth, Anne Mateer, Wendy Walters, Carolyn Simmons, Stacey Giles, Tiffany Millen, Rachel Bruce, and Ticcoa Leister. Thank you for your invaluable feedback, suggestions, and edits.

To all the helpers, teachers, counselors, mentors, coaches, pastors, friends, influencers, authors, Bible study teachers, volunteers, and program facilitators that shaped my life. What you do matters for all eternity.

Ruth Wariner, thank you for replying to my Tweet, and then for trusting me to help launch your *New York Times* bestselling book, *The Sound of Gravel*. I felt like I was doing reparations for the atrocities my dad committed against your family. Mostly, thank you for opening your heart and life to an "Ervilite." Four decades of fear and familial estrangement were undone when you messaged me back on Twitter that day.

ABOUT THE AUTHOR

ONE OF MORE than fifty children of infamous polygamist cult leader Ervil LeBaron, **Anna LeBaron** endured abandonment, horrific living conditions, child labor, and sexual grooming. At age thirteen, she escaped the violent cult, eventually gave her life to Christ, and sought healing. A gifted communicator and personal growth activist, she's passionate about helping others walk in freedom. Anna lives in the Dallas–Fort Worth metroplex and loves being Mom to five grown children.

To read more of Anna's journey—and access exclusive additional resources, please visit **www.AnnaLeBaron.com/TPD.**